CW00373618

When Radio Was the Ca

Music in your home! A 19th century plug for Electrophone.
(Evergreen, UK)

When Radio Was the Cat's Whiskers

Bernard Harte

ROSENBERG

First published in Australia in 2002 by Rosenberg Publishing Pty Ltd
PO Box 6125, Dural Delivery Centre NSW 2158
Phone 02 9654 1502 Fax 02 9654 1338
Email rosenbergpub@smartchat.net.au
Web http://www.rosenbergpub.com.au

Copyright © Bernard Harte 2002

All rights reserved. No part of this publication may be reproduced,
stored in a retrieval system, or transmitted, in any form or by any means,
electronic, mechanical, photocopying, recording or otherwise, without
the prior permission of the publisher in writing.

National Library of Australia
Cataloguing-in-Publication data

Harte, Bernard, 1918- .
When radio was the cat's whiskers.

Bibliography.
Includes index.
ISBN 1 877058 08 4.

1. Harte, Bernard, 1918- . 2. Radio broadcasting -
Australia - History. 3. Radio broadcasters - Australia -
Biography. I. Title.

791.440994

Set in 11 on 13.5 point New Baskerville
Printed by Griffin Press, Netley SA 5037
10 9 8 7 6 5 4 3 2 1

Contents

Dedication

To the memory of my close associates during wartime and outside it, many of whom have since left us. In particular, Brian Buzzard, who survived the war, then shunned a debilitating illness long enough to write his autobiography, *A Rascal and a Gentleman*. To Bernie Weisneski, who was shot down in 1944 during a bombing mission. I accompanied him over Japanese-held Portuguese (now East) Timor. His remains were never found. To Jack Dewhurst, with whom I flew on every mission over the South-West Pacific and the Timor Sea from 1941 to March 1943. We parted two days before he and the rest of the Catalina crew were shot down but survived, only to be caught by the Japanese off Gasmata (New Britain) and beheaded. To Gil Thurston, who joined our Catalina Squadron after meritorious service out of England with 10 Squadron Sunderlands. As our skipper, Gil brought us back safely from many sticky missions. He survived the war but died in Singapore on his first Sydney–London trip as a Qantas Captain in 1945. To my dear wife Jean, who suffered me during times of war and peace until her death in 1974. And finally, my thanks for the support given to me during the writing of this manuscript by my sons Bernie and Adrian, and to my daughter Dr Jane Harte-Daniel, for pulling me into line and bustling me along to complete it while I was still reasonably *compos mentis.*

Foreword

I suppose it is apt that I met Bernard through the radio network of friends, and that most of our communication has been across the spectrum bands of major radio-communication carriers. Bernard was there as wireless was still in its infant exploration of the world expanding around it, and he grew with it … sometimes having to invent, repair, 'make do', and otherwise use the inherent Australian trait of finding another way when something doesn't work, mainly when our country was at peace, but also in critical times of war—when time just didn't exist, it had to be done somehow.

My father was born in 1891, Bernard a generation later, myself in a later generation, and my children in the whizzbang world of IT. I am sure the twentieth century was the most exciting period ever experienced by one lifetime.

As the handshakes of our pioneers are slipping from our grasp, we must remember they opened the doors to a whole new world, to the whole world, even beyond in the space age of communication between man on the moon and his controller on earth.

Radio has opened up our nation, nurtured communities through times of rejoicing and disaster, brought a 'mantle of safety' for many decades to our scattered pioneers and those who carry on their tradition beyond the security blanket of major metropolitan centres.

Radio is the voice of comfort, of information, of melody and music. Radio can be with you wherever you are … at home, at work, on the move. Radio can soothe, infuriate, amuse, interact through talk-back, educate, cross vast barriers from studio to receiver; and it has the tentacles of ham, UHF, marine, short wave, long wave and medium wave; it also translates through the Internet. Radio is whatever and wherever you want it. It speaks to you in the day, and in the dark, it is as close as the flick of a switch without the need of landline power. I guess if you want to, you could listen to it underwater.

I am so pleased that someone with Bernard's breadth of experience in the radio industry, and his technical background, had also kept hundreds of tapes, files and other memorabilia. Bernard is a Virgo: the perfectionist, the preserver, the carer. And he cared for radio. It fascinated him from his childhood; he wanted to find out how it worked, and he worked with it.

In the ephemeral era in which we now live, where faxes fade, letter writing is a disappearing art, emails slide through the ether, are read, and disappear, I worry where the recording of our social and industrial history will be found in the decades ahead, as technology is rapidly overtaken by newer inventions and today is discarded for tomorrow.

When Bernard asked me to comment on his manuscript I was pleased. He knew I loved history and its context as it evolved. Indeed, as the Episodes started to flow, I often asked him to hurry up, as I wanted to see what vignette of development or anecdotal snippet he was going to wind into his research and memory.

I have been an interactive radio listener for many years, but I now have a greater knowledge and appreciation of that little square receiver sitting in my study. I laughed at the stories, and Bernard hasn't hesitated to tell them against himself. I hope the readers laugh also.

I never knew there were so many 'phones used for communication. There is the Electrophone, Racophone, xylophone, mulgaphone, gramophone, headphone, microphone, telephone, Palephone. But I am sure only the dedicated would ever have heard of the Blattnerphone. Fascinating.

The year of the centenary of Federation of our nation was also the centenary of the first official use of radio as a method of communication in Australia.

I commend Bernard for the blood, sweat, tears, frustration, and concentration he has put into recording the story of broadcast radio in Australia. He has documented history as he lived it, in both a researched and autobiographical way, in his own style of writing. You cannot hear his baritone voice, but it is modulated, trained and musical. It has the style and phrasing of an age we will not know again. It is the bridge between the days of early articulation and rounded vowels, which takes pleasure in the selection of pronunciation, and the speech which has evolved in a younger world as we enter the twenty first century. It is a radio voice. You can sense it behind the written words.

I will fight for the continuance of radio as a means of communication, especially in regional Australia, where distance and isolation by geography, poverty, personality or age may be more subtle but still exist without the major cities' ready access to other forms of developing technology. Radio is everybody's voice, regardless of who you are or where you are.

I have enjoyed the book. I am honoured to have been asked to write this foreword. Bernard was equipped to present and record this story, his story, our nation's story, because he was part of it. And he wanted to share his love of radio. Thank you, Bernard.

Gail Penrose (*'Magpie'*)
'Myalla', Bingara NSW

Prologue

The 'cat's whiskers', a term from the bygone era around which this book centres, refers to the small, coiled, fine wire that made electrical contact with the piece of galena crystal used in the wireless sets of the founding days of broadcasting early last century. By extension the cat's whiskers has come to mean 'excellent', the 'ultimate' or 'superlative'.

This book is about a period in the hundred years or so of radio's history when the medium was very much part and parcel of our lifestyle, the 'Golden Years' of the 1940s and 1950s in particular when radio serials, plays, comedy and audience participation shows dominated the airwaves on the broadcast band. Many personalities of the radio dial were raised, blossomed and praised during these years, becoming household names.

As radio stars are not enduring, I have touched but lightly on them in this narrative, preferring instead to cover other facets of radio communication, with emphasis on some of the behind-the-scenes people who played a prominent part in the saving and preserving of life at sea, on land and in the air, directly or indirectly through radio. In fact, it was the association I had with some of these unsung heroes during World War II that prompted me to write this book.

This is also the story of radio through my eyes, looking back on my 83 years; it is a testament to the wonderful people I have met and with whom I have worked. In what you will read I have aimed to recapture the wonder, innovation, innocence, love, humour, fear, bravery, camaraderie and general plethora of emotions and human endurance which dominated the era through which I have lived, and which radio, in its ultimately unique way, could represent to so many others.

And so over to the first Episode …

Bernard Harte

Episode 1

It wasn't wireless but it was still the cat's whiskers

It was called the Electrophone. Lauded by many as a revolution in the entertainment industry after its debut in 1899, the final year of the nineteenth century, it established a system of broadcasting mirth, music and monologues into homes in Victorian England more than twenty years before wireless ushered in a new phenomenon of broadcasting without wires.

The ingenious apparatus referred to above was actually a telephone with attachments of several headset receivers (earpieces) which enabled the telephone company subscribers to listen in to 'live' concerts and kindred entertainment coming to them direct from the stage of selected London theatres. This unique telephonic facility was provided by the Electrophone Company in conjunction with the National Telephone Company (now British Telecom) and channelled through the London and Bournemouth telephone exchanges.

To obtain the broadcasting service, telephone subscribers were charged an additional fee. There were two annual tariffs—£10 and £5. Subscribers who paid the higher fee were entitled to the loan of four headsets, plus a stand provided with hooks on which to hang the headsets when not in use and a choice of several concert programmes. The more modest fee of £5 restricted subscribers to the loan of two headsets, which could be hung on hooks attached to the wall when not in use. There was no choice of programmes.

The stand, often an elegant piece of furniture, was fitted with a mouthpiece (transmitter) of the type used in ordinary telephones of that time. This enabled subscribers to converse with the operator at the exchange, who would sometimes give her recommendation on the most suitable show of the week before making the connection.

To cover a stage show, a telephone mouthpiece (transmitter)—yet to be called a microphone—would be placed on the floor of the stage among the footlights. As it would have been several metres away from the performers and was of very low sensitivity, the efforts of the vocalists and instrumentalists would have been only just within the device's pick-up range.

The success of this revolution or, more correctly, evolution, in the presentation of entertainment must have been incredible—almost unbelievable—in those times. Certainly enough to cause quite a ripple among the artistically inclined gentry during the final and somewhat dull years of the reign of the ailing Queen Victoria. Indeed, listening to entertainment of an acceptable level via the Electrophone gave a good reason for the holding of social gatherings in many stately homes and hotels in England. On such occasions listeners would dress appropriately to give themselves the feeling of being part of the audience in the theatre.

The fact that several earpieces were tied together in parallel or some other bridging method for group listening would have resulted in a further diminution of the level of sound, making it rather difficult to catch every word, every note. Because the vacuum tube—or thermionic valve, as it was originally called—would not be invented until 1904 or improved until 1906, the only way of amplifying the minute electrical currents passing along telephone wires, to turn them into sound waves, was by magnetic means. This was in the form of a step-up transformer, which had its limitations. The situation was much improved when British scientist Sir John Ambrose Fleming invented the vacuum tube.

This device consisted of a filament and plate (also called an anode) encased in a glass tube. Acting as a diode or rectifier, it changed alternating current to direct current in the same manner as the crystal detector used in early wireless receiving sets. Two years after Fleming's invention, American Professor Lee de Forest modified the diode by placing a grid between the filament and anode in the form of a wire mesh which was activated by a small voltage. The effect was to increase the number of electrons reaching the anode through a regulator (the grid).

As there were now three elements in the vacuum tube, it was given the name triode (though sometimes referred to as an audion). A combination of the triode and a capacitor (condenser) greatly increased the strength of the weak signals reaching the wireless receiving set and also the sound level of the telephone—so necessary in long-distance communication.

These two inventions opened the door for the introduction of wireless broadcasting, and earned for Lee de Forest the title of 'Father of Radio (Wireless)'.

To return to the Electrophone. In 1911 the British Post Office bought out the Electrophone Company when it took over the telephone system and continued to provide this facility, which by then included concerts, solo items and church services.

The quality of sound reaching the home listener would have been a mere token of the original voice or instrument, due mainly to the limited fidelity of the telephone mouthpiece. Yet, in spite of the Electrophone's shortcomings, this on-line broadcasting service continued to bring a great deal of joy to subscribers until about 1922. By this time, wireless broadcasting was making a big impact in Britain. In 1925, the Post Office decided to terminate Electrophone broadcasting in the London area, but continued to supply the service through the Bournemouth exchange until the 1930s.

Even before Electrophone broadcasting was introduced in England in 1899, a similar type of service had functioned for a brief period in Hungary. Strangely, the Hungarian government failed to grasp the unique and important significance of the telephone as an instant means of communication, seeing it primarily as a system to convey music along telephone wires.

Eventually Hungary and other European countries got the message, and so the use of this instrument for person-to-person between homes, factories and offices soon became a priority.

From the time the telephone was first demonstrated in Boston in 1876 by Scottish-born inventor Professor Alexander Graham Bell, the United States had led the world in its acceptance as a utility. By the year 1887 there were more than 150,000 subscribers in that country, while the whole of Europe and Great Britain between them could muster a total of only 97,000 users.

The first telephone instrument employed the same type of earpiece (receiver) as the mouthpiece (transmitter), consisting of a coil of wire wrapped around the pole of a magnet with an iron diaphragm. When the sound wave from the speaker's voice—in the form of pressure—hit the diaphragm, it caused it to vibrate. In doing so, the magnetic flux created by the magnet varied in sympathy, causing a minute current to flow. This flow of current caused the magnet at the other end of the line to vary in flux, thus causing the diaphragm to vibrate, emitting an audible sound. In 1877, a year after Bell's invention of the telephone, another inventor, Thomas Edison, sought to improve the device with the use of carbon granules. Before long, the magnetic mouthpiece was replaced by a mouthpiece using carbon granules. But more on that subject in

Episode 18 on the microphones used in early wireless broadcasting and recording.

Less than two years after the invention of the telephone a few Australian experimenters were making their own instruments, using the publication *Scientific American* of 6 October 1877 as a guide, the issue in which Bell published details of his invention.

Alfred Biggs, an amateur astronomer and former school teacher, was credited with making the first telephone in Australia at Campbell in Tasmania. Hot on Biggs' experimental heels was William Thomas of Geelong in Victoria. The success of their experiments, and of other endeavours in this field of science, was certainly an extraordinary accomplishment in a mostly rural country at a time when initiative and improvisation were the mothers of invention.

Two years after the world's first telephone exchange opened in New Haven, Connecticut, in the United States in 1878, the Melbourne exchange began operating. Two months later, Brisbane exchange opened, followed by Sydney in 1881.

Marconi and his wireless

Guglielmo Marconi did not invent wireless. It was an existing phenomenon, embraced in the theory and discovery of electromagnetic induction, following experiments in the early years of the nineteenth century by British physicist Michael Faraday, and later by an American, Professor Joseph Henry of Princeton University.

Working separately with electromagnets, Marconi and Faraday noticed that when an electric current passes through a metal conductor it induces a current in an adjacent unconnected conductor. This revelation became known as the Induction Theory. In 1864, another British physicist, James Maxwell, took the theory a stage further by suggesting the existence of electromagnetic waves. A German physicist, Heinrich Hertz, proved Maxwell's theory to be correct. Fascinated by the discovery of electromagnetic waves (now referred to as Hertzian waves), the Italian-born scientist Marconi conceived the idea of utilising this medium as a vehicle to convey intelligence from one conductor to another conductor at a considerable distance.

In the year 1894, using an electric spark generator invented by Hertz, and an invention by French physicist Edouard Branly, called a coherer, as a receiver—to which he attached an electric bell—Marconi converted Hertzian waves into an electric current, causing the bell to ring. The sensation created by Hertzian waves was given the name 'wireless'.

Incidentally, a somewhat belated recognition of the achievements of the eminent scientist Hertz was made in the 1950s, when frequencies hitherto referred to as 'cycles' were renamed 'hertz'. Thus a kilocycle (being 1000 cycles) became a kilohertz, megacycles became megahertz, and so on.

Just one year after his successful experiment, Marconi transmitted a Morse code signal over a distance of 1.5 kilometres using an electric telegraph unit—the invention of two British scientists, William Cooke and Charles Wheatstone, thus fulfilling his ambition of using wireless as a new means of communication. Now 21 years old and still living with his parents in the Italian town of Pentecchio, near Bologna, Marconi continued to experiment and modify his findings, gradually extending the range of transmission and reception with the use of an aerial wire at both ends, communicating by Morse code. He also discovered wireless waves would travel over a hill.

Now convinced of the practical application of his discoveries in communication without wires, he sought the interest of the Italian government—to no avail.

In 1896 Marconi travelled to England to seek British backing to enable him to further develop and demonstrate his wireless system. He had a strong affinity with Britain through his mother who, before her marriage to well-to-do Italian Guiseppe Marconi, was a Jameson of the well-known Jameson Irish whiskey family.

Through his mother's influence, young Guglielmo obtained an introduction to the chief engineer of the British Post Office, William Preece. Preece and his telegraphic officials of the Post Office gave cautious endorsement to Marconi's achievements, keeping in mind, no doubt, that communication without wires could spell doom for the accepted landline telegraphy system. In that year, 1896, Marconi was granted the world's first wireless telegraphy patent. The registration of his own company, Wireless Telegraph and Signal Company, followed. This name was soon changed to the Marconi Wireless Telegraph Company.

Now well aware of the importance placed on the use of an aerial wire of suitable length and height to achieve long-distance communication, he returned to his native Italy in 1897, keen to endeavour once again to capture the interest of the government in the worldwide application of this wire-less form of communication. In 1899 Marconi established the first link by wireless between Dover in England and the French town of Wimereux, near Boulogne. Although this communication across the Channel was almost line-of-sight, a further demonstration some months later proved line-of-sight was not a prerequisite for successful transmission and reception—at least, not on the particular wavelength being used. In other words, wireless waves could travel up hill, over hill and through certain objects.

Emboldened by the success of his demonstration, Marconi embarked on a more dramatic ambition—to send a Morse code message over a long distance—persisting in spite of a shortage of funds and a wavering acceptance by some officials. Operating a crude receiving set in a room at an abandoned military hospital at St John's, Newfoundland, on 12 December 1901, Marconi and his assistant George Kemp picked up a faint signal—three dots of Morse code, making the letter S, transmitted across more than 3000 kilometres of ocean from Poldhu in England. Thus, transatlantic communication by wireless had proven to be feasible, leaving even longer distances to be conquered.

When he was informed of the transatlantic 'crossing' Marconi's rival, Thomas Edison, said that until he received more details he could not believe the report. The president of the Commercial Cable Company of America, whose company stood to lose the most if Marconi's invention were successful, declared his company would continue constructing new cables 'as though wireless messages were never heard of'.

In 1903 this new form of communication without the use of wires was well tested in an exercise between British Army Corps headquarters at Aldershot, south-west of London, and Royal Navy ships of the Channel Squadron. The exercise was a success, pointing the way to the advantageous use of wireless when waging war.

Across the Atlantic, the US press made a big thing of this new medium. In 1907, the Marconi Company established a transatlantic Morse code service with a dispatch to the *New York Times* carrying greetings from eminent men of the day, including the Duke of Argyle and Privy Councillor Lord Avebury. Messages originated in London, where they were transmitted to Ireland, on to Cape Breton in Nova Scotia, then by landline telegraphy to New York. The curtain-raiser to the establishment of this service was an exchange of greetings by wireless between President Theodore Roosevelt, then at Cape Cod on the Atlantic coast, and King Edward VII in Britain.

By now Marconi was pursuing a far more ambitious project; he dreamed of providing an Imperial chain of wireless stations to circle the globe, with transmitter/receivers strategically placed in countries of the British Empire, powerful relay stations placed about 2500 kilometres apart. He had already demonstrated to the British Government that such suitably positioned stations could reach more than 5000 kilometres during daylight and even longer distances at night, over water.

The British Post Office put a brake on the proposal for a few years while the possible effect on the cable service, and the practicability of such a revolutionary scheme, were considered. In 1913, approval was given to the Marconi Company to proceed with the project, but the agreement was cancelled a year later when Britain and her colonies declared war on

Germany. The installation of stations in England, Egypt and India had already begun, however.

In the event, it was just as well the scheme envisaged by Marconi was not put into service, as a more effective system of wireless communication was evolved after the end of World War I. This involved the use of short wavelengths in lieu of the longer wavelengths presently being used. Whereas long wavelengths tend to follow the surface of the earth, with a limited coverage, short wavelengths use an ionised layer around the globe, from which they are refracted, to gain an enormous distance. This fledgling communication system was put to use during the 1914–18 war, operating from warships and land bases—including Gallipoli in 1915. Wireless telegraphy had already been installed in some merchant ships.

Perhaps the most dramatic use of wireless occurred at 5.30 in the morning of 11 November 1918, when news of the proposed Armistice was transmitted from a small wireless telegraph unit located in the Eiffel Tower in Paris. The Allied Armies were instructed to continue in combat until the scheduled time of 11 am. Incidentally, one of the last salvos in that war was fired from a long-range battery under the command of an American officer called Harry Truman, who was to take office as the President of the United States toward the end of World War II, following the death of Franklin D. Roosevelt.

At the time that Marconi's successful demonstration of long-distance communication by wireless had captured the interest and imagination of governments and experimenters on both sides of the Atlantic, research had already begun in Australia. In 1897, Professor William Bragg of the Adelaide University gave a public demonstration of Marconi's Wireless. In 1899, the Chief Engineer of Telegraphs in New South Wales, P.B. Walker, transmitted a signal from one end of the Sydney GPO to the other, using a crude spark transmitter.

In Melbourne, another Government telegraph official, Walter Jenvey, constructed his own equipment which was 'aired' to the public when he transmitted from Bluff Head near Elwood, so located that he could make wireless contact with HMS *St George*—one of two escort cruisers accompanying the Royal Yacht HMS *Ophir*, carrying the Duke and Duchess of York to Melbourne to officially open Australia's first Commonwealth Parliament in May 1901. The other escort vessel was HMS *Juno*.

Wireless contact was made and a message of greeting passed on to the Duke and Duchess in the Royal Yacht by semaphore as she steamed into Port Phillip Bay to her Melbourne berth. This was an historic moment in Australian history, not only for the celebrations of Federation about to commence, but also because it marked the first wireless contact from shore to ship. (Melbourne's Parliament House contained both Federal and Victorian State Parliaments until 1927, when Canberra became the permanent location of the Federal Government.)

The first governmental interest in Marconi's achievements was shown in the Commonwealth Parliament later in 1901, when the possibility of linking Tasmania with Victoria by this means was raised. Frequent breakdowns in the cable service across Bass Strait were giving good cause to seek an alternative system. However, the reliability of wireless had yet to be proved to official satisfaction.

The Marconi Company was quick to submit a proposal to set up a wireless telegraph station in Tasmania, and another in Victoria, to provide Morse code communication across Bass Strait, without any funding obligation by the Commonwealth. This proposal followed several other approaches by the Marconi Company (one of which was to bridge the Tasman). But the Government, on the advice of the British Post Office, was now antagonistic to the inroads wireless was making at the possible expense of the established landline telegraphy, and rejected all proposals. A *Wireless Telegraphy Act* was passed in 1905, to give the Commonwealth Government complete control of the transmission and reception of wireless telegraphy.

With the speed of light ... and bike

Undeterred by such obstructionism, the Marconi Company continued to submit wireless proposals until 1906, when the Commonwealth Government gave approval for the erection of a demonstration station at Queenscliff in Victoria and another at Devonport in Tasmania.

On 12 May in that year the *Melbourne Argus* newspaper reported:

Queenscliffe was the scene of a technological sensation when the first official wireless message was sent 215 miles across the sea to Tasmania.

More than 200 guests gathered at the top of the hill beside the sea to attend the opening ceremony of the first Marconi Company wireless telegraph station. The Governor-General, Lord Northcote, had the honour of sending the first message, addressed to the Governor of Tasmania, Sir Gerald Strickland, declaring: 'The Commonwealth greets Tasmania and rejoices at the establishment of a means of uniting the people of Australia more closely together.'

This is how the *Argus* scribe explained how this method of communication worked:

> The operator tapped off the message in Morse alphabet, each tap being followed by the fierce crackling of the electric sparks in this little powerhouse. He operated at about 15 words a minute ... On the other side of Bass Strait, an operator received Lord Northcote's message. He wrote it out, and gave it to a boy on a bicycle. The boy scorched to a ferry and gave it to a boatman. The boatman rowed across the stream, and handed it to a telegraph office. Thence it was sent by telegraph to Hobart. Sir Gerald's answer came by the same route.

Official speeches ended with a forecast by the Prime Minister, Alfred Deakin, of the prospect of subduing distance in the future by 'enlisting the waves of the ether'.

Notwithstanding the success of this historic demonstration of using wireless, for the first time, for a commercial purpose, the Commonwealth Government did not renew the temporary licence given to the Marconi Company to establish the service; thus the underwater cable service was given a reprieve.

Episode 3

The government gets the message

Although the various Australian governments suffered from bureaucratic tardiness in recognising the enormous potential wireless offered for instant communication in times of war and peace, some Government members— after hearing of successful experiments and observing the outcome of several ventures in this field during visits to England—urged Parliament to take this fledgling medium under the Commonwealth's wing and push ahead with the establishment of ship-to-shore wireless links.

The enthusiasm described above led to the passing of the *Wireless Telegraph Act* of 1905. The Act gave the Postmaster-General's Department absolute control over the transmission and reception of all telegraphic messages— with the exception of those emanating from ships of the Royal Australian Navy. Under these proclaimed regulations the Postmaster-General was also given the responsibility for national wireless experiments, as a counter to the so-called 'proliferation' of unharnessed amateur and professional research.

Notwithstanding the fact the Marconi Company had failed to persuade the Government to replace the temporary licence for the Bass Strait experiment with a permanent one, the successful demonstration stimulated sufficient interest for the Federal Government to set aside £10,000 to be directed to wireless research.

At this stage Australia was but a small link within the British Empire, not a country ready and able to stand alone without worrying about being frowned on or directed by the 'Mother Country'. The British Post Office—

which was now actively keeping Marconi and his wireless at bay for fear of destroying its lucrative landline and cable telegraphic service—still had a strong influence on its Australian counterpart. This subservient attitude changed somewhat in the year 1909, following a conference in Melbourne to consider the use of wireless telegraphy in the Pacific region, close to Australia.

The Royal Australian Navy, born out of Federation, was now equipping its ships with wireless. Some merchant ships plying the Australian coastline were also carrying transmitter/receivers—but these could only be put to use from ship to ship, not ship to shore, as Australia had no official land-based wireless telegraphic stations.

Before long, however, a practical example of the need for emergency communication by wireless precipitated the Federal Government into a decision to establish land-based stations. This was the disappearance without trace of the steamship *Waratah*, en route from England to Australia. Two hundred lives were lost. The outcome of this tragedy was a decision by the Government to set up two powerful wireless stations, one on the east coast of Australia to cover the Tasman Sea and Pacific Ocean, the other on the west coast to cover the Indian Ocean.

Accordingly, tenders were called for the manufacture and installation of a wireless station at Pennant Hills on the outskirts of Sydney, the other at Applecross, near Fremantle in Western Australia, these sites being chosen by the Navy for strategic reasons.

The successful tenderer from five submissions was the Australasian Wireless Company of Sydney, headed by the German electrical engineer Walther Staerker. This firm had recently acquired the representation of the German Telefunken Company for Australia and New Zealand. The Marconi Company's tender price—the highest of the five bids—was £19,000 ($38,000). The Australasian Wireless Company's submission was a mere £4,150 ($8,300) per station.

This contract gave Telefunken a strong foothold in Australia, with a determination to keep the Marconi Company out of the communication picture.

Wireless war

The scene was now set for a dot-and-dash feud between the Australasian Wireless Company and the Marconi Company, in which the Australian Government was unwittingly involved. Marconi-equipped ship's wireless operators refused to handle messages from Telefunken-equipped ships. Apart from that, the Marconi Company sued the Australian Government over infringement of some of its many patents through the use of Telefunken equipment being installed at the two stations under construction.

The Marconi Company had already obtained judgment against a British company for infringement of patents; now the Australian Government was in the firing line. With this in mind, as soon as he took office in 1910 Labor leader Andrew Fisher decided to appoint a 'wireless expert' who was to be responsible to the Postmaster-General in all matters concerning wireless. The appointment went to a young Queensland electrical engineer and part-time scientist, John Graeme Balsillie, who had just returned to Australia after his involvement in the installation of wireless stations in Russia and China, following similar work in Britain.

Also at this time, a new Australian company was founded by an ex-PMG telegraphist who had entered the priesthood—Father Shaw. With the blessing of the Government, Father Shaw set up an experimental station and workshop in the Sydney suburb of Randwick. This led to the formation of his own manufacturing firm, Maritime Wireless, with the aim of providing wireless equipment for ships and for the network of coastal stations to be built as soon as Pennant Hills and Applecross were under way.

In the same year a young Marconi ship's wireless operator from the merchant ship *Otranto* stepped ashore at Sydney's Circular Quay. The operator was Ernest Thomas Fisk. Concerned at the dominance of the Telefunken company in the Australian communication field, he returned to Australia the following year, carrying his appointment of resident Marconi engineer. Fisk was destined to play a leading role in the development and acceptance of this branch of science as the principal vehicle for the conveyance of long- and short-distance communication and entertainment for the next 35 years.

Before the close of 1910, the Australasian Wireless Company had installed Telefunken equipment in three merchant ships of the Huddart Parker Line—*Riverina, Ultimaroa* and *Zealandia*. A few other local shipping companies were in the process of installing Marconi equipment. To communicate with Telefunken-equipped ships, Australasian Wireless set up a base station at the company's Sydney headquarters in Underwood Street. Some months later an improved site was obtained atop the Australia Hotel, using the call sign AAA. This was the first land-based station in Australia to carry commercial messages. The station was shut down as soon as Pennant Hills and Applecross began operating.

On his return to Australia in 1911 as the Government's appointed wireless expert, John Balsillie wasted no time in getting on with the job. A great deal of apprehension arose among the staff of the Marconi Company, Telefunken and several other overseas companies when it became known Balsillie was promoting spark equipment of his own design—known as the Balsillie System—to be installed in all coastal wireless stations. This news 'sparked' off a series of writs for patent infringements, which failed to immediately quench Balsillie's aspirations. As Government-appointed engineer, he quickly brought coastal stations at Melbourne, Brisbane and Hobart into service with equipment manufactured at Father Shaw's workshop.

After several delays occasioned by skirmishes between the Government and the contractor, Pennant Hills and Applecross were readied for a 1912 opening. The first to be completed, Pennant Hills, using Telefunken equipment, was allotted the call sign POS (later changed to VIS). The station was brought into service on 19 August 1912, followed by Applecross on 30 September, with the call sign POP (later changed to VIP).

The year 1912 was a momentous one for many reasons. In April 1912 the greatest seafaring disaster of all time occurred when the British luxury liner *Titanic* struck an iceberg on its maiden voyage from Southampton to New York, with the loss of 1517 lives. The fact that 712 people were saved as the ship quickly went to the bottom was undoubtedly attributable to the fact it carried wireless. The distress signal was picked up by several American amateur wireless operators, but more importantly by the operator aboard the *Carpathia,* which was some 100 kilometres away. Steaming in pitch darkness through seas studded with ice floes, the *Carpathia* reached the survivors some four hours later.

Ironically, another ship within visual distance of the doomed liner carried wireless, but the only operator was off duty and fast asleep. Officers of this ship had sighted the lights of *Titanic* in the distance, but when they disappeared from view had assumed the ship had moved over the horizon.

This tragedy put the spotlight on wireless as an emergency service. An international conference on Safety of Life at Sea, held in London in January 1914, made it mandatory for merchant ships carrying 50 or more persons to be fitted with wireless. (Sadly, many poorer nations even now do not enforce this regulation, and tragedies at sea still occur with dozens of lives lost.) About the same time, Marconi was working on the development of an auto-alarm system which would ring a bell on the bridge if a distress call was received when there was no operator on duty. Successful tests led to this system being adopted.

A distant relative of mine took passage on the *Titanic* and went down with the ship. A man of the cloth, he was travelling to Canada to join his brother in the spiritual field. Many years ago my mother told me he gathered several passengers and had them singing hymns as they were about to be engulfed by the Atlantic. His name was Byles (my grandfather Maynard's mother was a Byles). My wife and I called on one of his cousins, Marie Byles, when she was living in the Sydney suburb of Epping. A keen bushwalker, she was New South Wales' first female solicitor. Marie died in the 1970s after suffering head injuries when attacked by an intruder.

Every year of the first three decades of the twentieth century provided almost bewildering technological advances in the development of wireless and its kindred avenue of communication, the telephone. In 1912 the first public automatic exchange in Australia was brought into service—at Geelong, near Melbourne.

A change of name, no less

Although the new medium of communication without the use of wires was suitably called wireless from the time of Marconi's early experiments in England, in 1912 the US Navy decided the term was too inclusive and adopted the term 'radiotelegraph' to refer to the transmission of Morse code telegraphy from ship to ship and from ship to shore.

When the transmission of telephony began, the term 'radiotelephony' was used for a while in the United States and Britain, but soon gave way to the Navy term. 'Telegraphy' and 'telephony' also bowed out, giving way to 'radio'. The US Navy also originated the term 'broadcasting', as applied to this electromagnetic medium, stemming from the one message sent by the Admiral to all ships of the fleet. In other words, he 'broadcast' the one instruction in one fell swoop, as it were.

As for the good old term 'wireless', the British remained resolute that the word was here to stay, refusing to allow 'radio' into the communication vocabulary until well into the 1930s. In fact, the Admiralty *Handbook of Wireless Telegraphy* continued to give 'radio' the cold shoulder in its print run of 1939. However, the entry of the United States into World War II in December 1941 soon brought the British, and the Australians, into line, and thus 'radio' was universally adopted.

The political turbulence in Europe which was to culminate in the outbreak of World War I in 1914 had the Federal Government very concerned at the vulnerability of Australia, and greater emphasis was given to communication by wireless and cable. By the end of 1912 a network of wireless stations along the Australian coastline and on some nearby islands had been established. Apart from the interchange of messages, the stations were also used to send out weather reports and provide a news service for passengers at sea.

Some teething problems occurred, however. During the installation and testing of the Applecross station by the German engineers of the Telefunken Company, several problems had arisen. The contract stipulated that communication had to be made with Pennant Hills in daylight on a wavelength of 3000 metres to a ship 830 kilometres out to sea. The tests were not satisfactory due to an insufficiently sensitive receiving set.

Murray Johnson's story

It was left to a young Australian recently recruited by the Australasian Wireless Company to solve the problem. He was Murray Johnson, who worked on the installation with one of the German engineers, Mowens. Murray soon found out that the German-made receivers lacked sufficient sensitivity because of the detector used. Wasting no time, he made up a galena detector of the type used extensively in those days by Australian amateur wireless operators. It did the job! For the next 40 years Murray Johnson's history was really the history of radio in Australia, as his engineering accomplishments embraced every facet of telecommunication.

I met Murray during his twilight years when he was living with his family at Yarras on the Hastings River, near Port Macquarie where I was living at the time. Over a cuppa or two he told me a little of his long association with and accomplishments in the industry of radio, which I recorded on tape and published in the *Port Macquarie News* to preserve them for posterity. At the time I called, Murray was writing his autobiography for the eyes of his family, which he decided to call *G . Pop—My Life and Work*. With the permission of his family, I have included extracts from his writings in this volume.

Murray's involvement in the intricacies of wireless, as it was in 1910 —the year he entered the industry—until his retirement in 1962 was a far cry from the prospects of his early years as a boy at Hastings Park, near Wauchope, at the time when most country lads were destined to take their place behind their father's plough or to become bush workers.

Born at Coopernook in 1889, Murray spent his early days at Hastings Park and Wauchope. He was a six-year-old schoolboy when in 1895 the world learnt of the successful experiments with Hertzian waves by the 21-year-old scientist Guglielmo Marconi. Far too young to fully grasp the significance of that historic event, only a few years later Murray was destined to participate in another of Marconi's experiments.

They were halcyon Mark Twain days for a lad living in the bush with his friends, his animals and his favourite pets to keep him company. When Murray was eight years old, the Johnson family moved to Wauchope to be closer to the sawmill his father operated. The sudden death of his father in 1901 put the boy on a new path in pursuit of a career, however. It came about shortly after his mother sold the mill to merchant and shipper Nicholas Cain, and took her children to Sydney.

At the age of fourteen, Murray obtained work in a sawmill in Sydney tending the boilers. His job was to keep the steam up to operate the mill machine which in turn operated the saw benches. There was no electricity laid on at the time. Two years later, he became apprenticed to the engineering firm of Morris Bros. It was here that Murray put his foot on the first rung of the ladder to an engineering career. Filled with ambition, he commenced a diploma course in mechanical and electrical engineering at Ultimo Technical College, located just around the corner from Morris Bros, almost alongside the Grace Bros building in Broadway.

One of the lecturers took a personal interest in Murray's progress and one day asked if he would like to join the newly formed Australasian Wireless Company, which had just won the contract with the Australian Government to build the Pennant Hills and Applecross wireless stations; there was a position vacant. Young Johnson got the job as junior engineer and was immediately despatched to Pennant Hills to install the power supply unit. Before the station began operating, two buildings to house equipment and six cottages for families of employees had been built, and a 122 metre lattice steel tower erected.

This complex was the beginning of the Pennant Hills Radio Centre, which was to be the hub of wireless communication with ships at sea and the Pacific Islands in the early 1930s and later the location of a short-wave transmitter sending programmes overseas, using the call sign VK2ME. The first radio-telephone transmitter was also housed here. Sadly, little historical evidence remains at Pennant Hills to let future generations learn of the activities of this very busy, very important centre of early wireless communication.

From Pennant Hills, Murray went across to Applecross in 1911 to work on the installation of Telefunken equipment. With no thermionic valves in use at this stage, transmission was by brute force through a spark coil on the selected long-wave frequency. Transmission coverage was no problem but those insensitive receivers were. That's when Murray improvised. In the small mining town of Northampton, near Geraldton, he obtained some galena crystal. Mounting an insulator on a breadboard, he attached to it a copper spring to which he secured an ordinary darning needle. The point of the needle held its tension by the copper spring, pressed onto the galena crystal which was held in position by an ordinary china cup. With this haywire device, Murray maintained contact with ships at sea and with Pennant Hills without any difficulty. Eventually a detector (receiver) manufactured to Murray's specifications was sent from Sydney.

This successful experiment was eventually given mention in the archives of the Telefunken Company in Germany in a publication issued after the end of the 1914–18 war. More recently it was mentioned in a book compiled by Dr Desmond Thackeray, who wrote to Murray to inform him that the publication of the details of his detector clearly established his right to a place in history books.

Recreation for the installation staff at Applecross wasn't all beer and skittles—except occasionally. Fired with a few too many beers, the Norwegian rigger and the German mast engineer often traded hot words. This is Murray's description of one particular incident:

It was 1911. In the evening I would probably go to the open-air pictures, then meet Schubert (the German) and Neilson (Norwegian) about 11 pm on the last boat to Applecross. By this time, they were usually under the weather. On one particular evening I had great difficulty in getting them past the hotel at Applecross. We had about two miles to walk and when we reached a junction in the road, they wanted to turn the wrong way—back to Perth. Neilson spoke fluent German and he and Schubert talked constantly. They commenced to quarrel and Schubert had Neilson on the ground. Neilson was saying in English—'Shoot me, shoot me!' They finally decided that they would have a duel when we reached the station. I was hopeful that it would all blow over by that time. However they both brought out revolvers as soon as we arrived back at the station and I could see they were quite serious. For a time I was completely at a loss to know what to do. I then suggested that as they hadn't used their revolvers for some time, they should have some practice, to which they agreed. I drew a large circle in the sand and placed a lighted candle in the centre, at which they had to fire from about ten feet [3 m]. They took it in turn, shot for shot, but the candle burned steadily. At last Schubert ran out of ammunition, as I hoped he would. 'Bloody Australians!' he growled, knocking me over, and staggered into his room, slamming the door. We didn't see him again until well into the next day. Quite sober, I doubt if he had any memory of the previous night's events. Neilson appeared quite happy to forget. He had been a ship's Captain but lost his job due to drink. He was a most likeable man and normally was good company.

The Morse code alphabet

A •—   B —•••   C —•—•   D —••   E •

F ••—•   G ——•   H ••••   I ••   J •———

K —•—   L •—••   M —•   N —•   O ———

P •——•   Q ——•—   R •—•   S •••   T —

U ••—   V •••—   W •——   X —••—

Y —•——   Z ——••

1 •————   2 ••———   3 •••——   4 ••••—

5 •••••   6 —••••   7 ——•••   8 ———••

9 ————•   10 —————

Full stop •• •• ••   Comma •— •— •—

Episode 4

A dreadful story

In the last episode I made brief mention of my grandfather, Lewis Maynard, in referring to the Titanic disaster of 1912. I know I should be continuing the story of radio with unbroken continuity but I have to admit that my mind is inclined to wander off the track now and again, which could be understandable at my age of eighty-odd.

Mention of grandfather Maynard sent my thoughts back to the 1920s and the long association my family had with the Queensland city of Bundaberg and district until one horrific day in 1928, when Grandfather brought shame on the family, causing all six of his Bundaberg-born offspring to shun that beautiful city, never to return.

At 4 o'clock in the afternoon of 4 February 1928, Lewis Maynard murdered his wife, Alice Maud, by gunshot and then turned the gun on himself, dying some two minutes later.

Alice Maud was his second wife. His first wife died in 1915 from natural causes—or so it was deemed at the time. My father Thomas Harte, my mother Emily (nee Maynard), my sister Muriel and I were living in the Brisbane suburb of Toowong at the time of this calamity. I was then ten years old. Hidden away under our wooden-piered house at my workbench one Sunday, I was tinkering with my crystal wireless set when the phone rang. The sound of copious weeping overhead sent me for a walk down to the Toowong village. And there it was, splashed across the poster of the *Truth* newspaper—news of my grandfather's misdeed the previous day.

Feeling very mortified, I went home to a doleful mother and father, but I didn't reveal that I was fully aware of what had happened. Not a word was said to me. Not a word was said by me, pointing to a lack of family communication and sharing. I mention this as a typical example of parental attitude in those Edwardian days. 'Hide it under the bed and don't bring it out.' The non-discussion of sex was another example.

Some 60 years later, when my mother was in her ninety-second year, we got around to talking about Grandfather and a little about his life and sudden departure. I mentioned that I knew all about it at the time it happened.

'Good Lord!' exclaimed my mother. 'I had no idea you knew about his dramatic ending all these years, Bernard. You should have mentioned it!'

'Perhaps *you* should have mentioned it, Mother', I retorted.

Lewis Holden Maynard was born at Bradford in Yorkshire, England on 6 August 1860. At Bradford he was engaged in the family's wool milling interest as an engineer. It seems he got too friendly, in fact a good bit too friendly, with one of the female employees for his parents' liking. So they despatched him to the Australian colonies with the sole object of defusing their son's strong attraction to the young lady. To make sure he didn't hurry back home, he was provided with a reasonable remittance.

In the Burnett district, near Bundaberg, he acquired several properties of modest dimensions, which pleased his mother and father greatly. They saw their son following a righteous path as a gentleman farmer and marrying an Australian girl in 1885. His young wife produced the first of their seven children in 1886 while he was turning out a good crop of tobacco, maize and pumpkins. The third-born died in 1891 as a result of a snake bite.

Soon, deeply engrossed in local affairs, he became a prominent member of the local chapter of the Masonic Lodge and an alderman of the Bundaberg Council, serving as Mayor in 1912 and in 1914. He was eventually defeated in Council because of his stand over yellow fever. In the presence of strong evidence that mosquitoes were bringing the disease into the district via ships berthing at Bundaberg port wharves, he advocated a campaign of mosquito eradication, but his fellow aldermen gave the expenditure the thumbs down in the 'interest' of ratepayers. Thereafter he stood apart from civic life, devoting much of his energies to the School of Arts, the Technical College and the local museum, to which he was a large contributor, as he was to the Queensland Museum in Brisbane. He also gave encouragement and assistance to a youth who was to become Bundaberg's favourite son, the pioneer aviator Bert Hinkler, who began his career flying home-made gliders off the local sandhills.

Recalling her father's association with young Bert (he was born in 1892), my mother told me she could still 'see' her father walking up the gangplank of the ship about to depart Bundaberg for Brisbane, holding

Bert's hand: 'Bert was not only nervous about the boat trip. He looked most uncomfortable. He was wearing a brand new pair of boots. Father had just bought them for him. I don't think he had ever worn footwear before. His feet must have been very sore as he wasn't wearing socks.'

Although Grandfather brought in a few innovations in rural production in the Burnett district, including the introduction of the first Jersey dairy stock, 'Sir Kenmore' and 'Lady Norman', his heart and soul lay in the industrial arena. This gave him scope to give a good account of his training in the engineering field in the woollen mills 'back home'.

One of his accomplishments was to bring the first electric lamp to Bundaberg, worked by three bichromate cells. This lamp was one of the exhibits of the School of Arts Museum for many years. Later, he assisted in providing electricity for the Millaquin, Quanaba and Doolbi sugar mills. As a keen amateur photographer, he exposed the first dry plate in Bundaberg in a darkroom rigged up in a spring cart which he and a few enthusiasts had driven up from Brisbane. One of them—already a professional photographer—was to become a son-in-law and my father, Birmingham, England-born Thomas Harte.

At the time I was knee-high to a grasshopper I was taken to his home on several occasions. I can still picture the entrance foyer of that two-storey dwelling. Alongside the bottom of the staircase leading up to the next floor stood an upright leather cylinder, about the size and shape of a golf bag, which housed an umbrella, a walking stick and a rapier—safely in its scabbard. I was nearly frightened to death one day when Grandfather suddenly pulled the weapon out of its sheath and with a dramatic gesture playfully lunged at me. Muttering something like, 'You've got to be quick to live, boy', he shoved it back in its housing, to my great relief.

At the top of the staircase, diagonally opposite the main bedroom, was his gun room. Although not much larger than a walk-in pantry, this room held a large collection of firearms, including a small gold-studded gun. It was to go to his youngest son Harold, according to his will. As the family was not represented at the auction of Grandfather's possessions, the true value of the gun was not recognised, so it went for a mere 30 shillings.

Guns and swords aside, there were two aspects of my grandfather's lifestyle which always brought a gleam to my eyes. One was the magnificent queen cakes he would turn out for me whenever I paid a visit to his kitchen. (He was then living alone.) The other was the Fry's chocolate bars he would hand out to his children and their offspring in Brisbane. In those days those mouth-watering chocolate delicacies were about 40 centimetres long—if I recall correctly—and sheathed in a purple coloured wrapper.

Absolutely scrumptious! Even today I have lingering gastronomic thoughts—pleasant thoughts—of Mr Fry and his chocolate bars, long after he merged his business with Mr Cadbury's company.

Although his involvement in the employment of 'blackbirded' Kanakas on sugar plantations has been a little clouded over, my grandfather did spend a year or so supervising these Pacific Islanders in the clearing of land, at the time that Bundaberg was earning an infamous reputation as the principal exchange in the use of this cheap labour. In March 1887 it was estimated there were some 3000 Kanakas in the district, many of whom were taken there from their island homes by intrigue.

Worthy of mention

Writing in the *Brisbane Daily Mail*, just three years before our subject's death, a columnist had this to say about him:

> And despite an affected cynicism, which has on occasion caused comment, and which is possibly the mask adopted by a man shy of showing his real sentiments, the warm great heart of the real man and his humanitarian spirit, finds an outlet in the Society for the Prevention of Cruelty, in which as honorary officer in Bundaberg, he has done good service in the protection of children and animals. Occasionally some of Mr Maynard's quaint cynical sayings have raised doubts as to his orthodoxy among the 'unco quid', but when one gets beyond the spoken word to the bedrock of deeds, one cannot fail to recognise that there is embodied in his life the spirit immortalised by the poet Coleridge when he wrote in his 'Rhyme of the Ancient Mariner':
>
> > He prayeth best, who loveth best
> > All things, both great and small;
> > For the Dear Lord, who loveth us,
> > He makes and loves them all.

In his regular column in the *Brisbane Courier-Mail* about some of the Bundaberg personalities he came across in the 1920s, well-known local journalist and historian Clem Lack found Grandfather offered plenty of ingredients for his column:

> In my boyhood days in Bundaberg a notable citizen was Lewis H. Maynard, who was an enthusiastic naturalist and a generous donor to the Queensland

Museum. In his Norfolk jacket, leggings and a curved Sherlock Holmes pipe he was a familiar figure riding his bicycle from Bourbong Street, down Barolin Street, to his two-storied home in South Bundaberg. His fruit trees were a standing temptation to small boys and were frequently raided He had a wonderful collection of historic curios and articles of various kinds, and also possessed probably the best collection of firearms in Australia. This collection, from blunderbusses, flintlocks and horse pistols, Brown Bess muskets of the type used at Waterloo, to the Sharps rifle of the American Civil War, and the Snider rifles, as used in forays with the aborigines in the Queensland frontier days, are installed in the Queensland Museum. Lewis Maynard was a former Mayor of Bundaberg.

All this praise of Lewis Maynard's humanitarian spirit begs the question: Why did he murder his wife? It's too late to unlock his mind. I can only pass on the facts.

The young lady he left behind at Bradford came out to Australia some years after his departure to take up the position of family housekeeper, a position he made available for her, essentially to assist his wife with her domestic chores and help with the upbringing of the children. His wife, my grandmother, died in 1915 after a short illness. I didn't have the opportunity of getting to know her as I wasn't born until 1918. Grandfather then married his housekeeper, much to the chagrin of his sons and daughters. Soon the lovey-dovey stuff went out the window, and after a few years of unhappy matrimony the lady decided it would be prudent to catch the next ship back home. Grandfather didn't waste time in instituting divorce proceedings, as it took more than three years in those days for a decree nisi to be made absolute. As it happened, just three weeks before the dissolution of the marriage would have become legal, the second Mrs Maynard turned up on his doorstep and threatened to take Grandfather and his family 'for a row'. At that moment he apparently decided to end the unhappy relationship, with the gun.

When my mother eventually opened up and spoke about this shocking event, she expressed her strong dislike for her stepmother. Always a gentle soul, her outburst surprised me: 'Bernard, in my long life, I've never hated anyone—except that person. When Mother was in bed ill, Father insisted this woman look after her, nurse her back to health. All that was wrong with Mother was asthma. She would have a bout of it now and again but soon got over it—until this woman took over. We knew nothing about syringes and injections in those days, but looking back over the years, I'm convinced that woman gradually poisoned Mother until she succumbed. We had already decided she was an evil person.'

I wanted to get a bit more out of my mother, but she clammed up, leaving me to wonder if perhaps Grandfather had found out the truth in my mother's allegations, precipitating the action he took. I fully intended to put this to her the next time we had a little chat, but alas! a few weeks later we lost her.

I just had to get this story off my chest.

And now, where was I before I went astray from more storytelling about wireless—I mean, radio? Ah yes! The development of Australian coastal wireless telegraphy stations leading up to the 1914–18 war.

Over to the next Episode!

Episode 5

The Tin Lizzie and the cowbell

One very hot night in Darwin, the night of 11 November 1918, a Tin Lizzie and a cowbell came together to ring out the joyous tidings to the citizens of this shanty town that the Great War had just ended, ushering in 'everlasting peace'.

The driver of the Tin Lizzie, only recently acquired, was Warrant Officer Murray Johnson RAN, officer in charge of the coastal wireless telegraphy station at Darwin. He was responding to instructions received in code from the Navy Office in Melbourne to advise all the citizens of Darwin that an Armistice had been signed.

So, just after midnight, Warrant Officer Murray Johnson and his wife Doris set sail in their Lizzie—officially referred to as a Model T Ford—to pass on the good tidings. As there were no wireless broadcasting stations yet available to spread the news, the sound of Lizzie's horn in concert with the cowbell vigorously rung by Doris as she stood precariously in the back of their trusty steed was music to the ears of every household in the town, and a welcome distraction from the hordes of dive-bombing mosquitoes. By 5 o'clock in the morning, Lizzie decided she had had enough for one night and came to a sudden halt, leaving the messengers of joy to get home by shanks's pony.

Discussing this incident from his long life when I visited him in his garden bush-house at Mount Pleasant near Wauchope just a few years before he left us, Murray told me of rummaging in his large tool box one day many years later and coming across the cowbell. He mentioned it to Philip Geeves, then the official archivist of Amalgamated Wireless Australasia (AWA). Phil, a close friend and colleague of mine, suggested he offer it to the National War Memorial. And that's where it reposes today, an interesting exhibit for those seeking knowledge of the early days of wireless in this country.

Apart from the responsibility of operating a coastal wireless station during the war years, Warrant Officer Johnson had two other problems to deal with. The first was to find permanent acceptable accommodation in a town almost bereft of such facilities except for those provided for government officials. Befriended by the local Methodist minister and his wife, the Rev. and Mrs Pratt, the Johnsons and their newborn baby moved into rooms at the parsonage until a government-built house was provided. They resided there until they left Darwin in 1920.

The second problem was the industrial unrest at Vestey Brothers' meat works. There were eighteen union strikes at the plant during the first twelve months the Johnsons were in Darwin. A British firm owning a huge area of the Northern Territory, Vestey's was mainly engaged in producing meat for export, processing about 500 bullocks each day; the meat was canned and shipped to the fighting troops. The numerous strikes affected the local population, causing shortages of red meat. When meat was available, it had to be eaten the same day it was killed, as there was no refrigeration available and few ice chests.

The wireless chain

By the time the telegraphy stations at Applecross and Pennant Hills officially came 'on the air' in 1912, construction and installation of a chain of lower-powered stations was proceeding apace. This arose from the decision by the Commonwealth Government in 1909 to establish stations at strategic points along the Australian coastline for the threefold purpose of providing commercial wireless traffic between ships plying the coast and shore stations, improving the safety of lives at sea, and monitoring traffic transmitted from islands in the Pacific and East Indies controlled by foreign powers. In particular, the Government viewed with growing alarm the activities of Germany's island possessions in waters north of Australia. They were turbulent times leading up to the first Great War.

As I mentioned earlier, the Government had decreed that wireless telegraphy was to be placed under the control of the Postmaster-General's Department, which was to be responsible not only for its administration but also the staffing and operation of each station. By the outbreak of war in 1914, the PMG's Department had 20 wireless telegraphy coastal stations functioning. Apart from the 25-kilowatt Telefunken-equipped stations at Pennant Hills and Applecross, the other stations—operating on a power of 5 kilowatts—were using Balsillie-designed transmitters, manufactured by Father Shaw's Maritime Wireless Company at Randwick. The main design advantage of the Balsillie unit was that one electrode of the spark gap was shaped like a nozzle. Air under pressure was blown through this nozzle in the direction of the other electrode. This eliminated the raucous spark gap, thereby producing a sharp, easy-to-copy Morse code signal. It was quite an innovation, compared to the characteristic brute-force system of transmission which preceded the use of thermionic valves.

In 1913 the intense rivalry between the Marconi Company and the German Telefunken Company's Australian outlet, Australasian Wireless, found an amicable solution, merging their interests in a new company, Amalgamated Wireless (Australasia) Limited. Settling those differences gave the new company exclusive rights throughout Australasia to the patents—present and future—of both Marconi and Telefunken.

The foundation chairman of the new company (AWA) was newspaper magnate Sir Hugh Denison. The Marconi Company's representative in Australia, Ernest Fisk, was also appointed to the board and engaged as general and technical manager. The Marconi Company held half the shares, and the Commonwealth Government and Telefunken were the other major shareholders. On the outbreak of World War I Telefunken lost its shares. William Morris ('Billy') Hughes, who championed the development of wireless from its very beginning, represented the Commonwealth Government on the board for many years.

When Murray Johnson, in the employ of the Australasian Wireless Company, completed his work on the installation of the station at Applecross, he was offered a position by the PMG's Department as a wireless operator/installer for the coastal network, which he accepted. Early in 1913 he was sent to Geraldton, about 500 kilometres north of Perth in Western Australia, to work on the installation of the new coastal station there, and then to Broome and Esperance. In 1916 all coastal wireless telegraphy stations in Australia, and the few which had been constructed in Papua, were taken over by the Royal Australian Navy, an arrangement precipitated by a PMG operator unwittingly transmitting a message in plain language concerning the movements of a troop convoy.

Once coastal wireless telegraphy stations came under the control of the Navy, PMG staff were fitted out with naval uniforms. Three ranks were established—Warrant Telegraphist, Warrant Officer and Commissioned Warrant Officer. The officer in charge of a station held the highest rank, Commissioned Warrant Officer. That's how Mister Murray Johnson became Warrant Officer Johnson.

1914—the Navy goes to war

The RAN's Operational Order No. 1, issued aboard HMAS *Australia* on 7 August 1914, vividly describes this historic event:

To:
The Respective Officers
Commanding H.M.A. Ships
of the Seagoing Fleet concerned.

INTENTIONS
1. All indications pointing to the probability of German ships *Scharnhorst* and *Gneisenau* and *Nurnberg,* and perhaps *Komet* and *Planet* being in the neighbourhood of Simpsonhafen, New Britain, and to their being found either in that place or in Matupi Harbour, I intend to make an attack on those ports with the object of torpedoing any ships which are there and destroying the Wireless Station.
2. To effect this I intend to proceed with *Australia, Sydney* and destroyers to Rendezvous No. 3, arriving there at about 6 p.m. Tuesday, August 11th.

ATTACKING FORCE
3. *Sydney* will take charge of the destroyers and proceed as ordered in para. 4 and 5. Australia will move up to a position Lat 4.38S, Long 32E (Rendezvous No. 4) to support the above.

ATTACK ON SIMPSONHAFEN
4. *Sydney* and destroyers will be ordered to proceed at about 6 p.m. Tuesday, and will proceed to Simpsonhafen at 20 knots.

Should the enemy's heavy ships be met under way outside, the destroyers are to attack at once, *Sydney* informing me as soon as the attack develops, and retire to *Australia* with the destroyers.

The moon rises at 10.17 p.m., the attack is therefore be delivered at about 9 p.m.

It is probable there may be a patrol in St. George's Channel; this ship should be avoided if possible, otherwise *Sydney* will remain there to support; the destroyers will proceed into Simpsonhafen and attack any men-of-war found there, rejoining *Sydney* after delivering attack.

MATUPI HARBOUR
5. Should no men-of-war be found in Simpsonhafen or should only the

small ships *Planet* and *Komet* be there, the destroyers, after sinking the latter, are to proceed into Matupi Harbour and attack any ships found there, and rejoin *Sydney.*

The attack on *Planet* and *Komet* is left to Commander D.'s judgement, bearing in mind that the main objective is the enemy's heavy ships.

ATTACK ON WIRELESS STATION, RABAUL

6. Should no men-of-war be found in either harbours, the destroyers are to land a party and destroy the W.T. Station reported to be at Rabaul.

7. Having carried out the above, *Sydney* and destroyers are to rejoin me. Sydney is to inform me of the result of the attack as soon as possible.

INDICATION LIGHTS

8. If in action and being chased, *Sydney* on rejoining Flag is to burn her bow lights fixed before the Chart House vertically red above green 6 feet apart to show from right ahead to 5 points on each bow.

WIRELESS

9. No signals are to be made by W.T. before attacking the enemy.

GEORGE E. PATEY
Rear-Admiral

There were two incidents in this year close to home waters involving Australians, both of which had a meritorious outcome. The first occurred on Tuesday 15 September when the Royal Australian Navy succeeded in its attack on German wireless stations in the Pacific and claimed them for the King. The attacks were in response to a request from Britain to silence enemy wireless activity in the region. This is how the engagements, involving the Navy and Australian soldiers, were reported in the press:

Australia lost eight men and 12 have been wounded in the first serious wartime engagements at Kabakaul, Herbertshohe and Rabaul in German New Guinea over the weekend. Volunteers from the Royal Australian Naval Reserve were sent on the mission to attack Germany's strongholds in the Pacific and deprive them of overseas bases. The HMAS *Australia,* under the command of Admiral Patey, led the assault on the Germans' wireless stations. In an 18-hour battle over 6 miles of bush, Herbertshohe was captured, and later more Australian troops surprised the Germans at Rabaul and captured it. The two stations were garrisoned and a base was established at Simpsonhafen. One German officer was killed, two have been taken prisoner, and 30 German-trained native soldiers were killed. One of the Australian casualties was Captain Brian Pockley, 24, of the Australian Medical Corps. Recently graduated from Sydney University, Captain Pockley had operated on a captured German Sergeant-Major, who had been shot through the hand. Captain Pockley finished amputating the Sergeant-Major's hand then attended to the first Australian casualty, Able Seaman Williams, who had been shot through the stomach. Captain Pockley took off his Red Cross brassard and tied it around the hat of the soldier carrying Williams away. This cost Captain Pockley his life. He was shot dead 10 paces down the road. On Sunday the British flag was raised at Rabaul and the national anthem was played by the HMAS *Australia* band. Military occupation of the territory was formally proclaimed in pidgin English for the benefit of the natives.

This initial action by Australians received but scant attention in the annals of wartime history. What a pity! The name Pockley also earned fame in the second Great War for a much-decorated Air Force pilot whose most successful area of activity against the enemy in the Bay of Biscay became known as Pockley's Corner.

The other 1914 incident occurred on 9 November after the wireless operator on HMAS *Sydney* picked up a signal originating from Cocos Island that a strange ship was approaching. Acting on this alert, the commander of *Sydney* detached his ship from a convoy of four warships escorting Australian troops of the first Australian Imperial Force from King George Sound in Western Australia to Colombo and steered a course toward Cocos to investigate the sighting.

Meanwhile, the ship, the notorious German raider *Emden*, had anchored off Cocos and sent a party ashore to destroy the wireless station. At the time Cocos had both a cable and wireless station. *Sydney* arrived in the nick of time and engaged in combat with the raider and soon had the upper hand. Under the command of Captain J. Gossop, *Sydney* soon badly crippled the *Emden*, leaving her commander no choice but to run her onto the reef at nearby North Keating Island. Four RAN seamen were wounded in the engagement, which ran for two hours. The Germans lost 134 sailors and 65 wounded. The commander was taken prisoner. Putting this ship out of action was a triumph for the young Royal Australian Navy. Before she was brought to heel, *Emden* had sunk or captured 25 Allied ships and crippled the British sea lanes of the Far East. No less than nine Allied Japanese, British and Russian warships had been combing the seas for the raider. AIF commander General Bridges granted his troops a half-day off to celebrate the victory.

The year 1914 was also significant for the fact that in September Marconi returned to Italy from his home in England to serve in the Italian Government's armed forces.

In 1916, with the object of providing its own wireless manufacturing facility, the Commonwealth Government purchased Father Shaw's Maritime Wireless Company at Randwick for the sum of £55,000. The government also purchased Father Shaw's experimental station on King Island in Bass Strait. Not long after the sale of Maritime Wireless was completed, Father Shaw died suddenly. The manner of the sale brought on a Royal Commission whose report was highly critical of the transaction and led to the dismissal of a former Minister for the Navy and the resignation of a Member of the Senate.

Also in 1916, the Managing Director of AWA, Ernest Fisk, made a trip to England to sound out the Marconi Company about the possibility of a direct wireless link with Australia. As a result of his discussions with management and engineers, a series of test transmissions was made from the Marconi station at Caernarvon in Wales on the longwave of 14,300 metres for possible reception in Australia.

Returning to Australia, Fisk obtained Commonwealth Government approval to set up a receiving set at his home in Wahroonga on the North Shore of Sydney, with the object of establishing the wireless link. After much experimentation—eventually using a 10-valve set—he picked up a faint Morse code signal from the Caernarvon base. The fact that he could hear the station was enough to spur him on to continue his experiments with the assistance of his AWA engineers. Before long the reception was good enough to herald an historic event in wireless communication.

At precisely 3.15 am Greenwich Mean Time (1.15 pm Sydney time), by arrangement with the Marconi Company, a message was transmitted from the Caernarvon station to Fisk's receiving station at Wahroonga by Prime Minister Hughes, extolling the magnificence of the Australian fighting troops in France which he had witnessed on a tour of the battlefields just hours earlier.

Australian Prime Minister William Morris Hughes, affectionately known as the 'Little Digger' by the troops after he visited the battlefields, was born in Wales in 1864 and arrived in Australia 1884. Elected to the first Federal Parliament in 1901, he became Prime Minister in 1915, and served three times throughout the war, firstly as Leader of the Labor Party until he was expelled from it, then as Leader of the Nationalist

Party. His party eventually lost office in 1923, after three successful elections under two different names. He signed the Versailles Treaty in 1919 on behalf of Australia. It was a nice bridging of history for a Welsh-born Australian Prime Minister to be the sender of the first wireless message from Wales to New South Wales as the leader of this new nation.

At 3.25 am GMT (1.25 pm Sydney time) the Minister for the Australian Navy, Sir Joseph Cook, who was also on an overseas wartime tour, followed the Prime Minister with a message praising the bearing and achievements of members of the Royal Australian Navy, thus forming another bridge between the old and the new. Sir Joseph was born in England in 1860, coming to Australia a year after Hughes, and was also elected to the first Federal Parliament. He was leader of the Free Traders/Protectionist (Liberal) Party, and became Prime Minister in 1913, having been Minister for Defence at the time of the formation of the Royal Australian Navy in 1911, when its first vessels were ordered from the shipyards of the Clyde in Scotland.

Of course, the messages were transmitted in Morse code. The successful contact proved the practicability of direct wireless communication between England and Australia and encouraged Prime Minister Hughes to demand from England a direct wireless service rather than being at the end of a chain of global relay stations, as originally proposed by Marconi.

Incidentally, Hughes was not as popular at home as he was with the troops abroad, particularly with those who objected to his advocacy of compulsory recruitment (conscription). He resigned as Prime Minister in January 1916, honouring a promise to step down if the referendum held on conscription was rejected for a second time. However, he was quickly recalled by Governor-General Sir Ronald Munro-Ferguson and reinstated, to lead his fourth ministry in less than two and a half years.

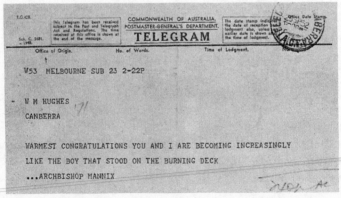

Telegrams were sent on all occasions, including this missive from the controversial Catholic Archbishop of Australia, Mannix, to Prime Minister Hughes in 1926.

Episode 6

'As you see, gentlemen, there are no wires!'

So said Ernest Fisk, managing director of Amalgamated Wireless Australasia Limited to an assembly of members of the Industrial Section of the Royal Society of New South Wales in the Society's meeting hall at 5 Elizabeth Street, Sydney.

The date: 13 August 1919. The occasion: a lecture on wireless telephony, augmented with slides, followed by a demonstration of the transmission of voice and music emanating from the Company's premises known as Wireless House, at 97 Clarence Street. The transmitter, a single-valve unit of small dimensions constructed by three AWA engineers headed by William Dowling Bostock, had been given a ship-to-shore test run a few weeks earlier. The success of this particular experiment had amazed the monitoring engineers with the clarity of the voice, heard as far distant from Sydney as Gabo Island in the Tasman Sea off the NSW–Victoria border.

A much-decorated war veteran, Bostock had recently returned to his post at AWA after overseas service, first with the Australian Imperial Force as a signaller, and later as a pilot in Britain's Royal Flying Corps, which became the Royal Air Force. In 1921 he left AWA to rejoin the services, this time in the fledgling Royal Australian Air Force.

At the time Pearl Harbor was attacked by the Japanese in December 1941—precipitating the United States' entry into World War II—Bostock held the rank of Air Vice-Marshal and was soon given command of the aerial defence of Australia and the Indies, serving under the American General Brett. Three days after his appointment, he heard that an officer junior to him, Air Commodore Jones, had just been made Chief of the Air staff—a promotion which rankled somewhat.

I had the pleasure of serving under this great Australian in World War

II, albeit briefly, when I was Staff Officer Radio Training Eastern Area and later 11 Group, South-West Pacific. After his retirement from the RAAF, Bostock took up a grazing property at Benalla in Victoria and was elected to the Federal Parliament as Member for Indi. He died in 1968.

Returning to the Royal Society's meeting hall in 1919: as wireless loudspeakers had yet to be produced, for the demonstration Fisk arranged a series of headphones to be slung in line from the ceiling of the hall. To obtain the maximum sound, a tinsmith was engaged to fashion metal funnels—in the shape of ice-cream cones—which were inserted into the diaphragm aperture of each headphone. Thus were the first loudspeakers created.

As Fisk ended his lecture, the moment came to demonstrate that sound could actually be conveyed to listeners without the need of connecting wires. A brief speech, followed by a musical rendition from a hand-wound gramophone (a machine which had then been available for less than 20 years) placed in front of a microphone, revealed an awe-inspiring achievement in Australian history, surpassing all other developments in visual and telegraphic communication—as the learned gentlemen of the Society were quick to attest. The rendition of the national anthem to conclude the demonstration was another milestone, as it was the first occasion on which a gathering had stood to attention as the strains of the anthem reached their ears by the almost supernatural phenomenon of wireless.

Not surprisingly, the newspapers, some of which viewed wireless telephony as a possible opposition medium, while others were sceptical about its permanent practicality, gave but scant attention to this historic event.

Melbournians enthralled

On the evening of 13 October 1920 a second demonstration of wireless telephony—soon to be referred to as broadcasting—was held in Melbourne at the behest of Prime Minister Hughes for the ears of Victorian and Federal politicians, gathered in Queen's Hall. At the time, Victoria's Parliament House was home to both the Victorian and Federal Parliaments, a situation which prevailed until 1927, when Federal Parliament and some government officers were transferred to Canberra.

The transmitter used for the Melbourne demonstration was a 500-watter manufactured in England at the Chelmsford works of the

Marconi Company, one of two units imported by AWA. It was installed in the home of AWA's Melbourne manager, Lionel Hooke. The programme, which came from the lounge room of Hooke's home, featured—for the first time in history—a 'live' performance in the form of Miss Hilda Walker, the recent winner of the Melba Scholarship. The same tin horns used in Sydney as makeshift loudspeakers were rigged up in Queen's Hall for this second demonstration. The audience, which included both Parliamentarians and their guests, was absolutely enthralled with the presentation and the manner in which it reached their ears.

The success of this venture even captured the interest of the reluctant press, especially in relation to Miss Walker's performance to an invisible audience. The singer had already been lauded in print for her fine rendition and success in the Melba Scholarship. The wireless-telephony demonstration was reported thus: 'a truly wonderful soprano voice was heard in our famous national song, "Advance Australia Fair", which was enthusiastically encored in Queen's Hall'.

Generously, the newspapers gave some mention to the technical side of this historic achievement. Miss Walker and her songs were well chosen and well timed for AWA's promotion of wireless telephony, as just a few months earlier—on 15 June, to be exact—the Australian prima donna Dame Nellie Melba had presented a recital, transmitted from the Marconi works at Chelmsford in England, which was responsible for a tremendous upsurge of interest in this new-found medium. Her singing had been heard as far away as Persia (Iran).

This was not the first occasion that Melba had sung to an unseen audience. A few years earlier she performed for the Electrophone Company, using the same type of microphone used for the Chelmsford recital: a standard telephone transmitter (mouthpiece) with a wooden funnel attached, made from a cigar box.

Another Australian singer, Peter Dawson, was also a pioneer of the airwaves. Born in Adelaide in 1882, he made his debut on the London stage in 1904, the year Melba was introduced to the technique of recording sound. Wireless did much to enhance the careers of both artists through both stage broadcasts and recording studios. Although one of the world's most prolific recording artists in his time, Dawson was never far from the breadline, blaming taxes for his impecunious position. When he died in Sydney in 1961 he left an estate of a mere £1,500. His most popular recording was of the 'Floral Dance'.

The year 1920 was important for the Postmaster-General's Department as well, for in that year all forms of wireless transmission in Australia came under its control. This included the coastal ship-to-shore service, much to the chagrin of the Navy, which reluctantly gave up the control it had exercised during World War I.

Mention of the Victorian Parliament House sends my thoughts back to 1940 when I was in the RAAF, training at Point Cook. Whenever I had a few days' leave I would make for Melbourne where I usually stayed with a relative who was the building caretaker at Parliament House. He and his wife lived in a large flat underneath the steps of the Spring Street entrance. Those familiar with the City of Melbourne will no doubt recall the numerous wide steps one had to traverse to get to the front door. Perhaps they were purposely designed for the benefit of politicians—any forthright citizen with a chip on his shoulder heading for the office of his local member to let off steam would have run out of puff by the time he had climbed that stairway! The flat was a large one, chock-a-block with antique furniture left over when Federal Parliament moved to Canberra. I always had a huge four-poster bed awaiting me.

AWA's Lionel Hooke had a very interesting career, commencing in the early days of wireless. In 1913–14 he served as the wireless operator in Shackleton's polar expedition. Back in Melbourne, he joined the Royal Australian Navy and spent the rest of World War I engaged in many sea dramas. He succeeded Fisk as managing director and later chairman of AWA. A charming and unassuming gentleman, I met him on one occasion when I was chairman of the Quarter Century Club, composed of radio people who have served 25 years or more in the industry. Fisk was our guest of honour at a function in Sydney to commemorate the 50th anniversary of radio broadcasting.

The United States leads the way

Well before Fisk's historic demonstration in Sydney, US engineers and company executives had awakened the public to the enormous home attraction of radio broadcasting, as it was now called, beginning with an experimental broadcast in 1910 from backstage at the Metropolitan Opera House in New York, featuring the voice of Enrico Caruso, the world's most famous tenor. The experiment was arranged by the scientist Lee de Forest, already acclaimed for his invention of the triode valve (vacuum tube).

Lee de Forest constructed a small transmitter for the experiment, calling his device a 'radiophone'. The broadcast was picked up by a wireless operator at sea aboard SS *Avon* in the Atlantic, and by and several amateur operators in Connecticut, who reported good reception.

In 1915—the year the term ANZAC was being forged on the battlefields of Gallipoli—the American Bell Telephone Company, of Arlington in the state of Virginia, conducted the first transatlantic voice transmission by wireless, but it was not until after the end of World War I that wireless broadcasting was brought out of the laboratory to provide a public service.

The most persistent advocate for a public broadcasting system was David Sarnoff, commercial manager of the Marconi Wireless Telegraph Company of America. Following the successful demonstration by Lee de Forest, and before him by another scientist, Canadian-born Reginald Fessenden, Sarnoff began experimental transmissions of music. In 1916 he sent a memo to the General Manager of the Company suggesting that radio be made a household utility by providing what he called a 'radio music box' as a home receiver for radio telephone transmitters broadcasting from as far as 50 kilometres' distance. Although music would be the main ingredient, sporting events could also be broadcast, he suggested.

Before the Company could give serious consideration to Sarnoff's suggestion it was 1917 and America had other things to think of, being at war with Germany. Besides, senior company executives continued to see radio—along with the telegraph and telephone—as systems of two-way communication between private persons, not for communicating material for 'all the world to hear'.

When the war ended, more experimental stations came on the air in the United States, transmitting voice. By this time the US government had become rather sensitive about the dominance of foreign countries operating in the communication field in America. The outcome was the formation in 1919 of the Radio Corporation of America, which took over the assets and business of the Marconi Company. Sarnoff was appointed a senior executive and rapidly rose to the high office of company President.

Meanwhile, at Pittsburgh in the United States an experimental station, which was later to carry the call sign KDKA, commenced broadcasting 'live' and recorded music as well as speech. The transmitter was designed and built by Dr Frank Conrad of the Westinghouse Company and operated from the garage of his home, transmitting mostly at night and weekends for a total of about four hours a week.

Although these broadcasts were on an experimental basis, KDKA programmes rapidly became a source of entertainment in local homes. Before long, livewire merchants saw the advertising value of placing a receiving set in their shop or showroom to attract customers.

Radio broadcasting was now approaching its threshold of viability.

In 1920 the Vice-President of Westinghouse—very much alive to the advertising potential of this new medium—instructed Dr Conrad to set up a radio station atop the Company's warehouse building in Pittsburgh. In August that year station KDKA, yet to be officially licensed, came on air and began regular broadcasting.

More changes came when on 2 November KDKA broadcast voting returns in the 1920 Harding–Cox presidential election, for the first time adding news to the advertising and entertainment mix generally heard on radio. The first broadcast of a church service was also heard in that year, along with a description of a boxing match, agricultural market reports and even a theatre performance. Station KDKA had begun a revolution in the radio industry throughout the United States—indeed, throughout the world.

Eighteen months after KDKA's first broadcast, 220 radio stations were on the air in the United States and the number of radio sets in private homes was close to a million. Radio performers became overnight celebrities.

Two other stations disputed KDKA's claim to be the first on the air. WWJ of Detroit was one of them, owned by a local. KQV, also of Pittsburgh, was the other, claiming it began transmission in 1919. It was part of the Quaker business network. Looking up its history I noted it would accept beer and wine advertising … but no liquor. This was still the situation in 1939. Funny mob, the Americans!

England well behind

Britain's depth of involvement in World War I hampered development of telephone, telegraphy and wireless there. The war over, Marconi returned to England to direct operations of the British Marconi Company and continue with his experiments in long-range wireless telegraphy. The Marconi Company's approach to broadcasting in England was on a much more conservative plane than in the United States, where the situation was rapidly becoming chaotic with new stations coming on the air almost daily, some of them just as rapidly going out of business for want of sufficient revenue.

Broadcasting in Great Britain was inaugurated from the Chelmsford works of the Marconi Company in January 1920. Talks, the playing of gramophone records and 'live' performances featuring vocalists and instrumentalists drawn from the company's staff provided programme material for what were then experimental broadcasts. The first paid artist was Winifred Sayer, an amateur soprano, who received five shillings for a performance broadcast in February 1920. The first professional artist to broadcast in Britain was the famous Australian, Dame Nellie Melba, who gave a 30-minute broadcast from Chelmsford on 15 June 1920.

Following these experimental broadcasts, several other operators came on the air with test programmes but it was not until 1922 that regular broadcasts were permitted. The first station was given the call 2MT Writtle. In that year the Marconi Company and several other manufacturers of wireless and electrical equipment formed the British Broadcasting Company, which became a public corporation in 1927.

The first BBC station was located on the roof of Marconi House, London, using the call sign 2LO. This station had actually been transmitting experimental programmes for several months before it was absorbed by the BBC. British old-timers, familiar with those early BBC broadcasts, always refer to 2LO, which became the key station for broadcasting in England.

Episode 7

It's as clear as a bell ...

So said a lady listener bubbling over with excitement as she telephoned from the Sydney suburb of Strathfield on the evening of 23 November 1923. The occasion was the official opening of 2SB Sydney by the Postmaster-General, Mr Gerrard Gibson—an event which ushered in public broadcasting in Australia.

At the conclusion of Mr Gibson's prognosis for the future of wireless broadcasting in the years ahead, listeners were treated to a studio concert recital featuring the lilting soprano voice of Miss Dorothy Deering and other gifted artists, including baritone George Saunders who went on to become wireless broadcasting's 'Uncle George'.

Although Dorothy Deering had participated in several experimental broadcasts from Paling's music store in Sydney some months earlier, she still suffered 'mike fright'. Warbling away to an unseen audience as she stood in front of a contraption known as a microphone, positioned on top of the type of hallstand usually graced by the family aspidistra, would have been enough to add a few unpredicted tremolos to the nervous lady's rendition on this momentous occasion. The tiny studio and home-made transmitter housing 2SB Sydney were located on the top floor of the Daily Guardian building in Philip Street, the home of Sir Joynton Smith's publication, *Smith's Weekly*.

The operating company, Broadcasters (Sydney) Ltd, was established by a group of wireless experimenters and retailers and a few people with other business interests in Sydney—including Sir Joynton Smith, who was appointed chairman of the company. In fact, a condition of Sir Joynton Smith's support for this enterprise was that the broadcasting facilities be located in the Guardian building—a condition heartily endorsed by his fellow directors of Smith's Newspapers, Robert Clyde Packer and Claude

McKay. Smith's Newspapers, by the way, was the outcome of an amalgamation of the publishers of *Smith's Weekly* and the *Daily Guardian*.

The Federal Government had given approval for the licensing of two broadcast stations in Sydney, one in Melbourne and one in Perth. Station 2SB was the first to get off the ground. Two wooden poles mounted on the roof of the Guardian building carried the transmitting aerial, sending the inaugural official broadcast to the four corners of Sydney suburbia. Well, almost to the four corners. There were a few 'dead spots' making it difficult, indeed almost impossible, to pick up the station on a crystal set with an unsuitable receiving aerial.

Weeks before the opening date—which was originally set down for 13 November—test transmissions had been carried out on the allotted wavelength of 350 metres (857 kHz), from the home of William John Maclardy. For some years an experimental operator using the call sign 2HP, Maclardy was the founder of the publication *Wireless Weekly* and managing director of the recently formed Broadcasters (Sydney) Ltd. The home-made transmitter used for the test had an output of a modest 10 watts. Maclardy engaged the services of engineer and technical manager of New System Telephones, Raymond Cottam Allsop, to assist in transferring his equipment to the Guardian building and to undertake a listener survey of the broadcasting of 'live' artists. This was the first listener survey carried out in Australia.

Although the result of the survey was encouraging, it was obvious a more powerful transmitter was required. Allsop immediately began construction of a 500-watter which he completed in time for the official date, with the assistance of a few wireless enthusiasts and AWA. Maclardy had five weeks up his sleeve to conduct the survey and obtain an official licence from the Postmaster-General's Department.

Raymond Allsop remained with 2SB as a consultant until appointed Chief Engineer under the new call sign of 2BL. Years later, Allsop formed a cinematograph company, manufacturing Racophone film/sound projection equipment for Australian cinemas. He was one of the first advocates for the introduction of frequency modulation (FM) radio.

And now, back to that momentous evening in November as the happy listener in Strathfield continued in telephonic communication with the 2SB manager, who let the lady know he was happy that she was happy with the reception and the wonderful studio recital he had lovingly prepared for the unseen audience.

'I could almost follow every word he said,' continued the excited lady listener, referring to the speech by the Postmaster-General. 'And Miss

Deering's voice sounded so natural in my headphones. It was as if she was here in my drawing room. My hubby made the crystal set for me. He's ever so clever, you know.'

At this moment an operator at the Sydney Telephone Exchange broke in to the conversation to tell the manager a trunk-line caller from Newcastle was anxiously asking to be connected and couldn't wait any longer on account of the fact he had soon to go on night shift at the steel works. Excitedly, the manager begged the lady listener's pardon, but would she please hang up so he could receive an urgent report from a long-distance caller. Sure enough the call came in from the Newcastle listener, congratulating the now preening manager on the success of the broadcast—but would he please ask the lady to sing a bit louder, as her voice was very faint on his receiving set!

Not all listeners to this inaugural broadcast were at home. Several Sydney theatres installed receiving sets to allow their patrons to hear the musical recital, which reached their ears from horn-type loudspeakers. The occasion also gave good reason for the holding of a concert in Martin Place, the programme being embellished by receiving sets fitted with loudspeakers to carry the proceedings from 2SB.

At the time of this first public broadcast there were less than 1400 wireless listeners in Australia. That is, official listeners, or—to put it another way—listeners who had paid the annual licence fee of 10 shillings imposed by the government in August that year. More on that later ...

By the time 2SB went on the air a second Sydney licence had also been allotted. It went to the long-established department store Farmer and Company, with the call sign 2FC. Two opposition department stores, David Jones Ltd and Anthony Hordern & Sons, had already allied themselves with Broadcasters (Sydney) Ltd as financial guarantors, a necessary arrangement for a station operating on a shoestring budget.

Less than two weeks after the opening of Australia's first broadcasting station, 2FC Sydney was launched from a studio in Farmer's Building in Market Street; the transmitter was located out of the city centre, at Willoughby. The date was 5 December 1923. AWA built and installed the equipment and then contracted to provide staff to operate the technical services. With an authorised power of 5000 watts, huge compared with 2SB's puny 500 watts, the listener coverage of the new station was understandably more widespread.

Two steel lattice masts at the Willoughby site carried the transmitting aerial. Constructed in the workshop of Mort's Dock under the supervision of AWA engineer Murray Johnson, these 60 metre masts soon became a well-known landmark among Sydneysiders.

The official opening of 2FC, on 10 January 1924, was a far more splendiferous affair than 2SB's opening, the highlight being a complete performance of the musical extravaganza *Southern Maid* direct from the stage of Her Majesty's Theatre, starring the darling of Bundaberg, Gladys Moncrieff. A few weeks later performances of *The Merry Widow* and *Sybil* were added to the station's repertoire. The level of programming, plus the higher authorised power of 5000 watts, consciously or unconsciously set a pattern for a degree of cultural snobbery that prevailed for a number years, as those who lived in the Twenties and Thirties would tell you.

The Sealed Set Scheme

The introduction of the Sealed Set Scheme was the outcome of a conference convened by Postmaster-General Gibson in May 1923, attended by people representing organisations concerned with wireless and, in particular, those plugging for the introduction of broadcasting on a business plane. Ernest Fisk of AWA—recently returned from overseas where he had been studying the introduction of wireless broadcasting in European countries and America—recommended a system of sealing receiving sets to a particular station, according to a fee paid to the company operating the broadcasting company. His recommendation was adopted almost without demur.

In August that year Government regulations were gazetted, providing for the licensing of broadcasting stations and for a listener licensing fee of 10 shillings per annum to be paid to the Government, plus a subscriber's fee, to be paid to one or more stations according to the listener's choice. This additional impost varied from 10 shillings to £4/4/- per annum. In Sydney, 10 shillings was paid to 2SB; a higher fee of £3/3/- was paid to 2FC in view of its higher power and higher production costs. The tuning condenser of all receiving sets was sealed by a representative of the PMG's Department, thereby restricting the listener to the station to which he paid the fee. Even home-made crystal sets were subject to the fee. An additional charge was made for inspecting and sealing the sets after they were taken to the station representative's office. There was no such thing as dial-twiddling ... well, almost no such thing.

Funny thing! Very few home-grown crystal or valve receiving sets were submitted for inspection. Apparently most of them disappeared into thin air. Take Adelaide, for example. According to Jack Ross' excellent book *Radio Broadcasting Technology*, during 1924 not one of these sets was submitted for approval. And I always thought Adelaideans were God-fearing people!

Apart from that little anomaly, any knowledgeable wireless experimenter would have had little difficulty in breaking the seal and setting sail to any station on the dial ... or so I was told!

It was obvious the Sealed Set Scheme was doomed from the start. Enter the class distinction—A, B and C Class stations. In July 1924 new regulations were introduced to replace the Sealed Set Scheme. Stations in the A Class category were to receive the main portion of the annual listener licence fees and retailer fees collected by the Government. B Class stations would not receive any of the revenue collected by the government, as they were to be self supporting through advertising. The category of C Class was provided for stations receiving corporate advertising from large sponsors, but no such licenses were issued.

The bogeyman

Although the Government dropped the Sealed Set Scheme, listeners still had to continue to pay an annual fee to tune in to any A or B Class station, an impost that didn't go down too well with the public—but of course, being the law-abiding citizens we were, we suffered in silence. But there were a few artful dodges to give the bogeyman, in the form of the radio inspector, a bit of a headache ... or so I was told!

In the days of crystal sets and one- and two-valve receivers, the installation of an outdoor aerial wire ranging from 6 to 15 metres in length was necessary for reasonable reception. Usually this meant erecting one or two wooden poles about 12 metres high to support the aerial wire. Sadly, the poles were a dead giveaway to any inspector on tour of suburbia. To worsen the situation, some proud home-lovers were inclined to paint their poles a brilliant white, thereby making them stand out. I did bring this situation to the attention of a few unlicensed listeners but they didn't believe me. Not that I ever condoned their thumbing their noses at the law, mind you! Visits by inspectors were always followed by an inundation of fines, the details of which were published in daily newspapers. It was most embarrassing ... or so I was told!

But of course, Australian citizens are renowned for their high degree of initiative, especially under adverse conditions, so it was not surprising to hear of intrepid non-licensed listeners quietly removing their poles just on sun-up and connecting the clothesline to the receiving set for daytime use. Monday was the only problem, when the lady of the house often tripped over the wires while she was hanging out the washing. Eventually, with the development of multi-valve superheterodyne receivers, the outside aerial became less important. Naturally enough, a goodly number of citizens of Sydney in particular breathed a sigh of relief ... but still kept a sharp lookout for any 'visitors'. Of course, in Brisbane no one ever got up to this kind of caper to evade the law—it was only the mob down south!

Before the A, B and C Class categories were applied in 1924, existing stations had to rely on subscriptions from retailers, who depended on the sale of wireless receivers and spare parts to recoup their contributions to the stations. The Sydney store Grace Bros was the first retailer to open a radio department and promote the wonders of radio telephony through demonstration broadcasts. However, subscriptions from retailers and some manufacturers were insufficient to keep the home fires burning. Station 2SB, which lacked the backing of a big company like Farmers, was heading for the wall until the Class System was introduced. As the call sign 2SB sounded very much like 2FC, in March 1924 the PMG approved a change to 2BL. The company name was altered to Broadcasters Limited.

The first station to be launched in Victoria was on 26 January 1924 when Associated Radio Company Australia Limited began 3AR Melbourne, to be officially opened on this Australia Day by Dr Argyle, Chief Secretary of Victoria. Like 2SB (2BL), this Melbourne station started with a city-based transmitter, in A'Beckett Street, operating on a power of 350 watts—well below the authorised power of 500 watts. Listener reception was rather poor in suburban Melbourne, so plans were immediately put in place to choose a more suitable site with higher power. In October 1925 the station began transmitting from a new site at North Essendon that provided much better reception and the almost complete elimination of a 'hum' that had been the bugbear of station engineers and listeners from the time Dr Argyle said his stuff. 3AR was now transmitting on a power of 1500 watts.

The next broadcast station to come on stream was in Western Australia, where 6WF took to the air on 4 June 1924, operated by the influential company Westralian Farmers Ltd. Under the engineering and managerial direction of Walter Coxon, 6WF was officially opened by the Premier of Western Australia, Mr Collier, backed by prominent instrumentalists and vocalists, including the Wendowie Quartet. Transmitting initially on 500 watts, the station quickly moved up to 5000 watts, charging a listener fee of £4/4/-, the highest listener impost so far. That was in addition to the 10 shilling Government fee.

On 13 October 1924, 3LO Melbourne came on air. The call sign and the programming suggested this new, somewhat pukka station was designed to walk in the steps of the now-famous 2LO London. Transmitting on a power of 5000 watts from a site at Braybrook, the studio was suitably located in the Cambridge Building in Collins Street. As it turned out, 3LO became the most successful station under the A and B Class system. By the time 3LO went to air, all the earlier stations were really feeling the pinch financially.

Managed by a Gallipoli veteran with entrepreneurial flair, Major Walter Condor, 3LO's official opening surpassed all other station endeavours with one of the several farewell performances of Dame Nellie Melba. This one was the opera *La Bohème*, broadcast from the stage of Melbourne's Her Majesty's Theatre. The pre-publicity given to this occasion by some newspapers and wireless did much to increase the sale of receiving sets in Victoria. 3LO, along with 2FC, was an A Class station.

A few weeks later a third Sydney station commenced transmission, on 7 November. Operated by Burgin Electric Company Ltd, with the call sign 2BE, it had an uncertain future from the beginning. It was undercapitalised yet had the distinction of being Australia's first commercial station, depending entirely on advertising revenue to keep in business. Less than two years after it commenced operation, insufficient advertising in hand or on the horizon forced 2BE management to reduce transmission hours to only two nights per week. In 1927 a fire at Burgin's premises put the station off the air for several weeks, spelling its demise. By 1929, on the eve of the Great Depression, 2BE Sydney was no more.

A few weeks after 2BE Sydney went to air for the first time, 5CL Adelaide became the first for South Australia. Licensed as an A Class station, it was owned by Central Broadcasters Ltd. Although this station was responsible for more than doubling the sale of receiving sets in Adelaide during its first year of operation, initially it was not all that popular, many preferring to remain tuned to 3LO Melbourne because of this station's more uplifting programmes, a high percentage of which were presented 'live' in contrast to 5CL's extensive use of gramophone records. One wag suggested it was because there was a dearth of talent in Adelaide during that period, but the comment was of course a furphy, as every forthright Crow-eater would no doubt hasten to tell you ... and me!

5CL commenced on a power of 500 watts, but when a 5000-watter came on air from a new site at Brooklyn Park on 16 December 1926, the extra local power made it more difficult to pick up interstate stations.

Tasmania's first station was 7ZL Hobart, opened on 17 December 1924 with a temporary power of 250 watts. Licensed to Tasmanian Broadcasters Pty Ltd, the station was managed by veteran wireless man Sidney Laws, who had been associated with John Balsillie's installation of some of the first coastal wireless telegraphy stations. Although sitting in the A Class category, revenue from listener licence fees was hardly enough to keep the pot boiling, considering Tasmania had less than 2500 listener licences compared to almost 200,000 in Victoria. An increase in power in 1927 to 1000 watts did help things along a little.

The first station to commence business in 1925 was 2UE Sydney on 26 January, followed shortly afterward by 2HD Newcastle, the first commercial station outside a capital city to be licensed. 2UE was founded by veteran engineer Cecil Vincent Stevenson, proprietor of the Electrical Utilities Supply Company whose address was Radio House in the Sydney city centre. Stevenson had assisted in the construction and launch of 2SB in 1923. The call sign of Stevenson's station was to be EU (representing Electrical Utilities), but it didn't roll off the tongue too well and was changed to UE.

The 2UE studio was the lounge room of Stevenson's home in the Sydney suburb of Maroubra. Music was mostly supplied from a gramophone placed in front of the microphone. Wooden poles erected in the backyard carried the transmitting aerial. Although the station began with little fanfare and a delayed mention by the press, it grew in stature and revenue to become one of the most successful commercial broadcast stations in the country.

The Stevenson family had much to be proud of. Most of their neighbours, agog at the novelty of this enterprise, were also proud to be living alongside to witness 2UE's progress.

In a letter to me from his Ramsgate home in 1993, after hearing my broadcast on the ABC's *Australia All Over* recounting the early days of wireless, Denis Brindle beautifully recaptured the Twenties era of the Stevenson family's 2UE in suburbia:

We were brought up at Maroubra, Sydney, where our father bought a house in Storey Street. Already there, and opposite us, was a big house owned by the Stevenson family. This would have been in 1923. Maroubra in those days was just about on the outskirts of Sydney in spite of the fact that we were only four miles from the GPO by tram. We grew up with the Stevenson family and because the father had one of the earliest cars in that part we often were taken to their weekender at Lilli Pilli on Port Hacking. About 1923 or '24 there was a lot of talk about a broadcast by Toti del Monte, a famous soprano at that time, who was going to broadcast a concert from Europe and it was going to be picked up and re-broadcast in Sydney by 2FC or 2BL ...

Well, my father wanted to be one of the first with a radio around that part of Sydney and he purchased, after much thought, what was called in those days a loose-coupler radio. This had a barrel with wire closely wrapped around it which one pulled in and out, evidently to get on to the different wavelengths. Of course, it also had what was called a 'cat's whisker', on which one had to try and find a spot with a small arm with a crooked piece of wire, which gave better reception and also more power. He then put up two tall poles about 50 yards apart with a wire running between them and connected to the pole each end by china non-conductors. We heard the programme and everyone was thrilled. Neighbours came in from all sides and were amazed at the reception. Not long after this, Mr Stevenson erected two very tall and strong poles above his house and established one of the first radio stations in Sydney. It was called 2UE. He used to broadcast every day (part) and every evening. Only gramophone records were used and of course, speech. My father was approached, as indeed were other families around, to lend Mr Stevenson records to augment his collection. By this time, the wind-up gramophone had come a long way and sound, although not good by today's standard, was still pretty good to us. I remember we had a lot of records of Peter Dawson, Nellie Melba and other famous singers. In a big storm one of the poles blew down and went through the roof of the house. Speaking to Norman Stevenson, his son, a few years back, he said it happened twice. Because we were just across the road from the station we could pick up the signal loud and clear. This was a handicap later on when more stations began to broadcast. The founder, Mr Stevenson, at the time of starting the station, was the owner of a substantial store in the city, called Radio House. Later he branched out with more stores in the suburbs. These shops sold everything for the radio fanatic. They have all closed down now ... I am 79 now but still vividly remember those good old days, which to me were better days than now. Days when neighbours were real friends and there was no crime—hardly, and no drugs.

Murray Stevenson, who carried on from his father, died in 2001 after an illustrious career in radio engineering.

Station 2HD Newcastle took to the air one day after 2UE made its debut on Australia Day, 26 January 1925. The licensee was Hugh Douglas, owner of a tyre-retreading works in Newcastle. As newspapers now considered wireless broadcasting a threat to their advertising revenue, there was no mention in the press about the official opening, modest as it was. The station changed hands in 1928.

Otto Sandel, a prominent experimental operator using the call sign 2UW, decided to go commercial on 13 February 1925 after operating an amateur station from the age of seventeen in his aunt's boarding house in Sydney's beautiful Manly. There, in a backyard shed, he had begun by making and servicing wireless sets. Transmitting initially from his father's property at Bellevue Hill, the new 2UW moved up from 15 watts to 400 watts with quite a flourish, using the slogan 'The little station with the big kick'. With selling receiving sets very much on his mind, Sandel moved his station into the T&G building in Elizabeth Street with a showroom to display the products of Sandel Radio Ltd. Within the next few years several changes of location in the heart of Sydney took place.

Queensland was the last state to establish a broadcast station, with 4QG Brisbane the first in line. The QG indicated it was a Government-owned station under the premise that broadcasting should be a public utility controlled by the State Government. After twelve months operating from temporary premises, 4QG was moved to the top floor of the Government Insurance Building on the corner of George and Elizabeth Streets in January 1926 with a 5000-watt AWA transmitter. The two steel towers mounted on the roof of this building to carry the transmitting aerial were a Brisbane landmark for many years. 4QG was, of course, an A Class station.

Many early broadcasters held to the theory that unrestricted height was essential for good transmission, but this really was a fallacy. Flat moist earth was more important. To explain in simple technical terms—a transmitting aerial system is, in effect, an electrical condenser. The aerial or insulated metal tower represents the 'top plate' of the condenser, the earth the 'bottom plate', the air or porcelain insulator between, the 'dielectric'. These components make up the radiating system.

Using 4QG as an example, there were two steel towers fastened to the roof of the building, not very far apart and supporting an aerial wire carrying the programme. A counterpoise in the form of copper wires strung out from the centre of the rooftop became the bottom plate of the condenser. Not a very efficient system. The two secured and well-earthed towers wouldn't help as they would tend to mask the radiated energy. Yet, knowing this, for years many broadcasters preferred to maintain transmitters alongside their studios in the city rather than seek open country.

2UW was the last station in Sydney to get the message. It was not until 1947–48 that a move was made from the city centre to a more suitable site between Concord West and the Homebush cattle yards. I should know—I worked on the installation and then the operation of two brand-new STC transmitters until I left Sydney in 1950 to manage 2KM Kempsey.

The 2UW site was ideal for broadcasting in that there were no buildings close by and the land was flat and moist. A single steel insulated tower was erected in the centre of the land and an earth-mat (the bottom plate of the condenser), consisting of copper wires radiating out every three degrees from beneath the tower and buried to a depth of about 10 centimetres, completed an efficient radiating system. But there was a snag. The swampy country, being on the edge of Parramatta River, was salty. Good for conductivity, but the salty soil ate into the copper mat. Coating the copper wire with bitumen paint gave some relief, but not for long. I suppose that site would now be part of the Olympic Village.

A mouthpiece

The highest power allotted to an Australian broadcast station up to 1938 was 10,000 watts, provided for several Class A stations. In the United States a power of 50,000 watts was not uncommon.

That reminds me of the story of a couple who lived close, too close, to one of those high-powered stations—a situation that dampened the harmony of domestic bliss somewhat, mainly on account of the wife's lack of sleep. It came about because of the strength of the electromagnetic waves floating about. Apparently her husband had a few fillings in his teeth, of two dissimilar metals. These two metals were actually in contact, creating a rectifier effect and converting radio-frequency wireless waves into an audio frequency—just like the rectifier of a wireless receiver. Whenever the husband opened his mouth at night, instead of emitting the customary snores out came music, advertisements and the voice of the announcer sending cheerio calls to sleepless listeners. In desperation the wife rang the station several times to complain, but each time was given the big laugh. There were only two solutions to her plight—change to another home or change to another husband. She changed to another husband and lived happily thereafter... or so I am told!

Perhaps I had better get on with the next Episode before too many questions are put to me ...

Episode 8

The turbulent Twenties
... and the flirty Thirties

The turbulent Twenties

This decade should not have been a turbulent period of Australia's history. The War to End Wars had just been won and our heroes—less the 60,000 left on the battlefields—were gratefully welcomed home by the Federal Government led by the 'Little Digger', Billy Hughes. Electricity and gas were rapidly replacing wood stoves in the home—except in the Outback. Electric refrigerators were making the meat safe redundant. Horse-drawn and cable cars were giving way to electric trams. Some wireless sets could now be operated from plug-in electricity. In the entertainment field, the availability of more gramophone records rapidly increased the popularity of the Salonola and the portable gramophone, while the piano and pianola still held their own. Yet—in spite of a better way of life science offered us, all was not well on the home front. Money was scarce. Strikes were many. Unemployment was rife. The Soldier Settlement Scheme was a failure, with many Diggers walking off their blocks. What's more, the wowsers had persuaded state governments to reintroduce 6 o'clock closing of pubs. Generally speaking, it was a dry argument.

This was the unhealthy situation confronting the fledgling wireless broadcasting industry in the Twenties, making it a struggle to survive. The A Class stations—dependent on a proportion of listeners' licence fees to operate—were finding it hard going, partly due to dissatisfied listeners refusing to renew subscriptions because of poor reception and poor programming. Country listeners in particular were left out in the cold due to the concentration of transmitters in capital cities.

The most successful station was 3LO Melbourne, which continued to enjoy a large wireless audience, much to the chagrin of the operators of 2FC Sydney, who considered *their* station was a cut above the others, including the first station on the dial, 2BL. This station was at a low ebb due to the disparity of its share of the revenue from listeners' fees, compared to the income received by the higher powered 2FC. A timely newspaper war saved 2BL's bacon when Sydney's *Sun* newspaper bought an interest in the company to offset the popularity of news bulletins supplied to 2FC by its rival, the *Evening News*.

Much the same situation prevailed in Melbourne, with 3LO receiving a greater proportion of listeners' fees than 3AR. This led to quite a deal of bickering between the A Class stations. As a result of a request from the management of 2BL for a bigger slice of the cake, the Postmaster-General appointed a King's Counsel to investigate this anomaly. This led to a Royal Commission in 1927 'to enquire into wireless broadcasting within the Commonwealth in all its aspects'.

On the commercial scene the B Class stations were also feeling the pinch, with only meagre revenue from advertising to keep them afloat. From 1925 to the end of the decade, applications for broadcasting licences were very sluggish, with only an additional eight stations coming on air. Two of them, 2MK Bathurst and 2XL Lismore, were short lived.

The first B Class station in Melbourne was 3UZ, founded by electrical merchants Oliver J. Neilsen & Co. A tiny studio in the centre of Melbourne was fitted out with a pianola and a gramophone to provide music. A microphone placed in front of the gramophone carried the sweet sounds to the ears of many appreciative listeners. Less appreciative were those Melbournians who took a dim view of 3UZ blotting out their favourite station 2BL Sydney at night, due to wavelength proximity. In the early days, the operating wavelengths of transmitters were not crystal-controlled to stop them wandering a little, nor could the dials of many receiving sets be finely tuned.

The honour of launching the first B Class station in Queensland went to Toowoomba wireless dealer Ted Gold. His station, 4GR, commenced transmission on 16 August 1925, under the name of Gold Radio Service. Ted Gold was to be closely associated with electrical and wireless merchant J. B. Chandler of Brisbane and gave him considerable encouragement when he started his own station, 4BC, in 1930. Gold and Chandler were both AWA dealers.

In October 1925, 2KY went to air from premises in the Trades Hall in Goulburn Street, Sydney, with the transmitting aerial mounted on the

This happy group (*above*), dressed to kill, were enjoying a concert coming to them from the stage of one of London's best-known theatres; more than likely, several telephone lines were used to cater for the number of listeners. (Evergreen, UK)

A young Guglielmo Marconi at his mother's knee, with his elder brother Alfonso. (AWA Archives)

The young Marconi photographed in London with some of his original equipment, soon after his arrival from Italy in 1896. (AWA Archives)

The official opening of station VIP at Applecross on 12 September 1912. (AWA Archives)

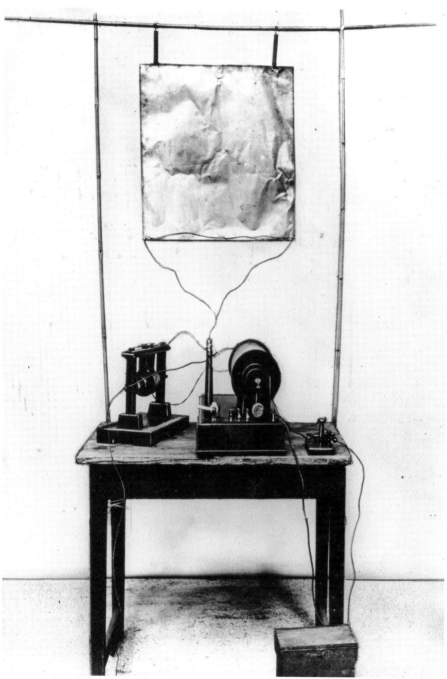

A replica of Marconi's first transmitting apparatus incorporating a copper sheet aerial, used in Italy in 1895 and on Salisbury Plain in England the following year. (AWA Archives)

RMS *Titanic* steaming out of Southampton towards a watery grave.

Grandfather Lewis Maynard (1860–1928) cogitating, when Mayor of Bundaberg.

Family group, 1923, including Lewis Maynard, rear left; the pensive boy in the centre is the author.

The Vickers-Vimy flown to Australia by Ross and Keith Smith in 1919, shortly after the plane landed in Darwin. Murray Johnson, in naval uniform, is standing just below the starboard engine.

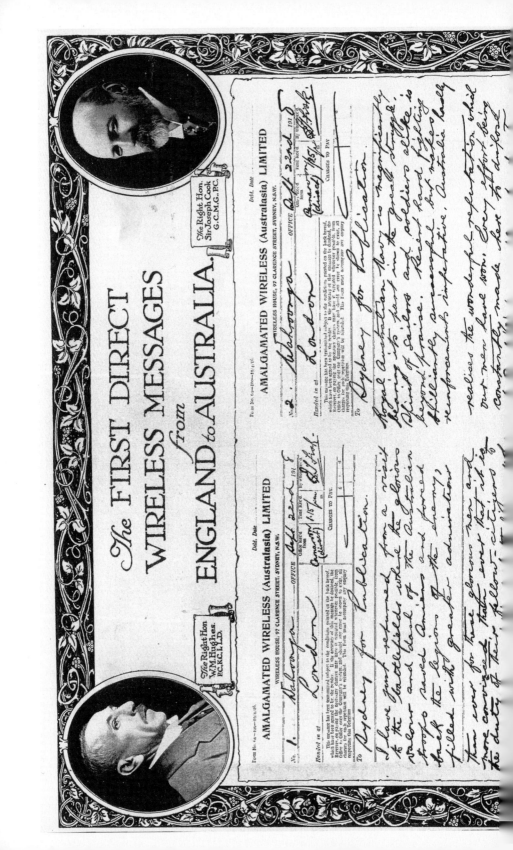

America's PIONEER RADIO STATION

Radio station WWJ was not only the *first station* in America, but it has maintained its position as the *first station* in listener interest in Detroit since it was established,—a fact proven by every survey that has ever been made!

WWJ

Established Aug. 20, 1920
NBC Basic Red Network

National Representatives
Geo. P. Hollingbery Co.
New York, Chicago, San Francisco, Atlanta

Advertisement for Radio WWJ Detroit—the second 'first' station to go to air in 1920.

(*Left*) The first direct wireless messages sent from England to Australia on 22 September 1918.

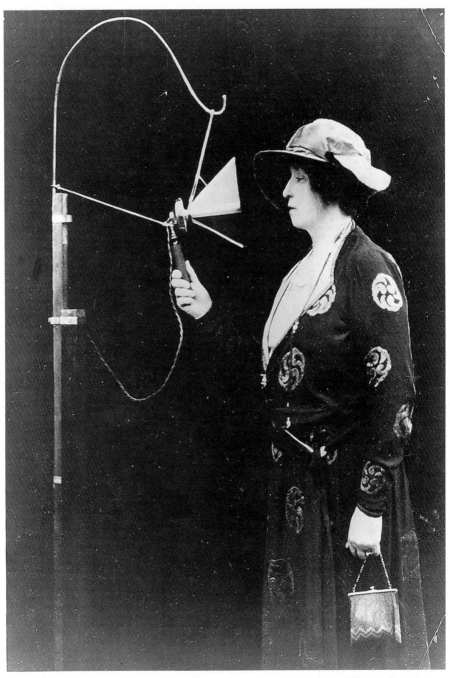

Dame Nellie Melba broadcasting from the Marconi works at Chelmsford in England in 1920. (AWA Archives)

roof of the building. The licence was held by the Trades and Labor Council with little capital—only £1,636. The objective of 2KY, under the direction of Labor Council secretary Jock Garden, was to provide the public with news of the 'goings-on' at the Trades Hall through direct broadcasts, as well as to provide sporting commentaries and easy-listening music.

On 23 August 1926, 2GB Sydney began operating. This licence was held by the Theosophical Society Ltd under the managership of chartered accountant A. E. Bennett, who made it clear from the outset that his station did not intend to fill the air with religious matter but rather, a good class of music, arts and science. The intended call sign was 2AB—to pay tribute to the British theosophist Annie Besant. As the letters AB were not acceptable, the licensee settled for GB, the initials of the sixteenth-century Italian Giordano Bruno, who was put to death for his beliefs. Engineers Beard and Shultz, responsible for the construction of 2KY, fitted out this new station. Len Shultz remained with the company as chief engineer. A well-known local aviator and engineer, he was held in high esteem by all who knew him.

2GB's first transmitter was located in the grounds of Bishop Leadbeater's residence at Mosman. In the 1930s a new site for the transmitter was selected on the southern bank of the Parramatta River opposite Meadowbank. The salt water and flat land made it ideal for broadcasting. For years the transmitting tower, sitting in a well-manicured lawn, has been a pleasing sight for train travellers crossing the Parramatta River. 2GB's studio was located in the head office of the Theosophical Society in Adyar House, Bligh Street. Nowadays it is located in Sussex Street.

In Melbourne, 3DB became Victoria's second B Class station when it commenced operating on 21 February 1927. The licence was issued to the Druleigh Business and Technical College Pty Ltd, but was transferred to a new company, 3DB Pty Ltd, in June that year. In 1929 the licence was acquired by the *Melbourne Herald* and the station went on to become a most successful enterprise in spite of the fact Australia was now wallowing in the trough of the Great Depression.

Although the A Class stations were going through a rough passage economically, 2FC and 3LO initiated many projects previously untried in Australian broadcasting. Under the direction of Oswald Anderson, 2FC made the first direct broadcast from an aeroplane as it flew over Sydney. Telephone landlines were also used to great effect, to broadcast events from the Jenolan Caves in the Blue Mountains and Mount Kosciuzsko, as well as a complete service from St Mark's Church at Darling Point. Interstate landline broadcasts were also on the agenda.

Station 3LO was more inclined to favour the arts, with direct broadcasts from the stages of several Melbourne theatres, and to foster studio performances by local artists and visiting celebrities. 3LO was the first station to invite their listeners into the studio to witness these 'live' broadcasts. Actually they were all 'live' in those days, as no suitable instantaneous recording method had yet been developed for broadcasting. Adopting the same presentation manner as 2LO London, 3LO announcers wore their 'monkey suits'—formal wear or dinner suits—and studio performing artists did likewise.

Adelaide and Hobart A Class stations followed much the same programme trends as their brothers. The Perth station's concentration was more on local programming as landline broadcasts were very expensive over such a long distance from the eastern states. Due to insufficient listeners and revenue, 6WF was withering on the vine.

When the report of the Royal Commission on Wireless Broadcasting was presented to the Federal Parliament in July 1927, in its new home in Canberra, there were some 20 broadcasting stations operating throughout Australia, comprising eight A Class stations and twelve B Class stations. Apart from rethinking music copyright fees paid to publishers and royalties paid to AWA for patents held, not a great deal came out of the inquiry. The decision was made that control of wireless broadcasting and the issue of listeners' and broadcasters' licences was to remain with the Postmaster-General's Department, in spite of a recommendation that a Wireless Committee be set up for this purpose. A more effective Royal Commission was held two years later, in 1929.

By this time, 1927, listener licence fees were 27/6 per year, the carve-up being 17/6 to A Class stations, 2/6 to the PMG's Department for administration, 5 shillings to AWA and 2/6 to the recently established Australian Performing Right Association (APRA) for the use of copyright music. B Class stations had a separate patent and copyright agreement. Operating the copyright agreement was rather complex. Every recording played by the duty announcer had to be accounted for (by the announcer) who had a large log-sheet in front of him on which he filled out titles, composers and publishers in longhand between announcements, which included advertisements and the usual guff. This procedure continued into the mid-Thirties.

Although only briefly involved at this period, I found this a chore and a half. In fact, I made a point of cursing APRA up hill and down dale for this imposition, while the office typist cursed *me* up hill and down dale for my almost illegible scrawl. As a result, I was instructed to print the log details. Funny thing that! Years later I was praising APRA for its contributions to musical culture and the pockets of composers and publishers when I did a stint as Licensing Manager of the Association for Australia and New Zealand. But that's another story.

Along with the complex and rather confusing system of broadcasting now in place across Australia, there was little brotherly love between the operators of A Class stations. Following a warning from Postmaster-General Gerrard Gibson that if disharmony were to continue he would consider not renewing licences when they reached their date of expiry, several station directors decided there was only one course open to them—amalgamation.

Accordingly, in Melbourne, a drawn-out lawsuit between the operators of 3LO and 3AR was defused when the stations agreed to amalgamate under the new company name of Dominion Broadcasting Co. Ltd on 1 March 1928. On 16 May 1928 the New South Wales Broadcasting Company came into being in Sydney to acquire 2FC and 2BL, with a capital of £100,000. The main interest of A Class operators thus switched from arguing to programming. Meanwhile, the Federal Government took another vital step, one that was to have considerable impact on the overall picture of broadcasting in Australia. On 25 July that year, Prime Minister Bruce informed Parliament the government would establish a national broadcasting service by acquiring all A Class stations, including 4QG, whose licence was held by the Queensland Government. Programming would be let out to a contractor and technical services would be provided by the PMG's Department. Bruce, referred to by many as an English Australian, wanted the Australian system to replicate the British Broadcasting Corporation.

The proposed national service would not affect the operation of B Class stations, which still depended solely on advertising for revenue, and the announcement stimulated interest in the establishment of more commercial stations. However, although 50 applications went before the Postmaster-General, not until 1930 did more B Class stations go to air.

Mentioning 4QG reminds me of a little mistake made one day in 1930 at the end of a religious session. The reverend gentleman before the microphone concluded his passionate sermon with a declaration that listeners could put their complete trust in Jesus, to which he added, 'I don't think.' Of course, the phones rang hot from listeners objecting to the reverend gentleman's change of mind. In those days the speaker's microphone was turned off and on by the control-room operator, but on this occasion the operator hadn't manage to switch off before the speaker began to add, 'I don't think I spoke too long, did I?'

There was another slip of a different kind a few years later in Sydney. Let me think now. Who was it? Was it that very popular 'Uncle' George? Or perhaps some other 'Uncle'? 'Uncle What's-his-name' had just completed a rather trying *Children's Session* and was probably thirsting for a beer. After kissing his tiny tots goodnight over the airwaves and calling on Mummy to tuck them into bed, he turned to the control operator sitting in his glassed-in booth and spoke thus: 'That'll do the little bastards for this week.' Although said only gently and without malice, he got it out before his microphone was switched off. At least he had the hollow satisfaction of knowing he had a large listening audience ... until that fatal Friday.

In May 1929 the Federal Government invited tenders for the supply of programmes for the proposed national broadcasting service, with technical facilities still to be provided by the PMG's Department. From eight tenders the combined submission from Union Theatres Ltd, Fullers Theatres and music publisher J. Albert & Son was accepted. The contractors then formed a company for this purpose, the Australian Broadcasting Company, with Stuart Doyle as Chairman. Veteran theatre man Frank Marden was appointed Superintending Manager of the new enterprise. The contract was for a period of three years. Under this company's regime three more A Class stations were opened.

The Australian Broadcasting Company played an important part in fostering the broadcasting of plays and serials, particularly after the improvement in sound quality brought about when the electric pick-up replaced the acoustic method of sound collection.

Sound-on-film—which followed sound on 16-inch (40-centimetre) transcriptions in cinemas landlined to studios—was an additional programme embellishment. 'Live' cricket broadcasts from England topped everything. In actual fact, the broadcasts were synthesised, the commentator sitting in a Sydney studio using cables arriving every few minutes to provide his 'description'. To give atmosphere to his commentary, whenever a bowler made a delivery the 'sound' of impact on the bat would come in the shape of a lead pencil tapped on the desk or against a hard-covered book. (Of course, the real thing was presented to listeners after the inauguration of the overseas short-wave service in 1932.)

Test cricket was then even more fanatically followed than it is today. It was a symbol of the competition between the Mother Country and her youngster. Radios, though rare and crackly, especially in rural Australia of the Depression, were a godsend to cricket followers. How closely the sport was followed is illustrated by a rural story which came to my notice.

A mere dot on the map was the village of Upper Manilla in the north-west of New South Wales, its hub the local post office and manual telephone exchange with less than 30 lines. One local grazier was the proud possessor of a battery radio. During the Test relays he organised with the post office to leave plugged in the telephone lines to his property and those of his two brothers after the exchange closed at 6 pm. At 4 am or whatever ungodly hour the cricket came through, he would ring his brothers and relay the ABC commentary as he heard it through the atmospheric crackle.

When the three-year contract with the Australian Broadcasting Company expired, the Australian Broadcasting Commission was born by Act of Parliament on 17 May 1932, to 'provide and broadcast adequate and comprehensive programmes and to take in the interest of the community all such measures as, in the opinion of the Commission, are conducive to the full development of suitable broadcast programmes'. The Commission received half of the £1/4/- radio-set licence fee. Of the rest, 9 shillings went to the PMG for technical services and 3 shillings to AWA for patent rights.

The Commission began operations on 1 July 1932 with eight metropolitan stations (2BL, 2FC, 3AR, 3LO, 4QG, 5CL, 6WF and 7ZL) and four regional stations (2NC, 2CO, 4RK and 5CK). Its headquarters were set up at 264 Pitt Street, Sydney. On 1 November regular national programme relays began between Brisbane, Sydney, Melbourne and Adelaide. The first Chairman was Sir Charles Lloyd Jones, the General Manager H. P. Williams. In 1933 Williams died and was replaced by Major W. T. Condor. In June that year a relay line was established between Adelaide and Perth.

... and the flirty Thirties

By the beginning of the Thirties, when most Australians were suffering from the Great Depression, wireless—now referred to as radio—was lifting spirits and leading the way in encouraging young citizens to kick up their heels on the dance floor with the foxtrot and quickstep and on the ballroom floor with the soothing waltzes of Strauss. Through radio many dance bands were born— Jim Davidson's Orchestra and later Jim Davidson's Dandies and Coglan's Band in Sydney, Arch Kerr's Black Cats and Ned Tyrell's Orchestra in Brisbane, to name a few. There was no doubt about it, radio provided a salve to the unhappy at this time of stress.

Communication by both telegraphic and telephonic means was improving in leaps and bounds; one of the most notable events was the opening of a radio-telephone service between Australia and England in 1930, inaugurated with a conversation between Prime Minister Scullin of Australia and Great Britain's Prime Minister Ramsey McDonald. This conversation was followed by the editor of London's oldest newspaper, the *Morning Post*, speaking to the editor of Australia's oldest newspaper, the *Sydney Morning Herald*.

Although Marconi, the man who started it all, never found the time to visit Australia, he kept in touch. On 26 March 1930, by arrangement with Ernest Fisk of AWA, as a demonstration of the wonders of wireless Marconi switched on hundreds of lights festooning the Sydney Town Hall—by remote control. The occasion: the 1930 Radio and Electrical Exhibition in the Town Hall.

The AWA engineer in charge of the operation was my latter-day friend Murray Johnson. The idea was for Marconi to press a Morse key to activate a transmitter located in his yacht *Elettra* in Genoa Harbour. The signal transmitted from the yacht was to be picked up at AWA's receiving station in the Sydney suburb of La Perouse. To ensure the reception did not suffer from atmospherics, AWA's other receiving station at Rockbank in Victoria was also used, the signal to be sent on landline to La Perouse to allow the duty operator to choose the stronger signal to be sent on landline to the Town Hall. But things didn't quite go according to plan. I'll leave it to Murray to tell you about the hitch:

A very sensitive telegraph relay was used at the Town Hall, which in turn closed the main power relay for the lights. As a precaution it was decided to leave the line between La Perouse and the Town Hall open to the relay, to avoid the danger of a spurious signal switching on the lights. About three minutes before Marconi was to switch the lights on, I closed the La Perouse line and the lights immediately came on. I had failed to realise that an open line would accumulate a static electrical charge, which of course activated the relay. I quickly explained what had happened to Mr Fisk (later Sir Ernest), who in turn told the large audience. All switches were restored to normal and less than one minute later, Marconi did in fact switch on the lights, on schedule. I think the majority of the audience were impressed and the papers next day hailed it as a remarkable feat.

Just 50 years later, on 12 October 1980, Marconi's daughter, Mrs Gioia Marconi-Bragna, as Chairman of the Marconi International Fellowship, organised a re-enactment of the 1930 event in conjunction with AWA Chairman John Hooke. It took place in the Sydney Opera House. Murray Johnson was invited to attend. He was the only person present who had been in the Sydney Town Hall on that special day in 1930. Once again, over to Murray:

> At 8.50 pm a signal was sent from the burnt-out wreck of *Elettra* at Bologna. The signal switched on coloured lights on the Opera House and on the Sydney Harbour Bridge which triggered a spectacular fireworks display in the harbour. The event was broadcast 'live' in Italy by a 40-minute satellite television link-up. We were able to see all the speakers on the television screen.

It must have been a very proud occasion in the long life of Murray Johnson, especially when he was asked to rise to enable the distinguished guests at the Opera House to see the man who handled the technical arrangements for the original event.

In 1964 Murray had the privilege of meeting Marconi's son, Marchese Giulio Marconi, Chairman of the Italian Marconi Company. Giulio had come to Australia to unveil a marble bust of his father erected at the AWA radio-electric works at Ashfield in Sydney. As Murray said: 'He seemed to be a shy and retiring man, but we enjoyed each other's company. We talked of historical times, people and of his father and family. I showed him my Marconi Veteran's Badge. This pleased him immensely ... two years after our meeting Giulio died in Italy. His father died in 1937.'

Sadly, the historic Ashfield works closed when much AWA's manufacturing activities were transferred to North Ryde. In 1989 the Ashfield buildings, which covered several hectares, were sold. The bust of Marconi was transferred to a new but 'temporary' home at La Perouse on Botany Bay, in the grounds of the former AWA Receiving Station, which had been taken over by the Overseas Telecommunication Commission. When the OTC station closed, poor old Marconi was bustled off to Queensland. He now reposes at the entrance to Telstra's Radio Brisbane site, some 50 kilometres north of Brisbane, almost out of sight, out of mind, as this marine communication unit is about 10 kilometres off the main highway. What a pity this bust is not accorded a more prominent position, or a place in a telecommunications museum. As the sculpture was a gift from the Lions Club of Turin in Italy to the Lions Club of Sydney, perhaps the Sydney club could get the ball rolling in a more appropriate direction. The piecemeal privatisation of Telstra in the foreseeable future would give such a move even more value.

The AWA works at Ashfield, for more than 50 years a living memorial to the development and manufacture of all facets of radio, has disappeared into oblivion. The complex represented the vision and enterprise of such men as Ernest Fisk, Lionel Hooke, Alec McDonald, Sydney Newman, Joe Reed, Jack Davis and Fritz Langford-Smith—lest we forget!

Frank Marden recalls

A few weeks before Frank died at the grand age of 95 years, I called on him at his home at Crescent Head on the mid-North Coast of New South Wales 'to chew the cud' over the good old days, while his devoted wife Olive put the kettle on. As I mentioned earlier, Frank—a long-time cinema man—was pushed into the broadcasting industry at short notice to manage the Australian Broadcasting Company onits formation in 1929. He said he had a feeling of trepidation over the move due to the fact he hadn't even the foggiest idea what broadcasting was all about:

> I was busy supervising the erection of the Company's new theatre in Perth when a telegram arrived from Sydney calling me back to Greater Union's headquarters. As soon as I arrived my boss, Stuart Doyle, told me I was now manager of the Australian Broadcasting Company and I'd better learn something about the game in a hurry.'

Although Frank's memory for detail faltered occasionally, the few sherries we shared helped to sharpen things up a little. 'Politicians,' he kept telling me, 'were my biggest bugbear, but I got around most of those who mattered by offering a job to one of their relatives or close friends. After all, they were all on my side—all the ones who mattered. We had to do a lot of wheeling and dealing in those days.'

But politicians and governments weren't the only obstacles that Frank had to hurdle in the development of the infant industry of broadcasting. The others included the press barons. One of them was Keith Murdoch (father of Rupert Murdoch) of the *Melbourne Herald*. The *Herald* had its own B Class station, 3DB, which had the sole rights to broadcast the Melbourne Cup.

Frank wanted Murdoch to allow A Class stations to take the broadcast but Murdoch firmly rejected the request. He wouldn't have any truck with a company with Union Theatres' Stuart Doyle on its board. (For some time Murdoch had been trying to persuade Union Theatres to advertise cinema attractions on station 3DB, but he kept getting the cold shoulder.)

One particular year (it might have been 1931), after Murdoch had turned him down again just a few weeks before the running of the Cup, the determined manager of the Australian Broadcasting Company moved swiftly. The first thing Frank did was to get on friendly terms with a trainer who had just built a beautiful villa alongside Flemington Racecourse. From the roof of this villa one could command a magnificent view of the course—even better than the view from 3DB's broadcast box.

With the friendly trainer's approval, Frank set up broadcasting equipment on his roof, and 3DB's commentator went to town with a colourful description of the Cup. A breakthrough had been made! A couple of days later, Murdoch called Frank into his office in the Herald building and offered him a job—which he turned down.

After the Australian Broadcasting Company's contract with the Federal Government was terminated in June 1932, Frank went back to managing cinemas for his parent company, now Greater Union Theatres. At one stage he had 43 cinemas under his wing, but his return to the celluloid industry was to be short lived. He was drawn back into the broadcasting arena when the Australian Broadcasting Company purchased 2UW Sydney in the name of the Commonwealth Broadcasting Corporation Pty Ltd (CBC) and appointed him General Manager. Following the formation of Commonwealth Broadcasting Corporation (Qld) in 1937, the company also purchased 4BC Brisbane, 4GR Toowoomba, 4RO Rockhampton and 4MB Maryborough.

By this time the Federation of Commercial Broadcasting Stations (FACB), which began functioning in 1930, had become a strong voice for the interests of commercial operators in all matters pertaining to the broadcasting industry. It would be fair to say that the influence of the FACB was responsible for eventually killing off the government-titled B Class stations in favour of commercial stations.

Frank Marden served two terms as President of the FACB, in 1939 and 1940. He remained as General Manager of the Commonwealth Broadcasting Network (covering all stations owned by CBC) until his retirement in 1946.

Episode 9

The lean years ...

The Great Depression had an enormous impact on all facets of the radio industry. Radio stations coming on stream during the first five years of the Thirties, and the commercial stations already established, found it really hard going, some falling by the wayside. During the first three years of this decade 45 new commercial stations and four national stations were licensed, making a grand total of 65 since the inception of broadcasting in Australia in 1923.

Although listener interest in broadcasting was growing apace, as measured by the rapid sale of receiving sets, there were still insufficient licensed listeners to attract applicants keen on providing stations in country areas. In the four years leading up to the Thirties only two stations were licensed, both city based—3DB Melbourne and 5KA Adelaide.

A well-known pioneer amateur operator led the field for country broadcasters as the first licence-holder in the Thirties. He was George Exton, whose station 2XN Lismore hit the airwaves on 6 January 1930 with a power of a mere 50 watts. Exton struggled to keep his station afloat for want of sufficient advertising and closed it in 1936 when Richmond River Broadcasters established 2LM Lismore. Station 2MV Moss Vale also had a very short life—folding just nine months after commencing on 15 December 1930. In Western Australia, 6BY Bunbury had high hopes when it went to air on 16 April 1933, but folded three years later. On the city scene, the *Melbourne Herald's* pride and joy, 3DB, managed to make a modest net profit of £129/18/- for the year 1933.

Although few national advertisers had seriously considered radio advertising as a supplement to press advertising, two agencies were taking an interest in this new medium—George Patterson Pty Ltd and J. Walter Thompson Pty Ltd. The incentive to place sponsored advertising on radio came from the great popularity of broadcasts of Australia's various bids for the Ashes in the late 1920s and early 1930s. Sydney station 2UW provided the vehicle for this coverage—which, in actual fact, originated in 2UW's studio with the doyen of Australian cricket, M. A. Noble, at the microphone. By arrangement with AWA's Beam Wireless fastened on England, a stream of messages by Morse code from the Oval enabled Noble to keep up a running commentary on a game he could not see.

The man behind this innovation was 2UW general manager Oswald Anderson, who had been involved in wireless broadcasting from the outset (he was concert manager of Paling & Co.'s music store when experimental broadcasts were made from there prior to the opening of 2SB in November 1923). Anderson went on to manage 2FC/BL. When Paling & Co. bought the licence of 2UW he returned to his old firm to manage this acquisition and remained at the helm until the Australian Broadcasting Company's Frank Marden replaced him.

By the end of 1930 Anderson had set up Australia's first commercial radio network, the Federal Radio Network. Initially consisting of 2UW, 4BC, 3DB and 5AD, less than two months later 4GR, 2HD, 2AY, 3TR and 3BA were added to the stable, with 6ML in Perth anxious to join the chain. The Perth station first planned to use a cable service to pick up programmes from the eastern states since there were no telephone lines available to convey them across the Nullarbor at the time. In the event AWA's experimental overseas short-wave station VK2ME relayed 2UW's coverage to 6ML.

Although the spread of telephone services across the rest of Australia was proceeding at a meteoric pace, in spite of the Great Depression, Western Australia was left out in the cold. The vast distance to be covered from east to west, plus the lack of revenue to be derived from a large state with a small and scattered population, made it difficult to justify the expenditure.

West Australian Premier Sir James Mitchell eventually inaugurated a telephone service between Perth and Melbourne, over one of the longest landline telephone circuits in the world, on 18 December 1930, but there was only one pair of wires. In 1933 a carrier channel for radio broadcasting was added to the same pair of wires, bringing much joy to West Australian broadcasters. The carrier method, by the way, is a system employed to enable several channels of high-quality voice transmission over one pair of wires, the channels being separated by different frequency levels. This system revolutionised interstate telephone communication.

Cricket broadcasts were the main factor keeping the Federal Radio

Network together, creating a larger listener pool and awakening advertiser awareness of commercial radio. However, once the Australian Broadcasting Commission got into full swing with interstate hook-ups the sun began to set on the Federal Radio Network. Oswald Anderson's innovative system of providing a running commentary of the cricket from England on 2UW and its associated stations was taken further by Charles Moses, sporting editor of the ABC. He extended these synthetic broadcasts with additional atmosphere, using a rubber-topped pencil hitting a piece of wood to more realistically simulate the ball hitting the willow.

Mentioning Charles Moses (later Sir Charles) reminds me of an incident which occurred during his long regime as General Manager of the ABC, which began in 1935. When world-famous pianist Solomon was engaged by the ABC for a concert tour, the General Manager was at Mascot aerodrome to greet him on his arrival. Apparently the trip out from London had been a bit rough, and as a result Solomon was not in a very good mood when he arrived. As the pianist stepped down from the plane, the General Manager, all smiles, stepped forward. 'Mister Solomon, I presume?' he enquired. 'Yes, I'm Solomon', replied the ivory-tickler, somewhat irritably. 'Well, I'm Moses,' said the genial GM. 'Don't be funny! I'm in no mood for jokes,' snapped the illustrious visitor.

Incidentally, before the Federal Radio Network got under way in 1930, the New South Wales Premier, Jack Lang, had envisaged setting up a network of radio stations owned by the state to spread the gospel of trade unions and his Government's activities. Cabinet approved the State Wireless Scheme, as it was called, but Lang was dismissed by the Governor Sir Phillip Game before it was given serious consideration.

In the spiritual field

Apart from the strong listener attraction of sporting coverage during the early Thirties, church broadcasts were also popular. Very much aware of radio's household penetration, in 1938 the Roman Catholic Church inaugurated regular religious sessions on the Sydney commercial station 2UE. The highlights of these programmes were a direct broadcast of the International Eucharistic Congress in Sydney in September of that year, followed by a series of weekly broadcasts from St Mary's Cathedral. Secretary of the Congress Management Committee, Father Meaney, was so impressed with the strong listener pull created by these broadcasts he successfully campaigned for a broadcast station licence for the Catholic

Church. On the eve of Christmas 1931, 2SM Sydney began transmission, with Father Meaney as General Manager. AWA provided the technical service.

The Protestant Council of Churches, noting the success of the Catholic Church's radio endeavours, also sought and obtained a broadcast station licence. 2CH Sydney began spreading the Gospel on 15 February 1932, following a splendid opening programme of musical items direct from the New South Wales Conservatorium of Music. As with 2SM, AWA contracted to provide the technical services. Financed by a prominent Methodist layman, Frederick Stewart (later Sir Frederick), 2CH concentrated on a better class of music than most commercial stations.

Stewart began his commercial career as a railway clerk in his home town of Newcastle. A very shrewd man, he acquired considerable real estate in Sydney, and launched a private bus service between Parramatta and Sydney which grew into a huge undertaking at a time when public transport was still the principal means of getting about. He also served as the Federal Parliamentary Member for the Parramatta electorate.

Initially the 2CH transmitter was located in the grounds of Stewart's home at Dundas. Although not a very good site for transmission, the tower provided an excellent landmark to remind listeners of the existence of 2CH. Citizens who lived in that area would no doubt still recall the home, which Sir Frederick donated as a hospital known as the Lottie Stewart Home in memory of his late wife. Located on a high point of Dundas, this 136-bed establishment enjoys a wonderful reputation for its nursing service. What a location! Visitors and able-bodied patients have a bird's-eye view of the new Sydney Stadium and surrounds prepared for the Sydney 2000 Olympic Games.

Frederick Stewart was my late wife's uncle, a relationship which was to our benefit during a short stay we had in Sydney during the war years when I was attached to Royal Australian Air Force Eastern Area Headquarters at Point Piper, and he kindly offered us the use of his unit at Manly.

Community singing

There was no doubt about it, community singing did more to promote commercial radio in Australia as an entertainment medium than any other form of programming. It provided an income for many vaudevillians who had fallen on hard times as a result of the Depression, some of whom later reached stardom as radio personalities. During the Thirties at least one radio station in each capital city organised community singing, an amalgam of audience participation, vaudeville artists and good compering to present a very earthy programme of entertainment. Just what people at home and in the theatre needed to cheer them up during those years when jobs were light-on.

4BH Brisbane made a big thing of weekly community singing held in the old Theatre Royal in Elizabeth Street. Compere, songster and punster Les Daley, assisted at the keyboard by his prankster partner Reg Staples, always kept the show going at a steady pace. The Les-and-Reggie combination went on for years. In fact, they would have been the biggest drawcard on Queensland radio. One particular community concert with Les and Reggie at the helm, the Christmas Show of 1938, was remembered for years by Brisbanites of that generation. As the date of the programme coincided with Les Daley's birthday, patrons were expecting a humdinger of a performance, one not to be missed.

The venue was the Theatre Royal, as usual on a hot sticky day. Fortunately the Royal Hotel next door was on tap for patrons in urgent need of a little internal comfort. Inside the theatre, the spotlight was on Les and Reggie, supported by a bevy of beauties dancing and kicking up their heels, a couple of song-and-dance men and the odd comedian. The audience made up the rest of the entertainment as community songsters.

Long before the show got under way people started streaming into the theatre. Within minutes the place was chock-a-block for this special occasion. In fact, police had to be called in to control the crowd. With dignified restraint, the *Courier-Mail* described the scene thus:

> Several women were led from the press while police officers guarded the side doors of the theatre. Streams of would-be patrons, mostly women and children, poured through the bar of the adjoining hotel in an effort to reach the auditorium while there was a general melée about the ticket boxes. Within minutes of the doors being opened, the seating accommodation was filled, the crush occurring when attendants attempted to turn away the overflow crowds from the entrances. Numbers of people unable to gain entry soon dwindled away.

In actual fact, not too many 'dwindled away'. A big percentage of frustrated husbands, fathers, boyfriends and what-have-you decided to leave their loved ones in the long queue outside the theatre for 'just a tick' while they went off to investigate the story about the seating accommodation. The most convenient spot to make their investigations, naturally enough, was the Royal. The pub, of course!

As the contingent of dissatisfied would-patrons stepped into the bar, regular imbibers were still recovering from the shock of seeing numbers of ill-mannered, thoughtless concert-goers invading their hallowed ground, cutting through the bar in a headlong rush to the theatre entrances, so—understandably—things were a bit frosty for a few minutes. To the regulars it seemed like a second invasion. However, as we all know full well, there's nothing like a glass or two to create a better understanding of our fellow man. Within an hour, give or take a few minutes, the regulars and the new arrivals were leaning on each others' shoulders with deep affection and common sympathy, during which time the aforementioned loved ones were still lining up outside the pub in the full heat of day. Before long, rousing songs, screaming recitations and other snippets of stagecraft could be heard coming from the depths of the bar, produced with a degree of professionalism that matched the standard of entertainment inside the theatre.

The theatre audience was also treated to this sudden outburst of new-found talent—it was so deafening they couldn't hear Les and Reggie or the other performers on stage. Then suddenly it was all over. The Theatre Royal and the Royal Hotel simultaneously disgorged their patrons and another 4BH Community Concert had passed. I did hear that Les and Reggie decided to give the show away toward the end of the programme and joined the other show in the bar—but that story was never confirmed. It was a pity the newspaper reporter missed all that. He could have picked up a good story.

Les Daley's mainstay on 4BH was *Topical Chorus*, a 15-minute segment presented 'live' each night, Monday to Friday, a programme which gave his wit full rein, ably assisted by Reggie at the keyboard. Using the same musical bed, each night he would come up with lyrics to describe daily happenings in Brisbane, which he laced with the doings of some of the characters about town. It was a very popular show. As well as *Topical Chorus* and the community concerts, this dynamic duo also organised radio picnics at well-known beach resorts during the summer months. As a staff technician, I was involved in most of these outside broadcasts.

Les had one problem. He was inclined to hit the bottle at the drop of a hat, which posed a bit of a problem for Reggie in keeping him sober for the next broadcast. Les couldn't have found a better keeper, however. Strange to say, the more Les sampled the amber fluid, the more he came up with ideas. His lyrics on the news of the moment flowed as smoothly as beer out of a keg. He had a happy disposition and, sober or not, was never without a smile wide enough to mask the tragedy of his life.

Les had a wife and two children to whom he was absolutely devoted. Whenever he could, he would take them along to community concerts and beach picnics, often leaving them in the care of Reggie while he went off to have one or two with the boys. Les had been through World War I, joining up at the age of sixteen and being wounded twice. But that was nothing compared to his postwar tragedy. Les's wife, whom I met on several occasions, was as thin as a rake with hollowed eyes and a faded prettiness that gave her a rather pathetic appearance. Sadly, she was riddled with tuberculosis and died a few years after their arrival in Brisbane. Their eldest child, a daughter, also died of tuberculosis. Doctors discovered Les's son was also afflicted with the disease, but he survived.

When eventually Les himself fell victim to the same malady, he dropped his bundle. One night he didn't turn up for his *Topical Chorus* broadcast. He was found in the gutter outside the Regent Theatre, blind drunk. He was sacked from his position as Brisbane's top radio man, and went on his way with his sick boy. Fortunately he managed to get a job with Sydney's 2UE. His *Topical Chorus* was another winner in that city but once again alcoholism limited his stay. Then he went back to his home state of South Australia, where he earned a modest income as an entertainer although most of his performances were 'on the house', entertaining World War II diggers in training camps around Adelaide.

Some years ago I bumped into Reggie Staples and his wife Betty at Port Macquarie. Next day, sitting over a cuppa in their home, memories of Les, stories about his popularity over the airwaves and his many acts of kindness during his period in Brisbane, came flooding back to us.

Reggie recalled one particular occasion when he was worried sick about Les's non-arrival at the studio in time for a quick rehearsal for *Topical Chorus*. It was to be a special broadcast, another Christmas programme. Reggie had just enough time to drive out to Les's place just in case he had forgotten what was to be *the* big show, so off he went like a bat out of hell. As it turned out, Les was still there, waiting for a taxi that didn't look like arriving. With just minutes to spare, Reggie bundled him into his car and headed back to the studio, taking every short cut he could find, including a one-way street. Halfway along this street he came face to face with an angry tram driver and a couple of motorists trying to press on in the other direction.

Reggie was stuck. Les was stuck. And the tram and a long line of motorists were also stuck—in a narrow street lined with tenement houses.

There wasn't enough room to swing the proverbial cat, let alone a car. Things were hotting up a bit, what with angry motorists and the tram crew and passengers saying their piece—until Les and Reggie were recognised. Everyone gathered around their car to wish them a Merry Christmas. Then a gent from one of the tenement houses wheeled a piano out onto the footpath. To the hooting of horns and lusty refrains from everyone and their dogs, another *Topical Chorus* was on! It was a good show, Reggie told me, even better than the one they had planned to broadcast from the studio an hour or so earlier.

I well remember when Reggie joined our staff at 4BH. He wasn't all that long out from England, and understandably carried a strong Pommy accent. He started off in Brisbane driving taxis by day and earning a bit more bread for the sideboard with his piano at weekends. A product of Birmingham (my father's home town), Reggie made his first broadcast in 1926 on the government-operated 5IT, playing piano and padding out the music with a few songs. This led to stage shows, but he was not a full-time professional. Then a friend mentioned a radio star from Melbourne had just joined 4BH and was looking for a 'piano man'. Reggie got the job and the two got on famously from the start. They really were the king pins of radio in their time. Reggie died in 1980, a few months after we had met again.

Episode 10

Spring ... and a young man's fancy lightly turns to ... Myrtle

Funny thing about spring. Every year it comes around, and for some unknown reason it invariably brings to mind a specific memory about something or other or someone or other in the passing parade of my almost forgotten past.

This year it was about Myrtle. Not the flower—a little lady with whom I had a brief association back in the Thirties. Lord knows why my thoughts should gallop back in time to Myrtle—there is neither rhyme nor reason for it. I hardly knew the girl.

Let me think now. When was it? Ah, yes, it would have been 1935. I was then but a callow pimply-faced youth, too polite, or too timid to set about sowing my wild oats according to custom. I was then on the engineering staff of Brisbane's 4BH.

Mixed with my technical duties was some air-work as the station's junior announcer. Being less experienced than my mature colleagues, I was relegated to the Saturday afternoon shift, considered a 'dead' part of the week as far as ratings went. That being the case, programme manager Howard Sleath was satisfied he had little to fear of my affecting the popularity of the station, one way or another. The programme was a music session, which merely involved playing records with a bit of natter about the artists and orchestras, interrupted occasionally by advertisements, presented 'live' of course ... they were all 'live' in those days.

One particular Saturday afternoon, a female listener phoned to let me know how much she was enjoying my 'learned' comments. I was so overjoyed to find that someone out there in wireless-land was actually listening to my presentation that, I kept her on the phone for ages. By the time the record had run its length, I had extracted the preliminaries from her—she was just out of her teens, she was single, had auburn hair and no current boyfriend.

By now, feeling rather excited in anticipation of a budding romance, I made a breathless introduction to the next record, placed the pick-up in the groove and continued with my charming listener, reluctant to let her go. She told me she was on the switchboard of a warehouse in Charlotte Street in the city, but had higher ambitions. She wanted to get on the stage and was already studying stagecraft and voice production. She also wanted to do some broadcasting. I told her I might be able to pull a few strings in that direction and suggested she keep in touch with me.

As for myself, naturally I told her I was in my late twenties, had been to the Old Country and was contemplating a trip to America in the near future, confident I would land a job in broadcasting in that country. Still hanging on to my listener—my voice at the end of the phone—I kept cross-fading from one record to another, having in mind to back-announce the titles and catch up with a few ads.

After a quarter of an hour or so, during which time we revealed more of our inner thoughts and aspirations, I manfully moved toward the next step, albeit with a gulp in my voice. A date. We fixed it for the following Friday night. I was to meet her in the foyer of the Wintergarden Theatre at 7 o'clock, which would give us ample time to get to know each other before the show began. The main attraction was John Barrymore and Greta Garbo in *Grand Hotel*. I chose this film as I had already heard it was a bit risqué. Reluctantly, we parted on the phone after a few kisses down the line.

Less than a moment later my happiness came to a sudden halt, so much so I would have been more than willing to drop dead. To my horror I discovered I had forgotten to switch off the microphone, which meant that for the past 20 minutes or so my wooing and kissing had been broadcast, accompanied by a rousing rendition of 'The Road to Mandalay' on HMV 12-inch by Laurence Tibbett, and records from other lesser-known artists.

Seconds later the phone rang. It was the manager calling from his golf club. His wife had been in touch. He really gave me a blast. Next, the chief announcer was on the phone. Another tongue lashing.

Cringing in front of the merciless microphone, bleating out a word or two as I valiantly continued with the music and unconvincing advertisements, I was so mortified that even the heap of phone calls from happy listeners letting me know it was the best show on air since wireless

was invented and would I do it again next Saturday arvo, failed to allay
my fears of being carpeted on Monday morning.

Not surprisingly, I was dropped from the Saturday afternoon show,
and any further air work, so it was back to the soldering iron for the next
few months, until I was called to the microphone once again, this time
for a fleeting career as an actor. But that's another story, best left alone.
And now back to my dearly beloved—Myrtle.

The fact I had put my age forward by about ten years and had given
Myrtle the impression I was a man of the world now had me a little worried.
The plain truth was that I had never taken a girl out socially. What will I
say? What am I expected to do with her after the show? These were just
two of the queries I put to myself as I approached the foyer of the
Wintergarden Theatre with uncertain step on that night of October 1935.

To make sure I didn't keep my date waiting I got there more than an
half an hour before the appointed time. A few minutes to 7 o'clock, I
noticed a group of young people assembled at the entrance to the theatre,
busily looking up and down the foyer as if seeking someone. Then, to a
man—and two women—their eyes fastened on me. I couldn't follow what
they were getting at. And why me?

I made a quick survey. Yes, my fly buttons were all done up, I was wearing
matching socks and my trousers were certainly not half mast. It was now
fifteen minutes past, with no sign of Myrtle. Ten minutes later I was
convinced she wouldn't turn up and was about to go home to Mum when
a meek little voice at my elbow asked if I was Bernard Harte. I swung
around with joyous anticipation, ready to give the voice my most courtly
greeting, but the words stuck in my throat. Surely this dumpy little person
with glasses and slightly buck teeth wasn't my Myrtle. But she was.

At this instant, the aforementioned group burst into applause
accompanied by ribald laughter, seemingly aimed at me—or us.
Fortunately they were off down Queen Street, still laughing like hyenas
as they disappeared.

It wasn't until a week later I found out they had heard me plighting
my troth over the air the previous Saturday and had decided to meet in
the foyer of the Wintergarden to find out if Myrtle would turn up and see
what we looked like in the flesh. Hence the laughter.

And now back to the foyer. We exchanged polite but stiff greetings
after which I excused myself and went to the ticket box to purchase our
tickets for the stalls. Catastrophe! Catastrophe! The only seats now
available in the house were in the dress circle—the most expensive.

As I reeled in shock at the cost, the ticket lady thrust two tickets at me, pursing her lips to indicate her displeasure at my holding up the queue, and asked for the money. I gave her all the coin I had with me and was still one shilling and sixpence short. With the lady in the box now very restless and the queue getting longer, I called Myrtle to my side, explained the situation and asked if I could borrow the shortfall.

Without demur, Myrtle kindly gave me the money and I grabbed the tickets. Now utterly humiliated, I hung my head like a dog as I trailed after Myrtle as she sought out our seats. I felt like a passenger, not an ambitious swain.

I just couldn't concentrate on the first half of the programme. All I could think about was the absence of money to buy my guest a box of Columbines. As if she sensed my problem, as soon as the lights came on at interval Myrtle suggested I allow her to buy a box of Columbines.

'Yes, I would be grateful, Myrtle,' I whispered, in a manner that didn't exactly exude the gusto and confidence of Brisbane's would-be leading radio announcer last Saturday afternoon.

To cut a long story and a brief romance short, after the show ended, I shook hands with Myrtle outside the entrance to the Wintergarden, thanked her for her company and apologised for having to borrow, adding an assurance that I would drop the one and sixpence into her workplace first thing Monday morning and looked forward to taking her out again. Before she had time to respond in a suitable vein, I was off. I didn't have the nerve to ask her for my tram fare home to Toowong, so I set off on the long walk, wondering if Myrtle would be tuning in for me next Saturday afternoon and perhaps a little curious about where I had got to.

Episode 11

Growing pains

By 1934 things were a little brighter on the radio broadcasting scene, with more homespun programmes, 'live' of course, with a few recorded shows— mostly American, like Eb and Zeb, Flash Gordon and Charlie Chan—adding a touch of canned mystery. But it was the enormous popularity of Children's Sessions and their associated 'uncles' and 'aunts' that did more than any other programming to take radio into Australian homes. And, as most of the sets were still switched on after nightfall, listening to the locally produced plays, talks on current affairs, and 'live' and recorded music became a must for the oldies. But it was still hard going for any station to reach profitability. Eventually the acceptance of radio almost as a member of the family meant prosperity was well on the way, bringing with it bigger, better and brighter productions.

4BC Brisbane

The first commercial station to be established in Brisbane was 4BC. As I mentioned earlier, it was founded by John Beale Chandler, who began business in that city in 1913 as a manufacturers' agent. In 1918, when few suburban homes had access to an electricity supply, and most were still using petrol or kerosene lamps for home lighting—apart from the few connected to the Brisbane gasometer—Chandler shot to prominence in the business world by acquiring the sole agency for the Gloria domestic lighting system.

This method worked on petrol vapour. Installation involved running fuel lines throughout the house to provide room-by-room illumination. When electricity became the main system for home lighting, Chandler was in position on the ground floor, so to speak, to contract for house wiring and to market electric refrigerators and, later, electric stoves. This led to the opening of electric-radio branches in Cairns, Warwick and Bundaberg, with the main showroom in Adelaide Street, Brisbane. When wireless broadcasting was established, direct association with this new industry was a natural progression—hence 4BC (Beale Chandler). Within three months of going to air in August 1930, 4BC was well to the fore technically with outside broadcasts by landline, starting with the arrival of the pioneer aviator, Charles Kingsford Smith, at Brisbane's Eagle Farm aerodrome after completing a flight from England to Australia in a record time of 9 days 21 hours and 40 minutes in his single-engine Avro Avian *Southern Cross Junior.* After covering the official welcome at the aerodrome, 4BC crossed to another point in the city to describe the procession and motorcade as the aviator moved toward another rousing welcome. A coverage such as this wouldn't raise an eyebrow today, but in 1930 it was an outstanding technical accomplishment.

In another pioneering effort, 4BC made the first comprehensive broadcast of an Aboriginal corroboree, which was relayed interstate and broadcast overseas by AWA's short-wave station, VK2ME.

The original 4BC studios were located in Adelaide Street, Brisbane, above a well-known and highly respectable funeral parlour. Naturally enough, a fair amount of chiacking went on about this location, especially among the staff of rival stations who had a tendency to refer to 4BC's 'deadly' programmes.

Very much involved in civic affairs, John Beale Chandler served several terms as Lord Mayor of Brisbane, and for a period of four years was a Member of State Parliament. In recognition of his outstanding contribution to state and civic affairs he was awarded a knighthood. He died in 1962.

4BK and other Brisbane broadcasters

The second commercial station to be licensed in Brisbane was 4BK, which went to air on 29 September 1930, just six weeks behind 4BC. The company was founded by electrical merchants Edgar V. Hudson Ltd, rivals of Chandler's business, in conjunction with the music store of King & King. The studios and transmitter were located in the old King & King building in Queen Street. The call sign was originally intended to be 4FO, which undoubtedly would have been perfect for sending-up by the locals; it was quickly changed to 4BK.

Some years later 4BK was purchased by the *Courier-Mail.* The studios and transmitter were transferred to the new Courier-Mail building opposite the post office in Queen Street, a most inefficient site for transmission, although any shortcomings were probably offset by the publicity gained by having a tall tower atop the building. Some years later a more technically suitable site was found in suburbia.

Brisbane's national station, 4QG, had a well-established listening audience by the time 4BC and 4BK went to air, and wooing them over to commercial radio was a big problem. Although talks, market reports and studio recitals were 4QG's main programme ingredients, the *Children's Session* had a big following, as did the *Breakfast Session*—especially when it was on relay from Sydney.

The *Breakfast Session* usually featured vaudeville artists. I well remember one of them—Will Mahoney. Will and his wife were already popular stage performers. If I recall correctly, as part of his comedy stage act Will had a dance routine which involved prancing on a xylophone. Later on, in the post-Depression years, a number of stage comedians made the transition from vaudeville to radio, including George Wallace and Roy 'Mo' Rene.

Broadcasting hours

With insufficient advertising to cover operating costs, many metropolitan stations restricted their hours of transmission. By October 1930, 2UE Sydney was the only commercial station transmitting regularly before 8 am. Most commercial stations closed at lunchtime and resumed some hours later, generally for the children's sessions. During weekends, transmission hours were minimal, more so on Sundays. Station 2KY, for example, came on the air for just four hours on Saturdays and remained closed on Sundays. The daily break in transmission was quite helpful for the staff of commercial stations, as most days the time was taken up with rehearsals for live studio performances that night, including plays.

Before Brisbane commercials began transmission on Sundays, some amateur operators were permitted to provide a non-advertising programme. The menu consisted of music, cheerio calls and birthday greetings. Many a child living in Brisbane during those years heard their name and birthday wishes called on the wireless from an amateur station. I well recall one station in Toowong opposite the fire station, and another at Kelvin Grove. In fact, I was a regular visitor to the Toowong station as I lived just around the corner from its studio.

The actor

He had only a short career, lasting about an hour, but he did cause quite a stir in broadcasting circles—especially 4BH. The 'he' was me—not by design or desire, I hasten to add, but by managerial decree. Settle back, and I'll tell you the sad story.

I was on the staff of 4BH at the time as a junior technician. The station was blessed with only one studio, then located on the top floor of Grice's music store in Queen Street. I remember the studio and that period of my life as well if it were yesterday.

The studio was neither soundproof nor acoustically acceptable, but some effort had been made to soften the intrusion of unwanted noise—like staff laughing and chattering during morning tea-breaks 'out the back'—by draping thick green baize curtains from ceiling to floor around each wall. Apart from serving as a part-audio barrier, these thick drapes provided a repository for accumulated dust. It was an old building, and of course not air-conditioned. With no fresh air inlet, breathing was sometimes a problem for announcers trying to get their messages out—especially on a hot summer day. Any Brisbane summer day was hot and humid!

Most days when the station was off the air for a couple of hours, the time would be taken up with rehearsals for the radio play to go to air that night. As there was no recording equipment available in those times every performance was live, so there was no room for slip-ups by the cast.

As a control-room operator, my job was to ensure that the actors gathered around our one and only microphone did not get too close, and didn't shout into the thing or bump the microphone stand while saying their piece.

The type of microphone used in those days consisted of loose carbon granules encased in a circular metal box fronted by a diaphragm, usually made of a thin sheet of mica. The microphone was held in position in a steel band or ring by four steel springs intended to absorb unwanted knocks and bumps, for which purpose they were quite useless. It was not uncommon for an over-enthusiastic actor to hit the microphone with his script as he emphasised his point. The result would be a hell of a din, loud enough to blot out the other voices and serious enough to throw the transmitter at Bald Hills off the air for a few minutes, transmitters not being equipped with overload protection relays in those years.

All this made my job very important as the sidekick to the producer, who would stand beside me in the glassed-in control booth as I grimaced at the actors in the form of a stern warning to watch their distance—and waved my arms, even my fist, at the appropriate moment. Indeed, I really had them a little scared, a situation I relished, more so because I had the cigar-smoking producer beside me who also happened to be the manager. And me—just a callow youth of little consequence—outside the booth.

The sound effects were mostly provided by mechanical means although occasionally we had the use of gramophone records especially manufactured for such performances. They mostly had half a dozen tracks, each carrying a different sound effect. I remember one particular sketch when the sound embellishment didn't go according to plan. The script called for the sound of twittering birds in the background as a love-sick couple ambled through a park. The lady made reference to the beautiful sound of the feathered accompaniment—according to the script. Her lover endorsed her remarks. The duty announcer—who doubled as the effects man—was slightly late in bringing in his 'birds'. Much mortified by missing the cue, the now very nervous effects man hastened to make amends by dropping his pickup into the 'birds' track. Trouble was, he dropped it into the wrong track—the one marked 'pigs snorting'. Suddenly realising he had made a slight error, the quick-thinking gent changed the revolution of the two-speed turntable to the higher speed. After a few initial grunts, the pigs quickly moved up to a higher pitch, sounding just like twittering birds, thereby debunking the theory that pigs can't fly! Of course, by this time the couple had already left the park—according to the script.

It was just as well the two actors weren't wearing headphones, as this little episode would have stopped them in their tracks. As I happened to be on duty in the control booth at the time, naturally I gave the effects man a solemn look of sympathy—as soon as the many hilarious listeners who phoned in, and I, had regained our composure.

To return to the story I set out to tell you ...

It came to pass one day as I was about to go home after completing my morning shift that the manager, Eric Harrison, called me into his office.

'Bernard,' he said. 'Have you ever done any acting?'

'No, Mr Harrison, apart from appearing in a Boy Scout play for our church,' I replied.

'Well, that's good enough. We need an actor in a hurry for tonight's episode. He doesn't have to say much, just a few lines. I want you to play the character. OK?'

Well, I nearly collapsed on the spot, but weakly agreed to the assignment—even though it meant getting home late for tea. The play was *One Man's Family*, which was being aired each week night. It was also being broadcast from some stations down south. It wasn't a bad play, but not worth writing home about. I had to play the part of a ne'er-do-well artist on a cruise ship on the Mediterranean, sitting on a deckchair alongside a lovely lady, wooing her passionately, if only with my eyes, while her suitably out-of-sight hubby was over the rails going for the big spit.

My reaction to the instruction to become an overnight thespian had me in such a nervous state I spent the balance of the morning running to and from the toilet, then tremulously joined the rest of the cast in the afternoon for the rehearsal. As it turned out, I didn't make a bad fist of my lines though I did find it hard to come to grips with my lady lover. She was a bit snooty, in my opinion, and so old—so very old. (She must have been at least 23!)

By three minutes to eight, when we had gathered around the microphone waiting for the opening theme, I was a nervous wreck. At one minute past my *big* moment came. I stepped up to the microphone to speak my lines, when lo and behold! I was shaking so much I got too close and whacked the microphone with my script—with such force the transmitter at Bald Hills was thrown off the air. Then came the deep silence as we waited the three minutes it took to bring it back on the air, during which time my fellow thespians were all looking daggers at me—but not a word of admonition. Just looks! Just looks that kill!

There and then I decided to terminate my new career as an actor. I bade the rest of the cast good evening, walked out of the studio and caught the next tram home to Mum, leaving the remainder of this episode of *One Man's Family* for the professionals to sort out.

The control-booth operator

After that little fracas, I endeavoured to keep my distance from rehearsals of *One Man's Family* and the like. When unavoidable, my performance in the control booth was somewhat muted. However, I did have an unexpected intimacy with the play on one other occasion. The studio performance was going smoothly and I was at peace with the world, just fiddling with the appropriate controls. Halfway through the episode, I decided to make a cup of tea to go with the sandwiches my mother had lovingly prepared for me. I slipped out the back, plugged in the jug, and went back to my control desk in the booth while it came to the boil. No sooner had I returned than I noticed the voices of the actors fading away in the loudspeaker—and then they disappeared.

'That's funny,' I thought. 'Must be a valve (tube) gone in the speech rack. That's torn it.' Then the penny dropped. At a great rate of knots I whizzed out the back, pulled out the plug of the jug, restored the other plug to its rightful place and ran back to the control booth to hear the voices of the players rise to their usual level. I should mention that the control equipment was rather ancient, almost out of the Ark. To light the filaments of the valves we used a chloride battery of three cells connected to the control booth by about eight metres of wire. A chloride cell consists of a glass jar about 50 centimetres in height filled with the chloride electrolyte. To keep functioning, the battery of three cells had to be continually charged. Our electric charger was plugged into the one power point we had, which usually carried a double adapter, but not on this particular night. To boil the jug, I had unthinkingly removed the charger plug. As a result, the battery immediately gave up its voltage. Seconds after I pantingly got back to my desk, the telephone rang. It was Mr Harrison.

'Bernard, did you have a blackout in there? My wireless set went off for a few seconds and then came on again.'

'No, Mr Harrison. We didn't have a blackout here,' I answered, truthfully but nervously.

'Must have been out here. We're always having power interruptions in this neck of the woods,' he opined. 'You OK? You sound as if you are short of breath,' he enquired sympathetically. 'Haven't been helping yourself to my cigars?' he added jokingly.

'No, sir, I'm OK. Thank you, sir. Can't take the smell of cigars,' I replied somewhat weakly.

'Goodnight, Bernard.'

'Goodnight, Mr Harrison.'

Mentioning microphones reminds me that the stands were heavy and cumbersome to lug around, which we had to do to set up for outside broadcasts. They had a cast-iron base and a heavy tubular stem to carry the microphone. You had to be in good physical nick to carry one. Carrying two at a time was an almost impossible feat—at least for me.

I recall a particular occasion in 1936 which really tested my endurance. It was a Christmas Ball, held in the Brisbane City Hall to raise funds for the Children's Hospital. The function was organised by 4BH and had the blessing of the Lord Mayor. My job was to set up the equipment to broadcast the official opening and some of the music for dancing. As our studio was not all that far from the City Hall—just a couple of blocks—I was not permitted to use a taxi to carry the gear, so it had to be shanks's pony. This involved carrying two microphone stands and a box carrying the line-amplifying equipment and accessories, committing me to three trips. It was a very hot and sticky night. By the time I had completed the installation and made a test down the line to the studio I was just about done in. On stage was an array of VIPs, including the Lord Mayor and Mayoress and our Managing Director, V. F. Mitchell, and his wife, all dressed in formal wear befitting the occasion.

With a minute or so to go before the broadcast, I was enjoying a slight breather, until the Managing Director came over to me. 'Bernard!' he said, 'Why aren't you wearing a dinner suit?' The fact that I was tucked away out of sight of the public was no excuse. As far as he was concerned, social etiquette had to be observed no matter which rung of the ladder one was on.

Queensland Premier Forgan Smith was in power from 1932 to 1941, leading a Labor government. A rather humble man, he lived in a modest cottage with his wife, shunning most of the social trappings that went with his high office. Each Sunday night he would broadcast a half-hour armchair chat from his home, which apparently had a good following. I was rostered to go to his house each alternate Sunday night to set up the broadcast equipment to send his chat down the line to the studio.

He was a very friendly chap and so was his wife, who would run to the kitchen and put the kettle on as soon as I arrived. Naturally I enjoyed the cuppa as an unseasoned, secret tea drinker. At home my mother wouldn't allow me to drink this beverage, declaring, 'Tea stunts your growth.' The fact I was heading for the six-foot mark was of little consequence. My dear mother held fast to several similar theories. One was, 'Don't burn the toast; if you do you could get cancer'; another, 'Have all your teeth pulled out when you're young, then you won't have any decay problems.' I must say these fallacies were shared by many mothers of those times.

Whenever Federal Parliamentarian and former wartime Prime Minister Billy Hughes came to Brisbane a broadcast was a must, as he had good listener pull. He stayed at the Bellevue Hotel on each visit, so that's where I had to go to set up equipment for a direct broadcast. Getting him on the air was a hell of a job. He had a raspy voice which didn't take kindly to the microphone. The fact he was deaf caused him to shout, which meant making him stand well back from the microphone to avoid distortion from his blast. An irritable man, he couldn't abide me pushing him back whenever he got worked up with his speech. Although he had really had his day in politics, he had been a great champion for the introduction and development of wireless in Australia, and for many years was a director of AWA.

The Big Broadcast of '37 ... that wasn't!

It was Christmas Eve 1937. The venue for the Big Broadcast was the SS *Koopa*, a pleasure steamer which had plied the Brisbane River and Moreton Bay, providing transport and happiness for many thousands of young and old Brisbanites since 1912. She was indeed Brisbane's *Sydney Queen*, that famous pleasure boat of the Sydney Harbour.

And this is how a Brisbane radio station's excursion into mobile broadcasting came about. Each Sunday night for well over twelve months, 4BH would broadcast a concert programme from the stage of the Regent Theatre, featuring Ned Tyrell's orchestra of about fifteen players and guest songsters. The programme, which was broadcast in the peak evening period from 8 to 9 pm, was sponsored by Stuart the Suit Specialist (SSS), and relayed to Rockhampton and Townsville where SSS had branch stores. It was a very popular programme and a big winner for the sponsor. In fact it was such a big winner, the management of 4BH and SSS hit on the idea of broadcasting the Christmas Eve programme from the *Koopa*— which, by the way, could take up to 1500 people. It was well organised and well publicised, indeed, a credit to our management and sponsor. Silvertails in the form of the Lord Mayor and a clutch of do-gooders around town and their wives were invited to this history-making festive event. A few tickets were also made available for others slightly down the social scale.

But there was just one tiny little thing which hadn't really been given much attention so far. How to get the programme to air, considering the fact our broadcasts were always by telephone landlines? A situation which called for a bit of quick thinking.

The predicament was solved when an amateur radio operator agreed to lend us his 5-metre portable transmitter, an offer gratefully received by management and studio staff but not the engineering staff, who had strong forebodings about the success of the venture, especially after the 'ham' wireless wizard turned up at our studio with his home-made transmitter loosely coupled together on an enlarged breadboard. It was arranged for one technician to take the equipment aboard the *Koopa*, with the second to set up a listening post at a suitable location along the Brisbane River bank to landline the programme to the studio.

The chosen spot for the best reception was the Cannon Hill Abattoir. As second technician, that's where I was sent. The exact spot—on top of a freezing chamber that put me in visual range of the proceedings. To get there I had to climb up an iron ladder on the outside of the building.

It took three climbs carrying the gear, which included an accumulator about the size of a car battery. Surprisingly, I wasn't a bit hot and bothered, on account of the fact the freezing chamber was badly enough insulated to give me an attack of the shivers. As it was supposed to be warmest night of the year, I hadn't brought any warm clothing along to combat the leaking freezing chamber, nor a gas mask to combat the aroma rising from the carcasses below me! Carcasses which I assumed must have long passed their use-by date.

However, it only took me a few minutes to get through to the studio, where the staff were all agog, waiting for the Big Broadcast, an excitement I didn't share. I had arranged with the shipboard technician for a test at 7.30 pm. At the scheduled time there wasn't a sound, not even a whimper, coming from the *Koopa*. By a quarter to eight, still not a sound. The receiver was as dead as a dodo. By this time the programme director, Howard Sleath, was on the phone demanding the 'presence' of the orchestra. He was really agitated ... and so was I agitated. I kept tuning the dial but not a sound. As it was only a one-way hook-up, there was no way I could communicate with my colleague. The only way he could ascertain if his jigger was working was to tune in to the station. It was now five minutes to the appointed hour for the cross. Howard Sleath had quietened down due to the fact he had lost his voice from shouting at me. I gathered he had completely run out of steam. Eight o'clock, just deep silence. Well, deep silence in the receiver. Just then the *Koopa* hove in sight, preceded by the sound of music for dancing by. I could see the lovely ladies being swirled around on the covered-in deck. It must have been a joyous occasion for everyone on board—except the technician and maybe the manager.

At five past eight o'clock, no sound, no cross. While the station manager insisted on showing the VIPs an extended view from the poop deck, my fellow technician had one more go to get the thing working. By this time the *Koopa* was abreast of me and the music was superb. As if especially for my benefit, the songsters started belting out my favourite carol, 'Joy to the World'. Less than a minute later the *Koopa* was showing me her stern, the music fading into the distance as she headed for Moreton Bay.

Then I heard the sound of a plop. Then another plop. Someone must have fallen overboard. Two must have fallen overboard, I thought. Next, a torch aimed at me from the disappearing stern. 'N B G,' it flashed. And another 'N B G'. And another 'N B G'. Although I could read Morse code I was unable to decode this message. (It meant 'no bloody good', the technician told me when he got back on dry land.)

As for the plops, I heard from another source that they were caused by my overwrought colleague venting his disgust at the useless portable transmitter by throwing it overboard. He was so het up he forgot to tell the compere, Mr Tyrell, and the orchestra that they weren't on the air. So everyone on board—but one—put their best foot forward to make the Big Broadcast of '37 a memorable event.

Meanwhile, back on top of the freezing chamber I was packing up the gear to return to the studio when I noticed one of the connections from the receiving set to the accumulator battery was lying loose! In my haste to get everything working, I must have accidentally knocked the clip off the terminal, rendering the receiver useless.

'Well, well,' I softly said to myself, 'No wonder I couldn't pick up any sound from the ship. Perhaps the little portable transmitter was working after all. That being the case, Mum's the word!'

2FC Sydney's very elegant studio; it left 2SB's studio for dead. (AWA Archives)

2FC's control room in 1924, in Farmer's Department Store, Market Street, Sydney. (AWA Archives)

Norman McCance broadcasting the arrival of Alan Cobham in Melbourne on Sunday 15 August 1926 after a flight from London, an event which attracted a crowd of 15,000 people. (National Library of Australia)

Major Hatfield with a group of Legacy children and (at left) the ABC's New South Wales manager, Basil Kirke, doing the 'daily dozen' for a programme which ran from 1937 to 1949. (ABC Archives)

Final rehearsal for *The Man who Stayed at Home*, 2FC, 26 March 1931. From left to right: Ethel Lang, Therese Desmond, unknown, Ellis Price, John Dunne, Laurence Halbert (directing), unknown, Nancye Steward, Bill Mitchell. (AWA Archives)

Marconi opened the Sydney Electrical and Radio Exhibition of 1930 by operating a key on his yacht *Elettra* in Genoa Harbour, which switched on 2,800 lights in the Sydney Town Hall. (AWA Archives)

Murray Johnson at the Marconi re-
enactment at the Sydney Opera
House in 1980.

At the opening of the new Parliament House in Canberra, Dame Nellie Melba
sings 'God Save the King' while Prime Minister Bruce looks on. (National
Library of Australia)

New South Wales Premier Jack Lang and Governor Sir Philip Game at the opening of the Sydney Harbour Bridge in 1932.

Inside an AWA-built Aeradio station, 1938–39. (Civil Aviation Historical Society)

Reggie Staples and singer on stage for the 1938 Christmas concert.

'Uncle Col' and Kitty broadcasting the Children's Session from 2GF Grafton in the 1930s, with vegetables and flowers gifted by children to the local hospital. 'Uncle Col' was C. E. Coldwell-Smith, foundation manager of 2GF. (AWA Archives)

Brisbane's welcome to Charles Kingsford Smith after his record flight from England to Australia in 1930. Far left, Russell Roberts, manager of the new 4BC, with future premier Forgan Smith looking over the aviator's shoulder; Premier Theodor (in bow tie) to the right of the Reisz microphones. Photographer Tom Harte (my father) was then working for the *Brisbane Daily Mail*. I was down the front somewhere. (National Library of Australia) [[*perhaps omit; author has not sought permission*]]

3YB on wheels, about to set off with Bert Rennie, Vic Dinneny and Bert Aldridge. (Ace Radio Broadcasters 3YB)

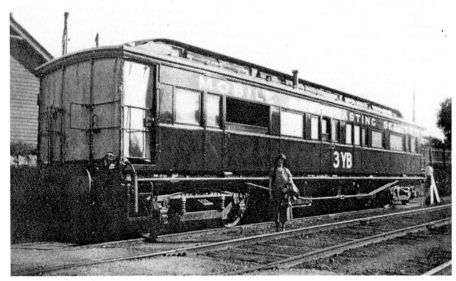

There was a busy half year ahead for Mobile Radio 3YB 'on the rails'. (Ace Radio Broadcasters 3YB)

MV *Kanimbla*, later HMAS *Kanimbla*.

Episode 12

The country scene ...
'It's just the wife chopping wood'

So said Marcus Oliver of 2MO Gunnedah, explaining that the knocking noise his listeners could hear in the background was not a fault in their wireless sets, just the sound of his wife chopping wood for the fire, the woodheap being just alongside the studio and in range of the microphone.

Although such an explanation was perhaps a little unusual, in country broadcasting in the early years the close link between the broadcaster and listeners was not. From the day Ted Gold set up Australia's first country station, 4GR Toowoomba in Queensland on 16 August 1925, non-metropolitan broadcasters were soon married to their listeners and the community through fire and famine, storm and tempest. The bad things and the good things—with emphasis on the good things—of country life were embellished with the novelty of canned and 'live' entertainment.

As for Marcus Oliver's comment about his wife, I doubt if she was ever committed to such a backbreaking chore as chopping wood. More than likely he was just airing his high sense of humour, an attribute that made him a popular figure in the area, both on and off the air.

Gunnedah, New South Wales

Gunnedah's station 2MO was one of the first country stations to be launched in New South Wales, on 16 January 1931; it was certainly the first to fare well in spite of opening for business in the trough of the Great Depression. In fact it first came on the scene some years earlier as the amateur experimental station VK2MO, Marcus being a pioneer in that field.

Born in the Sydney suburb of Neutral Bay in 1875, Marcus Oliver was educated at Sydney Grammar School and Aylesbury College, Hertfordshire, England. On leaving school he obtained an engineering apprenticeship to Seimens Bros of London. Back in Australia he joined the island trader Burns Philp and was soon on the island run as engineer on the company's schooner *Hercules*. He first became interested in wireless in 1911 and in 1912, the year he moved to Gunnedah with his brother Dalley to open a garage and engineering business, he obtained an amateur wireless station licence and began building his own transmitting equipment.

In 1912 he married a Londoner, Lucy ('Baby') Marcea, and set up a home in Marquis Street, Gunnedah, in which he was to establish 2MO nineteen years later. At the outbreak of war in 1914, the Government closed down all amateur stations for the duration of hostilities.

In 1928 Marcus re-established his amateur station with the PMG's permission, to broadcast music and cheerio calls on a restricted basis. Backed by the Gunnedah Municipal Council and several local citizens, he obtained a broadcast station licence and in 1931 immediately converted his popular VK2MO to professional status, with the call sign 2MO. With the help of his one and only staffer, his wife 'Baby', sharing the microphone, Marcus operated 2MO until 1936, when he sold the station to a newly formed company, 2MO Gunnedah Ltd. Rising from an initial power of a mere 10 watts to 500 watts, then 1000 watts, the station today operates on a power of 2000 watts, sufficient to cover a vast area and maintain the slogan coined by its founder, 'The Voice of the North-West'.

Marcus continued his association with the station as Managing Director of the company until 1939, when in search of a quieter life the Oliver family moved to Port Macquarie. Their two sons, Alex and Vivian, soon became involved in commercial affairs there. Alex operated a radio business which became a television outlet, and Vivian was a great worker for the Port Macquarie Historical Society.

Marcus Oliver died at Port Macquarie in 1946. I met his wife in the 1950s when music was her main local activity. Better known around town as Ollie, she was a member of a musical group for some years, scraping out a fair tune on her cello. I recorded the group for broadcast on the afternoon programme of local station 2KM, which I was managing at the time. Ollie died in 1969.

Wangaratta, Victoria

The first country broadcasting station to be established in Victoria, 3WR Wangaratta, had but a short life. Had 3WR survived, it would have been acclaimed as the first country station in Australia, as it commenced on 25 February 1925, some seven months before pioneer station 4GR Toowoomba went to air. The licence to operate 3WR was granted to the proprietor of a Wangaratta sports store, Leslie J. Hellier, in December 1924. Hellier saw wireless as an opportunity to promote sales of his sporting goods and, more especially, the sales of wireless sets and the kits to make them which he had stocked as an adjunct to his normal retailing display.

The studio and transmitter were located in his home in Rowan Street. As there were no electric pick-ups in those days to collect the sound from gramophone records, the music machines were a gramophone and pianola, the sound being picked up acoustically by a microphone. Revenue was well below expectations, so Hellier decided to close the station on 22 December 1925.

Six years later the station was re-established with the formation of the Wangaratta Broadcasting Company, using the same call sign. Hellier was appointed Managing Director. Although more professionally set up and with more transmission power and facilities than the original enterprise, the project did not prosper, and an application was made to the Postmaster-General to transfer the station to the bustling town of Shepparton. Approval was given and a new company was formed, named Goulburn Valley and North-Eastern Broadcasters Ltd. The licence was transferred to this company on 15 January 1935. In 1937 the call sign was changed to 3SR.

Ballarat, Victoria

The next station to come on air in Victoria was 3BA Ballarat, founded by two amateur experimental station operators, Alfred Kerr and Warne Wilson, who applied for a licence in 1929. With financial support from local businessmen, Ballarat Broadcasters Pty Ltd was formed and the station officially opened on 31 July 1930 by Jim Malone. Often referred to as the 'Father of Wireless', Malone was involved in broadcasting in this country from the ground floor, from the time he was transferred from his position as Chief Manager of Telegraphs in the PMG's Department to the fledgling Wireless Branch as Chief Inspector. Throughout his long career as a government representative he was well respected by members of the profession. Malone's nephew Kevin Freeman was Facilities Officer at 2GB Sydney for many years, with the responsibility of PMG landline bookings and facilities for the Macquarie Network.

Kalgoorlie and Western Australia

6KG was the first country broadcasting station in Western Australia. Licensed to Goldfield Broadcasters Ltd, the station's service began on 16 September 1931.

The second station to come on air in the west was 6BY Bunbury, opened with a flourish on 16 April 1933. Insufficient revenue caused its closure two years later, on 31 July 1935. Many years later, on 24 January 1953, the station was resurrected at a different location—Bridgetown—with the same call sign and licensed to WA Broadcasters Pty Ltd. Bunbury came into the news in the intervening years when 6TZ opened there on 11 October 1939. This time, the operating company decided to place the studios in the capital city—Perth—with the transmitter at Waterloo. The licensee, Nicholsons Ltd, also operated 6PR Perth.

Launceston and Tasmania

The first Tasmanian country station to be licensed was 7LA in the large town of Launceston. It was opened on 13 December 1930. The licensee company, Finlay & Wills Broadcasters Pty Ltd, later in its life included Sir Ernest Fisk of AWA on the board.

The next commercial country station on line in Tasmania was 7UV Ulverstone, the operating company being North-Western Tasmania Broadcasters Ltd. The service commenced on 6 August 1932. The transmission site at Ulverstone was found to be economically unsuitable, however, so on 9 March 1940 the operation was transferred to a new location at Devonport and the call sign changed to 7AD.

Crystal Brook and South Australia

Midlands Broadcasting Services Ltd obtained the licence to operate South Australia's first commercial country station—5PI Crystal Brook, commencing 7 January 1932. Apparently Crow-eaters preferred to 'weather' the static to listen to capital city-based stations, as it was not until 16 September 1934 that a second South Australian commercial country station, 5MU Murray Bridge, was established under the wing of 5AD Adelaide, owned by Advertiser Newspapers Ltd.

Mobile station 2XT

The Great White Train was the first complete mobile broadcasting station in Australia. Designed and operated by AWA, the Great White Train served both as a trade exhibition and to take the wonders of wireless to the 'bush' of New South Wales in the years 1925–26. In just twelve months, more than a hundred towns in country New South Wales were visited. As soon as the train came to a halt, the AWA engineers would be out and about erecting a transmitting aerial and within an hour or so station 2XT would be on the air, providing entertainment, rural reports and interviews from its well set-up mobile premises.

Although the audience was not all that large, as wireless broadcasting in Australia was then but two years old, this service stimulated the interest of country people in obtaining news of the progress of rural development in Australia and overseas on a regular basis. This led to more sales of wireless sets to those brave enough to withstand the static when they turned to Sydney stations after the departure of the Great White Train. Incidentally, in the call sign 2XT chosen to identify this station, X stood for 'experimental' and T for 'train'.

The Royal railway carriage

An association between engineer Bert Aldridge, ex-publican and man of great initiative, Vic Dinneny, several manufacturers and an accountant, led to the formation of a syndicate to apply for a mobile licence for Victoria, an idea dreamt up by announcer Jack Young from 3BA. The Y of the call sign referred to Young, the B to Ballarat. With some hesitation the Postmaster-General issued the group a restricted licence for mobile station 3YB, held in the name of Mobile Broadcasting Services Pty Ltd, based in Melbourne. The equipment was housed in two buses, one for the transmitter and the other for the studio/office. The power output was to be no more than 25 watts and the area of operation had to be outside the 50 kilometre radius of the five commercial stations currently operating in the district to be traversed (3BA Ballarat, 3GL Geelong, 3HA Hamilton, 3BO Bendigo and 3WR Wangaratta). A provisional licence was initially issued for a period of three months and later extended to twelve months.

Painted red and gold, the buses of 3YB—one a rather ancient Model T Ford, the other a more up-to-date Model A Ford—set sail for the station's first broadcast, which took place at Clunes in October 1931, with Vic Dinneny filling the roles of manager, advertising manager, announcer and cook. Bert Aldridge looked after the technical side of things, which included a power generator. Local support was given by Bert Rennie and Jack Young. All hands were on deck at each temporary location to erect and dismantle the transmitting aerial. Station 3YB was loudly applauded by listeners and advertisers, especially those living in towns without a local station. The only snag was the work involved in putting up and pulling down the aerial—a rather cumbersome and backbreaking procedure. Young decided to approach the Victorian Railways Commissioner, Harold Clapp, for the use of a carriage. Surprisingly, the Commissioner offered the Royal carriage—no less! Constructed by the Victorian Railways in 1899, the carriage had been especially fitted out for the visit of the Duke and Duchess of York for the historic event of Federation in 1901, and the celebrations that went with the occasion. Much to the chagrin of Sydneysiders, many of the ceremonial activities that marked this milestone in Australian history were centred in Victoria as Parliament House, Melbourne, was the seat of Federal Government from 1901 until Canberra was established in 1927.

After the departure of the Royal couple, the carriages stood idle for some years until hired for £12/10/- a week by 3YB and converted into an ornate studio/office/record library. Space was also provided for housing the transmitter and power supply and most importantly, living quarters. Dovetailed with various regular railway services, this luxurious carriage traversed a fair section of Victoria carrying loyal subjects in the shape of the crew of the mobile station, who hailed it as the ant's pants.

By 1935 a number of other commercial and national stations were on the air in Victoria, and a permanent home was sought for 3YB; in fact, three permanent homes. Two locations were approved by the PMG. One, at Warrnambool, carried the same call sign of 3YB; the other at Warragul, became 3UL. So ended this historic entity in broadcasting history, a wireless station on wheels.

In its new location, 3YB went to air on 18 January 1936, and 3UL commenced on 18 May 1937. Both stations prospered under the banner of Associated Broadcasting Services Ltd.

I must thank Peter Headen, manager of 3YB, for supplying me with photographs of this mobile station taken from a booklet compiled by an ex-staffer, Hugh Adams.

MV *Kanimbla*

The third, and final, mobile broadcasting station to operate, 9MI, was all at sea! Installed by AWA in MV *Kanimbla* before she left the Belfast shipyards on her maiden voyage to Australia, the station was beautifully fitted out to operate on two frequencies on the short-wave band, with a power of 50 watts.

The service commenced on 25 April 1935 as soon as *Kanimbla* cleared Ireland, with music provided by gramophone records augmented by 'live' performances featuring the shipboard Kanimbla Quartet. I managed to have a good gander at the station when the vessel tied up in Brisbane for a few days on this maiden trip to Sydney. The studio/transmitter was most impressive and so was its carrier. Mobile station 9MI was closed shortly after the outbreak of World War II.

Kanimbla was then seconded to the Royal Australian Navy and converted into a landing ship. In this capacity HMAS *Kanimbla* and her crew gave meritorious service in several assaults against the Japanese, including the landing of a large force at Tanaherah Bay, New Guinea, on 17 April 1944, heralding General Macarthur's 'Road Back' to fulfil his promise to return to liberate the Philippines from whence he had departed for Australia in early 1942.

HMAS *Kanimbla*'s next assignment was to take part in the landing at Morotai on 15 September 1944. Then followed assignments to send supplies ashore in the Philippines and Borneo (1 July 1945). A few days later, on the historic American date of the Fourth of July, General Macarthur announced that the Philippines had been liberated.

I had the privilege of viewing a huge armada of steel lying in Leyte Harbour (Philippines) on 22 June 1945 when I flew in to Leyte from

Biak (Dutch New Guinea, now Irian Jaya) via Peleliu (Caroline Islands) after the bloody capture of Iwo Jima and Okinawa. The armada was assembled for the final thrust. But that's another story.

South Burnett and Queensland

My first experience of country broadcasting was at Wooroolin and Kingaroy in the South Burnett district of Queensland, when I was transferred from 4BH Brisbane to the newly established 4SB. Although 4SB mainly relayed programmes from 4BC Brisbane, there was a small studio in Kingaroy used for local programming. The transmitter was at Wooroolin, some 23 kilometres from Kingaroy, which is situated in the heart of the peanut belt.

The Wooroobin transmitter was powerful, capable of transmitting 3000 watts, and designed to cover a large area although the permitted operating power was only 2000 watts. Communication with the Brisbane control room at 4BC was by Morse code. The Chief Engineer, Jock Cruickshank, was an ex-submariner of the Royal Navy who had served in the 1914–18 war. I was his offsider, but working an alternate shift that meant staying overnight, for which accommodation, kitchenette and shower room were provided. It was quite a good set-up, the technical operation being run very much on Navy lines. We got on very well together and I have to thank Jock for teaching me a lot about housework.

The people living in the district were rather conservative in my book, with strong family links. One particular custom, concerning retirement, was rather unique. It was not unusual when a local farmer and his wife decided to seek a softer life after many years of backbreaking toil—which included stooking peanut bushes year after year—for them to hand over the farm to a married son and move in to the nearest town, *taking their home with them.* On one particular occasion I was caught up in one of these moves. Read on ...

An oddly moving Christmas tale

I've been in some strange situations and some odd places at Christmas time, but nothing matched the occasion back in 1938, when I helped to celebrate Christmas Day with a family I'd never met before. It was on the road—in their house.

About 11 o'clock in the morning of Christmas Day I was driving slowly along what is today known as the Bunya Highway in the direction of Kingaroy, where I was living at the time.

It was a typical hot, sticky Queensland summer day. I was finding it hard to keep awake. I was sleepy on account of the fleas at the boarding house where I was an inmate—I had spent most of the previous night scratching, scratching and scratching. By dawn I was just about done in from lack of sleep. A quick cold shower in the laundry under the boarding house gave me but temporary revival. I would have preferred a hot bath, but that would have meant stoking up the copper and carrying buckets of water as there was no hot water system laid on in the premises; not even a chip heater.

My bedroom was just a partitioned-off section of the back verandah, with no door. Whenever I was away for the day, or part thereof, the friendly boarding-house landlady allowed her dog to doss down on my bed—a procedure I deeply resented because of the fleas the dog left behind. She was a big dog with big fleas. I also resented being asked to chop firewood on most weekends to feed the copper for the weekly laundering and the kitchen stove. Occasionally my landlady managed to snare one of my fellow inmates for this and other chores, but as most of the other boarders were at sport or some frothy occasion at weekends, jobs around the house usually became my lot.

During the previous week I had been desperately searching the town for alternative accommodation but there was nothing available to match my thin wallet, so I was stuck. With smouldering discontent at the thought of spending Christmas Day at the boarding house, I passed through the township of Tingoora, endeavouring to fix my sleepy eyes on the red gravel road ahead of me.

Less than half a kilometre on I almost ran into the back verandah of a house. For a moment I thought I must have dozed off for a second and inadvertently followed a track to the house. But now, fully awake, I took in the scene. Here was a house on the move.

Shifting houses from one set of stumps to another was a fairly common occurrence in the Burnett district in those years. Oftentimes I would be scooting along in my 1927 Baby Austin and come across one being trundled along, sitting on a trailer or spread across the trays of two trucks operating side by side.

I recall one house removalist who boasted in his advertising that he was such a perfectionist he could move a house from one location to another without upsetting a glass of milk or needing to shift one stick of furniture.

This particular house in transit really captured my interest. It was being moved along at a slow pace, I assumed in the direction of Kingaroy, and occupying most of the width of the road, leaving little room for motorists to get around it. On the back verandah, hanging from a roof support, was a big meat safe, placed to catch every breeze that might come by. Between each verandah-post was stretched a wide green ribbon as Christmas decoration. Tacked on one post was a happy cut-out face of Father Christmas.

Every now and again the lady of the house would come out on the verandah, take something out of the meat safe and disappear inside again. I was so intrigued by the scene that I moved my Baby Austin as close as I could get to the verandah within the bounds of safety, chugging along at snail's pace rather than attempting to squeeze around the house and be on my way. Now I could hear the sound of a pianola and some voices raised in song, beefing out a Christmas carol.

What a lovely family situation, I thought. If only I could be part of it, instead of having to go back to the boarding house and face the lady and the tough, aged turkey I had brought to heel after a lengthy chase a few days earlier.

As if reading my thoughts, the lady of the house and her husband stepped out on the verandah and beckoned me to come on board. I was surprised to note they were middle aged, in their prime so to speak. I yelled out at the top of my voice something about being unable to accept their invitation on account of the fact I happened to be driving my car— which, by the way, rejoiced in the moniker of Egbert, a name bestowed by one of my fellow inmates. In less than a minute the trailer driver had brought his load to a halt and was around the back with a length of thick rope.

Without a word, he wrapped one end of the rope around Egbert's front bumper and, with the added strength of the man of the house, lashed the other to the back of his trailer. By this time I was aboard and meeting the family.

Then we were away again, with my little Egbert prancing along behind on his rear wheels, like a dog on his hind legs begging for affection. A minute or so later and I was sitting with the family at the dining room table, tucking in to a magnificent meal of cool turkey and warm salad, after which came the sweets—fruit salad and hot custard. The lady of the house apologised for the custard, having been unable to cool it in the meat safe in time.

In response, I declared the whole meal absolutely scrumptious. So far, hubby hadn't partaken, preferring to delay his repast until he had cleaned up a couple of bottles of beer in honour of the occasion, a situation I could see had his one-and-only a little perturbed. I politely refused his offer of a beer, declaring I was a devout Methodist—but I did accept a bottle of ginger ale which I shared with the couple's comely daughter. By this time we had reached the township of Memerambi, which was the cue for the driver to give his motor a chance to cool down.

Being somewhat parched after a long haul, and with a few kilometres still to go, he hopped into the pub for a refresher, more than willingly accompanied by the man of the house. The driver considerately parked as close as he could get to the entrance to the pub to allow motorists to get around the big load. For the next half hour or so, mother, daughter and yours truly sweltered in the midday heat, to the background of Christmas carols and songs of a more ribald character emanating from the bar. Then, thankfully, the batwing doors swung open and out came the driver in cheerful mood, and the man of the house in even happier mood. As soon as the driver noisily sorted out his gears, we were on our way once again—with a jerk.

Less than an hour later we were moving along the street leading to the new site for the house. My host had already mentioned the block he and his wife had selected. It was on a slight slope overlooking the town, chosen, he said, to capture every cool breeze in summer and to avoid the winter westerlies. He was obviously very proud of his block of land. By now the driver was manoeuvring his huge load with some difficulty through an avenue of cars and a few sulkies lining each side of the narrow street outside a little wooden church. The church, directly opposite our destination, must have been jam-packed, judging by the number of vehicles.

Demonstrating the skill which only comes with considerable experience as a long-distance haulier, our driver commenced the delicate task of backing his load off the street onto the block, humming as he did so one of the carols his ear had just captured coming from the church. What a magnificent Christmas Day, I muttered under my breath. A first-class meal with a friendly family, an unusual experience, ending with a congregation in full voice to greet us. I was at peace with the world. But my reverie was quickly shattered by the raucous, almost hysterical, voice of my host.

'Where are the stumps? Where are the flamin' bloody stumps?' he yelled (to the accompaniment of the second verse of 'Abide with Me'). Continuing his outburst for all the world to hear, he looked across the street to the church as if challenging someone inside to arrange a miracle.

'He told me not to worry,' my host yelled. 'He said everything would be jake and the stumps in place. No sign of the builder. No bloody stumps. Nowhere to put me flamin' bloody 'ouse! I'll kill the bastard! That's what I'll bloody do. I'll kill 'im!'

At this moment an elder or some other official, who looked as though he could do with a good feed, emerged from the church and declared that such blasphemy, the like of which had never before assailed the ears of the congregation, would give my host an assured place in Hell, if not replaced with a prayer at this instant.

Inside the church, all was deep silence as the preacher and his flock followed every audible move of the drama without. Making it clear he was not able to accede to the instant demand of the churchman, my host kept ranting on until the driver let it be known he wanted the house unloaded before nightfall, as he had to be on the job early next morning to haul another house.

Unable to offer any worthwhile solution, I quietly unleashed Egbert and pushed him along the street until we were well out of earshot. I then started him up and steered a course for the boarding house where I was greeted with a frosty stare. Mumbling something about a flat tyre causing me to miss Christmas dinner, I made a beeline for my bed—too tired and too sleepy to combat the fleas the dog had left behind. Actually, that night I had my best sleep since becoming an inmate of that establishment.

As for the stumpless house episode, it was such a long time ago, I am not sure of the outcome on that Christmas Day. I recall seeing the house some years later, sitting on stumps in the grounds of the little church. It was being used for Bible gatherings and other worthwhile church happenings. I am unable to tell you whether my host gifted his house to the church to provide him with a place in Heaven or if the gift came too late to make amends.

Episode 13

War and peace and the Golden Years

Although radio broadcasting had passed its formative years by the end of World War II, it was not until about 1948 that it reached what we called the Golden Years—aided and abetted by the widespread use of instantaneous disc recording, the development of magnetic recording, an escalation in the production of soap operas/radio plays and audience participation shows, and the spread of network broadcasting.

During the war years many innovative outside broadcasts—including stunts—were made to counter somewhat the restrictions imposed on broadcasting. These programmes, the continued popularity of community singing, the participation of Australian and American servicemen in audience shows, plus news coverage on the progress of the war, albeit heavily censored, combined to make listening a must. And there was no one more gratified by the growing number of listeners than the advertising agencies, led by George Patterson Pty Ltd and J. Walter Thompson Pty Ltd, which went a little soft on print media expenditure to place more national advertising on radio. A shortage of newsprint during the war years also contributed to radio's good fortune.

However, the imposition of National Security regulations—for which the puritanical Postmaster-General of the day, Senator A. G. Cameron, carried the flag—gave quite a few station owners a rough passage on the way to prosperity and caused the demise of several companies. On the premise they posed a threat to the security of fellow Australians, four commercial stations were ordered off the air and their broadcast licences terminated. They were 2HD Newcastle, 5KA Adelaide, 5AU Port Augusta and 4AT Atherton. All four were owned and operated by the Jehovah's Witnesses.

Bowing to pressure from the established churches and growing adverse public opinion, Attorney-General Billy Hughes had promulgated a Commonwealth Gazette in January 1941 which declared this church an 'unlawful organisation' on the grounds of its outspoken pacifist philosophy which, the government considered, could pose a threat to security and possibly provide some advantage to the enemy, in particular Nazi Germany. The Jehovah's Witnesses appealed the decision and took the matter to the High Court, but lost the case.

These four stations did not set out to deliberately breach security regulations. They did so unwittingly, giving the enemy a possible opportunity to home-in on coastal Australia. In the case of 2HD Newcastle, in response to a query sent in to a popular quiz show by a listener to which the panel was unable to provide an answer, the quiz master had informed the listener this had earned him a prize of 2/6 which he was invited to collect at the 2HD office the next time his ship was back in port. The seaman happened to be a member of the crew of the *Iron Monarch*, a BHP-owned iron ore carrier, more than likely steaming along the coast at the time, heading for Newcastle. It was a dead giveaway!

In the case of 5KA, a gossip columnist let slip the news that there was a Royal Australian Navy minesweeper in dock and about to depart for the high seas when she commented that a former manager of opposition station 5DN looked resplendent in his naval uniform when seen to go aboard his ship.

The Jehovah's Witnesses operated a farm on the Atherton Tablelands in Far North Queensland near the church-owned station 4AT. It was here a drama was played out when police and the military swooped, wanting to know the location of the searchlight that was supposed to have been used for the enemy's benefit. It so happened that workers had been employed for several nights with a spotlight shining on a dam under construction on the farm. Another charge was that the church was supposed to have a field of corn arranged in code so as to be read by the enemy when flying over. Both charges were proven false, being examples of wartime hysteria and fertile minds.

In June 1943, Mr Justice Starke of the High Court declared the regulations on which the ban was based were 'arbitrary, capricious and oppressive' and had it lifted. Actually the Jehovah's Witnesses were a good thing for radio in the early days, being pioneers in the use of this medium from 1924. Over a period of some 20 years Australian commercial stations enjoyed weekly revenue from the church, broadcasting a programme under the banner of the *Watchtower*. Several other religious organisations followed this example, and evangelist Billy Graham was also a big user of radio. I had a great deal of empathy for the churches. The money was good, and there were no bad debts. Lovely people!

Several other stations were either reprimanded or put off the air for 24 hours during the war years. One incident concerned the sinking of the cruiser HMAS *Sydney* after a battle with the German raider *Kormoran* in the Indian Ocean. Although widely headlined in the press, a certain station got a lacing when the news announcer read a cutting from a newspaper referring to the sinking. In those years many commercial broadcasters used newspaper cuttings to compile news bulletins, sometimes by arrangement, sometimes without permission.

Mentioning weather conditions was also taboo as soon as the Japanese entered the fray. Identifying the location of an outside broadcast was another. Station 3GL Geelong was asked to terminate its coverage of a big bushfire because the smoke—seen for miles—could pinpoint its location, making the town and district vulnerable to attack. Certain aids to broadcasters were also banned—including binoculars. Ken ('London-to-a-brick') Howard got around this imposition by using a telescope for his horse-racing descriptions.

A long-running imported American programme, *Frank and Archie*, was given the chop because one of the characters, Frank Atanabe, was a Japanese houseboy.

Although commercial stations copped most of the hidings, the ABC also had to suffer the dictates of the Censor. National station 3AR Melbourne got into hot water after broadcasting the national anthem from a school when the headmaster called for 'renewed fervour' in singing 'God Save the King' on this occasion, as a mark of respect for the crew lost in the *Sydney*.

The licences of three of the four Jehovah's Witnesses' stations were allotted to applicants in waiting with a commercial interest; that of 4AT was assigned to the National Broadcasting Service, thus providing the Australian Broadcasting Commission with an outlet in Far North Queensland.

Chaste broadcasting

Maintaining the moral fibre of fellow Australians in times of war—and possibly peace—was another objective of Postmaster-General Senator Cameron. His aim was to remove all moral impurities from the airwaves, even before they reached the airwaves. Scripts for broadcast had to be scrutinised by his staff, and the lyrics of songs presented 'live' or on recordings had to conform to a moral code, which meant dropping some popular tunes of the times or altering words of songs considered offensive.

Nowadays such lyrics wouldn't even raise an eyebrow. Likewise in the late 1940s. But the good Senator wouldn't risk sullying the mind of radio listeners. The song 'She Had to Go and Lose it at the Astor', played on air many times before the war, was banned because of its suggestiveness. Veteran comedian and songster Gracie Fields was instructed to alter the last verse of her popular song 'He Wooed Her' before going to air during a wartime visit to Australia.

Alfred Paddison, who was President of the Australian Federation of Commercial Broadcasting Stations at the time, quickly responded to Cameron's morals campaign by declaring 'Australian radio was the cleanest in the world'.

If I may digress from the subject for a moment to say a little more about Paddison, known to the industry, unsurprisingly, as Paddo: for many years he was a great stalwart for the unified development and operation of commercial radio. A great orator, he had no problem in getting his message across. He was my chief when I took over the managership of 2KM Kempsey in 1950 and later when I took 2KA Katoomba under my wing. Retired in 1966, he continued a strong interest in radio broadcasting and print media until his death a few years later.

A former teacher of mathematics at Canterbury High School, Paddo was a close associate of the former New South Wales Premier Jack Lang and edited the Labor publication *The Century* until it closed about 1969. Lang's book *The Big Bust* was partly written by Paddo, and his follow-on book *The Turbulent Years* was completely written by him. I can vouch for that. When I took over from Paddo on his retirement, precipitated by a stroke, I provided him with an office alongside mine in Stanway House, King Street, Sydney, so he could concentrate on production of *The Century* and Lang's latest literary 'effort'.

It was a most remarkable effort on his part as the stroke had left him severely handicapped, with the entire right side of his body paralysed. Typing was a laborious one-finger job thereafter with many letters, even sentences, left out. As soon as he caught a cab home each afternoon, I made a point of slipping in to his office to retype and make corrections as best I could before the lady from *The Century* called to pick up the copy for the newspaper and the proposed book, usually late in the afternoon.

I well remember the day the book was completed. Lang phoned Paddo from his home in Blackheath in the Blue Mountains, as he did most days.

Being very hard of hearing he would yell into the phone, and in response Paddo would have to yell back.

'How's it going, Paddo?' I heard him say.

'It's all finished, Jack,' Paddo yelled back, 'but we haven't got a title for it yet.'

That's when I put my two bob's worth into this high-level discussion.

'How about *The Turbulent Years*?' I shouted.

'Bernie suggests *The Turbulent Years*, Jack. What do you think?'

'Right! *The Turbulent Years* it is,' shouted Lang.

I never got around to reading the book, but believe it was well received by Sydney booksellers.

A few weeks after settling on the title, Paddo had a bad fall as he was leaving his office and heading for the lift. He struck his head and bled profusely, requiring ambulance attention and admission to the casualty section of the nearest hospital. Next day, quite unperturbed, he hobbled back to work, but I decided he was another accident about to happen and that he should continue to work at his Elizabeth Bay home rather than coming in to the office. 'Very well, Bernie,' he said meekly after I told him of my decision. Months later another stroke carried him off.

I lost a good boss and a good friend. He had backed me all the way when I proposed to lift 2KM Kempsey from a small country station fettered by an ill-chosen transmitting site and a shared frequency to a new location and a new frequency of 530 kilohertz, a frequency which had yet to be embraced on the broadcast band. 2KM was to be a directional station; this involved the purchase of a large parcel of land, just over 20 hectares, and seeking the cooperation of manufacturers to extend the tunable range of their receiving sets to include this frequency. The advantage of 530 kHz is that it is the longest wavelength. The longer the wavelength the longer the geographical coverage for the same power, in this case 2000 watts. The area was doubled by installing a directional radiating system involving two steel towers instead of one and an extensive earth-mat system.

As soon as the new Kempsey project was functioning I opened additional studios at Port Macquarie and Coffs Harbour.

The ABC at war

Along with the commercial stations the ABC was very active during the war, programming many outside broadcasts at home and from the war zone. Mobile broadcast units were used to bring the latest news of Australian forces—most times using portable disc-recorders, not easy to keep functioning with dust and many loud noises in the air. War correspondents were appointed to go with the mobile unit which was attached to the AIF in the Middle East from 1940.

At home many new programmes were initiated during the war years, including the popular children's programme *The Argonauts*, begun as a segment of the *Children's Hour*. The Argonauts Club, which rewarded contributions from children across Australia with on-air mention and elaborate certificates, was launched in 1941 and continued for many years. More publicity-conscious than previously, in 1939 the ABC began publishing the *ABC Weekly*, a small magazine containing programme schedules and news items about programmes and announcers, which continued through the war and for some years thereafter—no mean feat considering the shortage of newsprint at the time.

With the appointment of a Parliamentary Roundsman in Canberra, Australian news, including Parliamentary capers, became an important ingredient in programming and raised the ABC's stature in this field in preparation for the beginning of the independent news service which was soon to follow.

During the war years revenue for the operation of the ABC, gleaned from the public purse, was increased to 55 per cent of the takings from listener licence fees following the findings of a Joint Parliamentary Committee of Inquiry on Broadcasting. The extra revenue allowed the national broadcaster to extend its range of services, particularly in the cultural sphere. This included the fostering of more concert and vocal competitions, the founding of the Sydney Symphony Orchestra and the increased use of permanent landlines to network sporting and other events throughout the continent.

War over, the independent news service was fully operational by June 1947. On 1 April 1950 Radio Australia's short-wave service, which had been an adjunct to the ABC during the war years, was transferred back to the Department of Information.

Soap operas, comedy and 'live' drama

Serials and radio shows were very much part and parcel of day and night programming by the mid to late 1930s, but the war provided a great impetus to 'live' and recorded productions of this facet of radio entertainment. Australian productions gradually eased out American canned dramas and comedies, including *Charlie Chan*, *The Air Adventures of Jimmy Allen* and *Chandu the Magician*, partly because of the difficulty in importing them in wartime and partly because the stable of radio actors on tap at home was growing. And they were not all from the uncertain stage. For many performers, young and old, radio provided the vehicle to carry them into the Arts.

By the end of the war several production houses were already functioning, including Artransa, Columbia Graphophone Company, Grace Gibson Productions and Australian Record Company in Sydney, and Feature Radio, Legionnaire and Broadcast Exchange in Melbourne. Colombia was part of the giant Electrical Musical Industries group of England. The Australian production headquarters were based at Homebush where most of Australia's 78 rpm records had been churned out under various labels since the early 1920s. A few radio networks also produced 'live' and recorded productions.

Grace Gibson, an American, worked in sales for the US company Radio Transcription of America, which supplied some material for Australian radio. The Manager of 2GB Sydney, A. E. Bennett, met her during a visit to America. Bennett persuaded the company to send her to Australia on loan to help set up a production company fostered by 2GB.

Grace came to Australia, liked the place and settled in Sydney, and so Artransa was born. In 1944 this very smart and popular lady decided to set up her own company, Grace Gibson Productions, which she retained until 1978, during which time GGP churned out 30,000 quarter-hours and several hundred five-minute featurettes for the Australian and overseas market. In recognition for her services to radio Grace Gibson was awarded the Order of Australia in 1987.

The company was taken over by her right-hand man, Reg James, who was still reselling many GGP productions a few years ago. During its years of activity GGP produced far more soap operas than any other production house in Australia and provided work for many actors and writers. Much of the output was adapted from American scripts.

At a function in Sydney to celebrate the 50th anniversary of radio broadcasting in Australia, Grace spoke to the old-timers sitting at the festive board from her new home at Waikiki Beach near Honolulu where she was busy soaking up the sun.

As for the artists, George Edwards led the field from the 1930s, producing and acting in such productions as *Inspector Scott of Scotland Yard* and *Dad and Dave*—based on Steele Rudd's book *On Our Selection*, published in 1899. A stage adaptation in 1912 featured Bert Bailey, who had purchased the dramatic rights from the author, born Arthur Hoey Davis.

Martin's Corner was another of many productions from the George Edwards Players made during the wax-to-vinyl cutting days at Columbia's Homebush studios. George Edwards, whose real name was Harold Parkes, adopted his pseudonym as a tribute to a famous actor of that name on the London stage. His own acting career began in the early 1920s when he trod the boards with his wife in a vaudeville act around Sydney.

Mary Hahn, whom I had the pleasure of meeting in Port Macquarie some years ago, worked for George Edwards as his secretary and doubled as publicity officer, wardrobe mistress and 'dogsbody', to quote her. As she said:

> His wife died so he joined his brother Lou Parkes to form a theatrical company, taking shows around the suburbs of Sydney. They had a new show about every two or three weeks. I remember some of them. There was *Charlie's Aunt, Up in Mabel's Room* and *Getting Gertie's Garter*. I had to go along to most of them. When the Great Depression came along, the business folded up. I had already left the company to get married and never saw him again.

To keep the pot boiling until he went into radio, George Edwards conducted community singing in picture theatres, sometimes during the interval at screenings. With his new wife, well-known stage actress Nell Stirling, he quickly took to this new medium, earning the title of 'the man with a thousand voices'. His scriptwriter and co-producer was the very talented Maurice Francis, who began his working life as a milkman.

Dick Bentley was another early radio star. He first faced the microphone in 1929 as a violinist in an amateur orchestra. He now lives in London.

Australia's Amateur Hour was launched during the World War II years under the sponsorship of Lever Brothers, through the J. Walter Thompson agency. The idea of an amateur hour had its genesis in the United States. John Dunne of 2SM was taken with the idea when he visited the United States and began a small edition of it when he returned, paving the way for fostering talent with a show he compered in the late 1930s he called *Amateur Night*. Now a big buyer of radio, JWT had a winner with the comedy sketch *Mrs 'Obbs*, for Bonnington's Irish Moss cough mixture. The intro to each commercial, 'Sip ... Sip ... Sip', accompanied by a sympathetic violin, soon had many listeners 'Sip ... Sip ... Sipping' their way through the day.

The George Patterson agency surpassed JWT as the biggest buyer of radio time, placing many spot advertisements and sponsored sessions on behalf of such national advertisers as Colgate-Palmolive. To handle radio productions the Colgate-Palmolive Unit was formed, with Ron Beck as manager and the young Jack Davey as an early producer/director. Under the umbrella of the Colgate-Palmolive Unit, a glittering array of actors, comedians, instrumentalists and producers were soon reaching for stardom. The *Cashmere Bouquet Show, The Quiz Kids, Colgate Cavalcade* and *Calling the Stars* were just a few of the many productions for radio instituted by the George Patterson agency.

As the war drew to a close, it was time to put out the red carpet to usher in the Golden Years of radio.

Mister Radio

By this time Jack Davey had far outshone all other performers to become the biggest listener drawcard, and also the biggest earner, in the history of Australian radio, accumulating what was then the staggering sum of more than £30,000 a year at the time of his death in 1959. Rightly he had earned the title of 'Mister Radio'.

Arriving in Australia from New Zealand in 1932, his radio career began when A. E. Bennett of 2GB gave him a position as a junior announcer. He quickly clicked on the airwaves, with his bright microphone presentation and fast-talking ad-libbing opening the door to better opportunities. This led to Colgate shows and the climb up the ladder to the pedestal as the top quiz master, the top compere and the top showman.

While his radio career was blossoming, he managed to include a weekly newsreel commentary, which was no hindrance to getting through more than 250 half-hour recorded shows a year and some charity work as well.

I only met the gentleman once. It was about 1955, when I was engineer/manager of 2KM Kempsey. He was a driver-competitor in one of the famous Redex or Ampol car trials of the time. The route, coming down from Armidale to Kempsey along the Armidale Road, included a brief checkpoint at Greenhill, some 13 kilometres west of Kempsey. By good fortune our studio/transmitting station was less than a hundred metres off the Armidale Road at Crotty's Lane, not far from the checkpoint.

As we had only short notice of the arrival of the cars, in particular Davey's car, I had to move quickly to tee up a landline. The Postmaster-General's Department, responsible for all telephone and landline installations, rejected my request for a temporary line at the proposed broadcast spot, the stopover point, on account of the short notice I'd given. As we had already plugged the fact we would have Jack Davey 'live' on air with a direct broadcast, I decided to hell with it—we would provide our own temporary landline, knowing full well it would incur the wrath of the PMG's Divisional Engineer and Telephone Manager.

As it happened, the cow paddock alongside the checkpoint was blessed with a barbed wire fence which continued along Crotty's Lane. With the assistance of my offsider, Jack Conry, I set up the outside broadcast gear at the spot, attached it to two strands of the barbed wire and ran a length of flex from the studio across Crotty's Lane to make the second connection to the fence. Five minutes later we were in business. A quarter of an hour later, after many station pointers about the coming of Jack Davey and the proposed direct broadcast, we had him on air.

Just as we closed the broadcast a carload of PMG executives arrived to read the riot act to me about infringing the PMG's given right. I meekly received the blast and crossed my 'Harte' that I'd never do it again. Of course we had planned a few more direct broadcasts that day when other newsworthy competitors were due to check in …

I knew I had already been reported to PMG headquarters in Melbourne, so I wasn't surprised when I was phoned from the highest echelon and given another blast, which included a recital of the dire circumstances which would follow if the infringement was repeated. The caller ended the conversation wishing me all the best, and added a little chuckle as he signed off. Nice to know someone in the PMG had a sense of humour.

But the matter didn't end there. I decided to continue with the broadcasts and sent Jack Conry to the point with our recently arrived, very first portable tape recorder. As it took less than two minutes to get the tape back to the studio and on air, we were able to simulate a direct broadcast when the same carload of PMG executives arrived back on the scene. Unable to catch us out and somewhat crestfallen—I thought— they headed back to base in Kempsey after I had exchanged pleasantries with them about the weather.

Last of the hillbillies

He was Bob Dyer, Jack Davey's biggest ratings opponent. An American, Bob Dyer came to Australia in 1938 with the Marcus Show. He was billed as the 'last of the hillbillies', using a mouth organ and guitar to run with his singing. The Marcus Show was the most risqué entertainment to grace the stage of a Brisbane theatre. Purely for professional reasons I decided to attend the first performance, managing to get a seat in the second row and sitting goggle-eyed to the end of the last act.

Dyer decided to settle in Australia and soon made a big name for himself as a compere. Although he lacked the ready wit of Jack Davey, his shows were highly professional, helped along by his beautiful wife, Dolly. One of his best shows was *Pick A Box*. It was one I couldn't get out of my mind—or out of my sight—for some years.

It was like this. In those years the advertising range of 2KM Kempsey extended north-west as far as Bellingen and Dorrigo. We had an agent in each major town on the way. The nearest was Macksville, where the agent was a close friend, Ron McNeill, who ran a real estate and stock and station agency. A well-respected family, the McNeills had been in the Macksville–Nambucca district for donkey's years.

On one of my monthly visits to agents, during which I hoped to pick up some advertising and record some material, I took Ron along with me to Bellingen. On the way home, as I was negotiating a slight bend in the highway a guide-post jumped up and smacked my little Ford Prefect in the snout with a loud bang, which was most off-putting. More so because the guide-post happened to be located on the wrong side of the highway.

The impact caused Ron to gash his head on the rear vision mirror. I was thrown onto the road with enough force to render me unconscious while my little Prefect turned on her side, somewhat damaged.

When I came to, Ron had my head cradled in his lap and was speaking with great anguish, assuming I was now a departed broadcaster. His deep concern turned to joy when I sat up and spoke thus:

'What the bloody hell happened?'

At this moment a policeman arrived and put the same question to me.

'You've been drinking!' he declared.

Sitting up, I answered him with as much dignity as I could muster. 'I'll have you know, Constable, I'm a devout Methodist. That right, Ron?'

'That's right, Bern,' said my friend. 'A devout Methodist.'

'Well, how come you've pissed yourself? Look at your left trouser leg!'

While I was trying to think of a suitable response in my confused state, as luck would have it Johnny Hunter, a motorcycle highway patrolman, turned up. The area from Kempsey to Urunga was part of his beat.

After one look at my distressed condition he suggested to his colleague that my condition could have been caused by shock. His diagnosis was accepted and his mate went on his way while Ron and I were given ambulance transport to the Bellingen Hospital. As it turned out I had only suffered a mild dose of concussion and was discharged next morning and driven home to Kempsey by my wife.

Poor old Ron, who had been worrying his guts out about me, was kept in hospital for a week while they dug out some glass and then more glass before sewing up his gash.

Now back to *Pick A Box*. When I left Kempsey that disastrous morning I took with me three cartons full of leaflets (now called 'flyers') publicising Bob Dyer and the show, which I intended giving the agents to hand out, but had forgotten to do so. When my little Prefect took a tumble and the doors burst open, these white leaflets were scattered over the highway at the accident scene ... into long grass, into bushes and even up trees. Thousands of them!

On the way home I managed to collect a few hundred, leaving the rest to the whims of nature. As a result, every gust of wind would send them scattering. At one stage, passing motorists could have been forgiven for thinking they must have been passing through a freak snowstorm. This situation prevailed for months, causing me to wince, almost cower, each time I passed through the accident scene.

Mentioning quiz shows reminds me of the story of the quiz master who was having some problem getting through to one of his contestants.

Quizmaster: I want you to tell me two days of the week beginning with the letter T.

Contestant: Today and tomorrow.

Quizmaster: No! I wanted Tuesday and Thursday. But I'll pay that one ... This is an easy one for you. Name two animals native to Africa. I'll give you a hint. One of them precedes the screening of all MGM films.

Contestant: That's easy. Two lions.

Quizmaster: No! I wanted two animals, not one. A lion and a tiger, or an elephant or a leopard, for example ... Name the famous French general who defeated the English umpteen times, until defeated at Waterloo. Before you answer, I want you to go over to that lovely big refrigerator standing in the corner of the stage, open the door and look inside. (Inside the refrigerator, sitting on the middle shelf and staring the contestant in the face was a bottle of Napoleon brandy.)

Quizmaster: Come back to the microphone and tell me the name of the French general.

Contestant: General Electric!

Once upon a time I used to compere a show in 2KM's auditorium in West Kempsey. One particular session caused me some concern. I had a visiting hypnotist on stage who was grateful for the opportunity to plug his coming stage show and happily gave the audience and listeners at home a sample of his skill. Not completely convinced he had the knack to mesmerise, I arranged to have a listener—our agent from north of Kempsey—occupy a couch in the window of a store while the hypnotist said his stuff, aiming to put him to sleep.

To my utter surprise he had his subject asleep on the couch in no time, to the applause of everyone except the far-away 'victim', now reposing on the couch obtained on loan through a contra deal with a local furniture retailer. I thanked the hypnotist; he went on his way and I continued on with the show.

When I got home I suddenly realised I had overlooked asking the hypnotist to snap the subject out of his trance. It was an empty shop but I did have a telephone installed beside the couch for the occasion, which I rang and rang. I couldn't wake the sleeper. So there he reposed for the night, visible to passers-by wondering what the hell was going on.

Not knowing whether he was actually asleep or was by now a very dead agent, I had become so concerned for his welfare—and mine—that by daylight next morning I was getting ready to catch the next bus to Timbuktu when the telephone rang. It was the victim—er—my agent. Apparently the traffic noise had woken him.

'What the hell did you do to me, you bugger? There's a heap of people gaping at me through the window and laughing their heads off. And, I'm bloody hungry. You can pay for me bloody breakfast, you bugger!'

I was so relieved to hear he was still alive I even arranged a quick contra deal with a local cafe to feed him.

Episode 14

1923 revisited

On 20 November 1993, some 50 veterans of radio broadcasting got together in the RSL Club in the New South Wales town of Port Macquarie to have a chinwag about the Good Old Days—their most momentous years—and to celebrate the 70th anniversary of the industry in which they had played such significant parts in their various spheres.

It was fitting that the organising committee of the function should choose as the guest of honour a senior member of the fraternity who had made an outstanding contribution to the furtherance of this medium. This recognition went to Bert Button, who entered the industry in the 1920s as a junior salesman and left with the rank of managing director. In actual fact Bert never really left the industry. A lingering nostalgia has kept him busy and very much in demand as a guest speaker at meetings, conferences and dinner functions in Sydney and on the Central Coast of New South Wales.

Born in 1907, Bert Button was educated at London's Westminster School and migrated to Australia in 1928. In that year he landed a job with Ernest Fisk's AWA as a salesman. When 2CH Sydney was founded in 1932, he was appointed salesman/sports commentator.

Although the licence was held by the Council of Churches, the operation and technical facilities were provided by AWA, giving Bert a firm foot on the ladder of broadcasting. His ability in these two facets of the industry was quickly recognised and led to his appointment as Official Announcer for the Empire Games held in Australia in 1938. After a stint in the RAAF, he occupied the position of sales manager of 2CH until 1945, when he joined 2GB as assistant manager. In 1950 he was appointed manager of that station, retiring in 1961.

During the years he spent with 2GB, Bert's contribution to radio was remarkable—almost revolutionary—in the way his drive and initiative forged new programme ideas, so vital to sustaining the pull of commercial broadcasting at a stage when television was appearing on the horizon. This was the period when listener-participation programmes and quiz shows peaked in popularity, giving full rein to performers such as Jack Davey, Bob Dyer and the loquacious Eric Baume.

Through his association with the formation of the Macquarie News Service, Bert projected news not only as a vehicle for information but also as entertainment. The many country stations invited into the fold were not only rewarded with the Macquarie News Service but became participants in it, providing network segments. In this way metropolitan listeners were made more aware of country life. The introduction of the half-hour daily *Macquarie Newsreel* and *2GB-Monitor*, based on a successful American NBC idea, gave additional magnetism to commercial radio.

Born in New Zealand in 1900, Eric Baume was a seasoned newspaper journalist, editor and war correspondent. As a distinguished scribe with a distinguished voice, it was logical he would take to radio like a duck to water. Controversial material became his game. He was also a good actor. Bert Button made a point of encouraging 2GB-Macquarie personalities to visit country radio stations. Eric Baume was always happy to oblige and was a welcome visitor. I hosted him on several occasions, which were pleasant events and good for public relations—and good for the coffers of the local RSL Club. Eric took such a liking to the poker machines that often enough he would play them until he had 'done his dough'. As a director of the Club at the time, naturally I cherished Eric's avid interest in the Club's welfare.

One of the last recorded interviews Eric Baume made, just before he died, was with Raymond Allsop, whom I mentioned earlier as an engineer concerned with the construction of 2SB, the first official broadcasting station. Allsop was not only a pioneer in the construction of broadcasting stations but also a pioneer in the manufacture of cinematograph sound equipment. Shortly after the 'talkies' came to Australia he set up a factory and went into the production of Racophone sound-projection equipment to reproduce sound-on-film. By 1938 close on 500 cinemas in Australia had been fitted out with the Racophone system.

For many years Allsop was a great advocate for the introduction of frequency modulation (FM) broadcasting, pursuing the idea while a member of the engineering staff of the Broadcasting Control Board, the authority which took over the supervisory role of the PMG's Department in 1949. Born at Randwick in Sydney in 1898, he died in 1972, sadly just a few years before FM broadcasting was introduced.

And now, back to the Port Macquarie RSL Club in 1993 ...

As Chairman of the organising committee, I intended to open proceedings around the festive board with an address covering the last 70 years. Trouble was, I had been so involved with the legwork, and yelling instructions to all and sundry in getting things organised leading up to the big event, that I was left rather hoarse.

In fact, when I faced the microphone with copious notes in hand, I could only muster a whisper, so I just had to apologise for being unable to say my scheduled piece. The response to my pathetic bleating was electric. The ovation which followed was deafening, after which everyone got stuck into the long-awaited meal, unhindered by such interruptions as long speeches!

The highlight of the programme was a re-enactment of the official opening of 2SB Sydney in 1923 by the then Postmaster-General, William Gerrard Gibson.

As we didn't have his written speech to hand, we had to dummy up what we thought he would have said on that historic occasion ... perhaps with tongues in cheeks. At the time there were only 1400 citizens in Australia licensed to listen to the PMG's utterances. But of course there were thousands more citizens with crystal sets placed in unobtrusive spots, like under the bed, some using the steel bed-frame as an aerial, and others daring to erect an outdoor aerial ... but I wouldn't know about that so I won't mention them.

'Official' opening speech by the Postmaster-General, The Hon. William Gerrard Gibson, MHR

This speech was ably presented on the Postmaster-General's behalf by Hugh McCrindle of Taree.

> Ladies and Gentlemen of this vast unseen audience. It gives me much pleasure in officiating on such an historic occasion, being the introduction of public wireless broadcasting in Australia, through this wireless station, 2SB Sydney.
>
> First of all, I must congratulate Sydney Broadcasters Limited—represented here tonight by the Chairman, Sir Joynton Smith—for the company's enterprise in bringing this about.
>
> I understand that during the past three weeks experimental transmissions have been carried out, with marked success, in giving those fortunate citizens

who own receiving sets the opportunity to adjust their apparatus to obtain maximum reception conditions.

I also understand wireless receiving sets have been installed in some theatres in Sydney, to enable patrons to hear this broadcast through loudspeakers, rather than having to use headphones.

Special arrangements have also been made at an open air concert in Martin Place for the audience to also hear this historic broadcast through loudspeakers.

I believe the day when a technical knowledge was necessary on the part of those citizens engaged in operating their wireless receiving sets, is past. I have been told such sets can now be operated by any citizen—any man in the street, so to speak. Great interest is already being shown in the utterance of public men and overseas visitors.

I am confident wireless broadcasting will provide the one and only means by which practically a whole continent will be able to hear, not a reproduction but the actual utterance of the speech or item which citizens wish to hear.

As you are no doubt well aware, in the interest of fellow Australians, our Government recently introduced a most practical scheme to obtain sufficient revenue to sustain the operation of wireless broadcasting.

A listener's licence is now granted to owners of wireless receiving set or sets on payment of an annual fee of ten shillings. In addition, a subscriber's fee is also applicable to listeners tuned to a selected station.

For example, the annual subscriber's fee to authorise citizens listening to this station, 2SB, is ten shillings. The applicable fee to listen to station 2FC, which is expected to begin transmission less than four weeks hence, will be two guineas a year. This higher fee will apply because programmes emanating from the studio of 2FC will be of a higher cultural nature than those transmitted by this station, 2SB.

Receiving sets will be tuned, locked and sealed to the chosen station, by officers of my Department, to prevent them being tampered with by unscrupulous citizens bent on tuning to any station they choose without payment of the necessary fees. Of course, fines will be imposed and prison sentences considered on any miscreants caught by my officers.

I am sure you will applaud this simple, practical means of giving listeners to wireless broadcasting, maximum enjoyment.

Although there must be many, many citizens listening to my utterances tonight, according to the figures just handed to me, there are only one thousand four hundred licensed listeners, which surely must be a clerical error, Australians being the law-abiding citizens they are, with a gift for fair play.

The large number of poles in back yards, carrying receiving aerials, which I witnessed when taken on a tour of Sydney suburbs by motor car this afternoon, would confirm this clerical error. Naturally, in the interest of Sydney citizens, I have ordered an investigation.

In conclusion, I offer all concerned in this enterprise my heartiest congratulations and express the hope that the public will avail themselves of the up-to-date speedy means of communication this station offers.

I hereby declare 2SB Sydney, the first public broadcasting station in Australia, officially open.

A rousing rendition of 'Vilia' from Franz Lehar's *Merry Widow* by Robyn Butler, representing the original vocalist, Dorothy Deering, ushered in an hour of enjoyable entertainment. Robyn Butler was accompanied by Penelope Evans at the pianoforte and Allan Wright at the cello. The Master of Ceremonies on this auspicious occasion was Edward Webster, formerly of wireless station 2KO Newcastle.

The musical items were introduced by James Dibble, formerly with ABC Television and 2GB-Macquarie, whose career blossomed when he joined ABC Television as senior news presenter. Along with Ed Webster and Hugh McCrindle, former manager of 2RE Taree, James read his hastily prepared script by yours truly, without fluffing one word, one line. A real professional!

The re-enactment ended with a toast by all present to the 'good health' of our late monarch, King George V.

No arrangements are yet in hand to celebrate the 100th anniversary of broadcasting, but I hope another group will get together to carry the flag. If such an occasion does come about, I think I may have to sit it out …

Episode 15

Amateurs, pirates and piddlers

Amateur wireless operators—or experimental operators, as they rightly preferred to be called—made an enormous contribution to the development of all facets of the science of wireless, more especially in the years from 1919 to the 1930s. Their experiments hastened the introduction of a public broadcasting system and a greater appreciation of the capriciousness of the ionosphere and its positive and negative effects on long-distance communication.

Most of the amateur operators were hobbyists until the wireless 'bug' overwhelmed other interests, a situation their better halves would no doubt sadly have vouched for. Some of these 'amateurs' actually came from professional ranks.

Joe Reed was one of them. Employed as an engineer with the PMG's Department, many of his home hours were devoted to designing and constructing 'rigs'. He left the Department to join AWA as a design engineer and in that capacity was closely involved in the development of the company's radio-electric works in the Sydney suburb of Ashfield.

Ray Allsop was another professional, whose interest in this newfound medium had begun by the time he grew out of short pants. Under the guidance of pioneer wireless man Father Shaw—who had his own manufactory at Randwick—Allsop went on to assist in engineering the construction of Australia's first official broadcasting station, 2SB Sydney, and remained as Chief Engineer until he left to pursue other interests allied to his work. One of Allsop's notable achievements was the first demonstration in Australia of stereophonic sound to a distinguished audience attending the 1938 convention of the Institution of Radio Engineers held in Sydney. But that was many years after he went on air with his experimental station in 1911. The station was dismantled on government edict when World War I broke out.

Marcus Oliver, then living at Neutral Bay in Sydney, was another experimental operator who had to dismantle his rig when World War I broke out. Allsop served with the Royal Australian Navy during the war years and, along with Oliver, resumed his experimental work after the war when the RAN handed back responsibility of controlling the Australian airwaves to the PMG's Department.

Charles Maclurcan was one of Sydney's early experimenters to concentrate on constructing a radio-telephony transmitter for broadcasting. Operating from his shack at Strathfield and also atop the Wentworth Hotel, owned by his family, he broadcast regular concert programmes each Sunday to a grateful and growing audience, using his call sign 2CM. Gramophone records provided most of the entertainment. In February 1923, 2CM broadcast a recital by Miss Josie Melville, the reigning musical comedienne in Sydney and the first professional artist to take to the airwaves.

Jack Davis, another AWA engineer, Oswald Mingay, Otto Sandel and William Maclardy were also among the band of Sydney experimenters who contributed significantly to the development of a broadcasting system.

Queensland medico Dr Val McDowall established an experimental broadcasting station adjacent to his surgery in Queen Street, Brisbane, in association with another pioneer, Tom Elliott. Commencing in 1921 the station operated mostly at weekends until 1924, broadcasting speech, gramophone records and the occasional stage show landlined from local theatres.

Dr McDowall and Tom Elliott maintained their pioneer spirit with experiments in television. Operating from the old Observatory building in Wickham Terrace, they used the scanning system invented by Logie Baird in 1925 to send images for a distance of about 30 kilometres, taking advantage of the height of the building. Most of their experiments were made in the years 1933–35. I well remember them, and itched to have a 'look-see', but that was not to be. As radio was very much the popular medium in those years, little general interest was evinced by McDowall and Elliott's endeavours.

Incidentally, the Observatory building was constructed by convicts. Fitted with sails, it was originally used to grind corn, although often convict manpower was used to turn the machinery through means of a treadmill. Early last century the mill was converted to use as a weather observatory. If memory serves me right, Tom Elliott was the foundation engineer of 4BC Brisbane, the Chandler-owned station opened in August 1930.

In Victoria, one of the most prominent experimental operators was Max Howden of the Melbourne suburb of Box Hill. Born in 1899, he was educated at the Brighton Grammar School where he was equal dux of the school in 1916. Although ambitious to make a name for himself in the field of wireless communication, his plans were fettered by wartime restrictions, although he did manage to obtain a permit from the Navy to operate a receiving set.

On 3 November 1924, Howden made wireless history by transmitting to America, making two-way contact with an experimenter at Tomona in California. This was the first Morse code contact between the two countries. A few days later, on 14 November, Howden made the first contact with England by establishing two-way communication with another experimenter, a Mr Simmonds at station G2OD at Buckingham, England, the prefix 'G' indicating the station was in Great Britain. Howden's call sign was A3BQ, the 'A' indicating an Australian station. Contact was strong, and maintained until sun-up, when G2OD faded out.

A cable to Howden from England the next day, reading, 'Congratulations on first two-way communication between England and Australia. Simmonds G2OD', confirmed this historic event in long-distance communication. Shortly after making this contact, which was by Morse code, Howden communicated with 2GOD by wireless telephony. Simmonds in England heard every word and confirmed this voice reception by Morse code.

After a long and meritorious career as an amateur wireless operator and a professional design engineer, Max Howden passed away in 1980.

In Western Australia, pioneer experimenter Walter Coxon was active before and during World War I, when he served with the British Admiralty as a research officer in the field of wireless. After constructing an experimental station in Perth following the cessation of hostilities, he emulated Maclurcan of Sydney's achievements by transmitting musical entertainment for the people of Perth through the playing of gramophone records.

Coxon was chief engineer and manager of Perth's first official public broadcasting station, 6WF, owned by Westralian Farmers Limited, an influential group of rural producers anxious to provide wireless news and entertainment to the scattered rural population. Under his guidance, the company was responsible for introducing and marketing a wireless receiving set known as the Mulgaphone.

Jack Milner of Tasmania and Vic Coombe of South Australia were two other experimenters to make a significant contribution to the world of wireless.

Some amateur operators were given PMG permission to transmit on the broadcast band when the national and commercial stations were off the air. On Sundays, for example, none of the Brisbane stations came on the air before noon, giving plenty of air space for the friendly amateur broadcasters to do their stuff, which was mainly a programme of gramophone records interspersed with cheerio and birthday calls, and an occasional recital.

After church on Sundays I was a regular visitor to the station in the Brisbane suburb of Toowong, opposite the fire station in High Street. Frank Nolan of Spring Hill and Ces Morris of Rosalie were also active Sunday broadcasters.

On the outbreak of World War II, the PMG terminated all amateur permits, although by then there were very few amateurs on the air as most of the national and commercial stations had extended their hours to include an early Sunday start-up.

Undoubtedly the driving force for government recognition of the achievements of amateur-experimental operators was P. George Taylor of Sydney. Pioneer aviator and wireless experimenter, Taylor came to prominence in 1910 when he demonstrated wireless communication to a group of officers of the Australian Army at the Heathcote military base, near Sydney.

Taylor was also a great advocate for the introduction of public broadcasting in Australia. In 1922 he called a conference to lobby government to get moving in this direction. He was also the founder of the Wireless Institute, which rapidly grew in membership and strength to become a potent force for the betterment of all things wireless. Today, the Institute enjoys a large membership of amateur wireless operators and is still very active.

Enter the pirates ...

To obtain permission to operate an amateur station, the enthusiast had first to obtain an Amateur Station Licence through an examination conducted by the PMG's Department. The examination comprised a section on the theory and practice of this branch of science and a demonstration of the sending and receipt of Morse code by key to a designated speed and standard.

However, sad to say, there were some operators who shunned the imposition of an examination, preferring to operate their stations surreptitiously. Wireless inspectors were kept busy trying to locate them. To be caught meant a fairly hefty fine and the threat of imprisonment. Fortunately, these miscreants were few in number—at least, in the Brisbane area.

... and the piddlers!

I recall one pair of villains and their many escapades on the amateur band. Both teenagers, they had been bitten by the wireless 'bug' and looked upon themselves as major contributors to science. But they were not ready to sit for the Amateur Operator's Certificate for several reasons, one being they had not as yet, acquired the minimum age! One of them had recently been in strife with one of his neighbours and was pleased to divert his thoughts to other things—like wireless.

The reason he fell out with his neighbour was due to his obsession with the telephone. Not the usual telephone, just the that surfaced during boyhood. It consisted of a couple of empty jam tins, one for each end of the line. The line was a long thread of strong cotton, held taut between two trees a hundred metres or so apart. Each end was attached to the base of an ordinary IXL jam tin with the bottom knocked out and replaced with a piece of stiff brown paper as a diaphragm. The taut cotton was connected to the diaphragm by piercing a hole in the centre and using a matchstick to hold it in place. Talking into the jam tin would set up a vibration on the stretched length of cotton, which in turn would set up a vibration of the diaphragm of the jam tin at the other end of the line. With this method this boy and his mate at the end of this dead-end street could talk to each other—just like Alexander Graham Bell.

Trouble was, left overnight, the cotton line would droop almost down to the ground. This particular neighbour, who left home just before dawn each day to walk to the Toowong terminus to catch the first tram of the day to the city, got tangled up in the 'telephone' line—so tangled up couldn't free himself in time to catch his tram and so was late for work. Although not seen to cry he took a dim view of being trussed up. When observed just on daylight, he was very het-up and still entangled. That day all traces of the 'telephone' apparatus were removed and the citizens of the street settled back to their normal, boring suburban routine.

Like most wireless enthusiasts, the two boys of our story made most of the transmitting and receiving gear for their pirate station. They even made their own A batteries to light the filaments of their transmitter. The method of making these batteries was passed on to them by a veteran of World War I who had served in the signalling unit of the AIF. As he said, 'This is how we made them in the trenches. We called them piddle batteries!'

Each A cell consisted of a glass jam jar or pickle jar into which the boys would urinate whenever the urge was there. A carbon rod taken from a discarded Eveready or Diamond dry battery would be dipped into the liquid—which served as the electrolyte—followed by a strip of zinc. Molten sealing wax, taken from the discarded dry batteries would cover each jar. Enough jars would then be coupled up to provide the current and voltage required to light the filaments. However, there was just one little anomaly in the set-up. On a hot day the sealing wax was inclined to split, leaving a distinctive aroma in the room under the house that the boys used for their nefarious activities.

These two scallywags got away with their unlicensed station until the day one of them inadvertently used the call sign of a licensed operator who had recently passed away. The lad was chatting away to someone up north near Townsville when the someone enquired—not without good reason—why he happened to be on the air a few days after his obituary had appeared in the newspapers.

'Yes, I came good, and I'm feeling much better now, thank you,' was the quick and foolish retort. After all, what did the word 'obituary' mean?

A deep silence at the other end was the cue for the boys to shut up shop before they were nabbed by the wireless inspector. In great haste they dismantled their gear and hid the leftovers in the ceiling upstairs when mother was out.

As it turned out, Tom Armstrong—the chief inspector no less—called a few days later, not directly because of their foul-up but in response to a complaint from a woman across the street who didn't take kindly to the lads completely blotting out reception on her pride and joy—her new dual-wave set—whenever they went on the air.

As luck would have it, the lads were all innocence when the inspector called. The only tell-tale evidence was a few QSL (greeting) cards pinned to the wall and the lingering aroma of piddle batteries well past their use-by date. With a friendly nod and appropriate warning about the dire consequences if caught, he departed. With a smile, they thought.

Naturally enough, on the way to school next day the lads acknowledged the neighbour's concern for the welfare of her dual-wave set, and her interest in better reception, by showering her galvanised iron roof with stones.

Let me think now. What *were* those two scallywags called? I'm sure one of them was Smith, or was it Jones? But for the life of me I can't remember the name of the other villain … can I? But of course, it was such a long, long time ago.

Episode 16

The day Mary had a little lamb

The year was 1877. The place, a barn in Menlo Park, New Jersey, in the United States of America. It was here an inventor of Scottish-Dutch ancestry with a penchant for nursery rhymes used the well-loved words 'Mary had a little lamb' to announce the success of his experiments in the preservation of sound. The inventor was 30-year-old Thomas Alva Edison, known to the locals and others as the Wizard of Menlo Park and to his ex-schoolteacher mother as the Little Question Box because of his more than usually inquisitive mind—which certainly made up for the fact her son had little formal education.

The rhyme was engraved on tinfoil wrapped around a small cylinder about four centimetres in diameter and made to rotate by hand. Edison called his invention a 'phonograph'. Although the recorded voice was but a piping sound of limited range, the phonograph ushered in a revolution in a facet of science which was to lead to the almost exact reproduction of the human voice, musical instruments and other sounds, the effect of which was to have a profound influence on the way of life these past 130 or so years.

This simple device recorded sound and reproduced it through a conical funnel shaped like an ear trumpet, the narrow end of which was secured to a diaphragm to which was attached a stylus (needle). Sounds going into the funnel, or 'horn' as it was then called, set the diaphragm vibrating which set the stylus vibrating in a side-to-side movement that was impressed on the tinfoil.

After his successful sound-recording experiments, Edison turned much of his attention to the development of the incandescent lamp, which became the electric light bulb and even more than the phonograph affected lifestyle and households after it was lit up in 1879.

Before the advent of recorded sound, the musical box, which made its tinkling presence known as far back as 1796, the polyphon, which made music from a rotating disc, the barrel organ and the pianola were the only means of producing musical sounds without actually playing an instrument—and they produced only the set pieces incorporated in their mechanisms.

The first movement toward recorded sound came in 1857, when the French inventor Leon Scott de Martinville produced a device he called the 'phonautograph', which recorded wavy lines from sound vibrations onto paper coated with lampblack wrapped around a cylinder. But he had no way of reproducing the music from these wavy lines.

Two years later another Frenchman, Charles Cros, improved on Scott's design by demonstrating that sound vibrations could actually be engraved on a layer of graphite but he, like Scott, was unable to find a method of converting the grooves into sound. Undaunted, in 1877—the year Edison's phonograph was patented—Cros deposited a sealed package with the Académie des Sciences des France, supposedly describing a method of recording vibrations on a lampblack-coated disc. The completed patterns could then be photo-engraved on metal. Theoretically, the original sounds could be reproduced using a diaphragm. Sadly for Cros, he had not constructed a model to provide a practical demonstration. He called his would-be device a 'palephone'.

After Edison's tinfoil phonograph, the next step in the progression was made by two US scientists, Chichester Bell and Charles Tainter, who engraved sound vibrations on a waxy substance covering a cylinder similar to Edison's, using a sharp stylus carried by the diaphragm. A distinct improvement on the method of engraving on metal foil, this system was patented in 1885.

Incidentally, the word 'phonograph' was not used first by Edison. In 1863 F. B. Fenby of Massachusetts was granted a patent for an 'electromagnetic phonograph', as he called it. The model was never completed but the name survived.

The flat disc

The most significant improvement in quality and method of recording sound occurred in 1888 when the German-born inventor Emile Berliner substituted a flat round disc for Edison's cylinder. The metal disc was wax coated. Unlike Edison's cylinder, which required a feed-screw or threaded spiral to move the recording head along the surface to create the sound track, Berliner used the sound track to move the head across the disc. Furthermore, the sound track was etched through the wax surface into the zinc base of the disc, creating a hard track suitable for playing with a needle on a gramophone.

Berliner was now on track to develop a method of multiplying the original flat disc recording. After trying rubber and other soft material for making duplicate copies he settled for Durenoid—a shellac material, strong but brittle. By 1900 a system of pressing many copies had been perfected which, with several embellishments, is still in use today.

By this time the Italian tenor Enrico Caruso and the Scottish singer-comedian Harry Lauder had made their debuts in the recording industry.

Caruso and other artists were confronted with a big obstacle, which unfortunately did little to enhance the quality of their voices. To make a recording, they had to stand very close to the horn—which captured the sound—almost shove their heads inside and bellow loudly enough to activate the diaphragm at the narrow end of the horn and cause the stylus to engrave a groove of enough amplitude to reproduce an acceptable volume. Accompanying musicians and solo instrumentalists had to stand almost shoulder to shoulder around the mouth of the recording horn to make an impression.

Berliner's method of churning out copies was a step-by-step process and rather time consuming. Usually a diamond or other highly polished hard stylus was used to cut the wax grooves to give a clean cut, to minimise the scratch level and distortion and thus obtain the best possible frequency range. The soft wax offered little impediment to the lateral movement of the clean-cutting stylus.

The recordist would follow the cutting for any irregularities by observing with a microscope. The shavings from the cutting stylus's journey were removed by a suction motor placed alongside the stylus, operating like a vacuum cleaner, in those early years. After the recording had been completed, the artist or orchestra would have to wait in the studio until the recordist made a final groove inspection and gave the thumbs up.

The wax recording was known as the 'master'. And so the journey began. The master was lightly dusted with a graphite powder to make the surface electrically conductive. Pursuing a higher fidelity of reproduction to meet the demand for a better sound in the 1930s, some record manufacturers would use gold dust in preference to graphite dust to achieve the ultimate electrical surface.

The next step was to submerge the master vertically in an electrolysis bath. After a given period a layer of metal would be deposited. This metal deposit or plate became a negative copy of the positive original master. That is, it carried ridges instead of grooves. The next step in the process was to provide metal backing to give it strength. This reinforced metal copy of the original was known as the 'father'. Although it could be used in the press to stamp out copies as a matrix, a new master would have to be cut whenever it showed signs of wear or became damaged. For that reason another copy would be made, referred to as the 'mother'.

The mother, being an exact replica of the master, was positive (like a real mother). The mother would be placed in the electrolysis bath until a layer of metal was deposited on it. This layer was referred to as the 'son' and, like the father, it carried ridges, not grooves. Hardened by coating it with a thin film of chromium, the son was now ready to go into the record press as the matrix.

Meanwhile, the mother remained on standby to produce more sons should the firstborn suffer from wear as the result of high record sales. As for the father, he was shelved, being of no further use unless the mother became damaged.

Two matrices would go into the press, one on the bottom table and one on the moveable top table. A dollop of shellac with lampblack was placed on the table, the press closed, and under steam pressure the recording would be moulded, then—hey presto! Another 78 rpm was made.

Are you still with me? If this chain of events is a bit hard to follow, don't blame me. Blame Emile Berliner. He started it all ... and went on to found the Berliner Gramophone Company.

The shellac composition had the disadvantage of being brittle, so the record was easily broken. But it had one advantage—under hot water worn-out discs could be shaped into delightful hanging baskets! My mother had several of them hanging in the bush-house during the Twinkling Twenties. Rather an inglorious end to the Black Bottom and the Charleston and other popular tunes of the times, but they did serve a good purpose in our fernery. The manufacturers overcame the problem of brittleness in the 1930s by laminating the records, placing a thin disc of paper in the centre of the mould before pressing.

To complete Berliner's gramophone, a means had to be provided to spin the turntable to play the record. A spring-wound clockwork motor was devised and kept at constant speed until the spring wound down, by a governor system. Of course, the music came out of the horn in sufficient volume to fill a lounge room. The shape and size of the horn played a big part in reproducing 'natural' sound after designers folded it inside a large wooden cabinet, which became an ornate piece of furniture in many homes in the first three decades of the twentieth century. Like the piano and pianola, the Salonola gramophone became a symbol of affluence.

Hill and dale

I mentioned earlier that the wax surface of the master offered little resistance to the lateral movement of the cutting stylus. Nevertheless, there was a measure of impediment, sufficient to dampen the side-to-side vibrations and in so doing restricting the frequency range.

The answer was to cut a vertical groove rather than a lateral groove.

In 1913 Thomas Edison demonstrated he had found the solution when he launched the New Edison Disc Phonograph, which played only vertical cut grooves. World War I intervened so it was not until 1926 that the machine, which employed a finely ground diamond stylus (needle) was marketed. It was called the Diamond Disc Phonograph but was better known in Australia as the 'hill-and-dale' gramophone because of the up-and-down movement of the needle during playing.

These machines were more expensive than the popular gramophones, the console models selling for close on £400.

Some citizens owning a Diamond Disc machine considered they were a 'cut above the others' on the social scale, to coin a phrase. My aunt had one, bought, she said, 'because of the superior tone'. As the machine and the discs (records) were imported, her favourite music was hard to get, so her library was limited.

As the groove was vertically cut there was more space available for music—about 150 grooves per inch. The turntable speed was 80 rpm, which provided for four minutes' playing time on a 10-inch record, slightly more than the usual 78 rpm. Certainly these machines produced a better sound but they were not popular, partly because the hill-and-dale movement rendered them incompatible with the lateral-cut record. By the mid 1930s very few were still being marketed.

At this point we say goodbye to the mechanical age in the field of recorded sound, and usher in ...

The electrical age

When the eminent scientist Lee de Forest invented the audion (triode) vacuum tube just prior to the commencement of World War I, a revolution in the wireless and recording industry was about to begin.

With the addition of a metal grid to Fleming's diode a means of amplification was provided. Sadly, before this discovery could be put to use commercially, World War I largely stymied its development, although some research continued. Thus it was not until the 1920s that the transition from the old technique to the new took place.

There was no more shouting into a horn for Dame Nellie Melba and other artists of the time. The horn was replaced by a microphone, and the mechanical recording head was replaced by a magnetic device which responded to an electrical current much magnified, thanks to de Forest.

As a result, a much greater sound was put on the wax surface of the master and a much greater sound was produced than through the un-amplified mechanical gramophone. Now it came through a loudspeaker, picked up from the grooves by an electrical pick-up and amplified by a vacuum-tube triode amplifier.

The next step was to replace the spring-wound turntable with an electric motor. Notwithstanding this vast improvement in the recording and reproduction of sound, there was still a long way to go to reach the ultimate in fidelity, however.

After the introduction of the electric pick-up, one of the first considerations in pursuit of a better quality of sound was changing the shape and angle of the playing needle to avoid what was referred to as the 'pinch effect', a situation which occurred when the point of the needle didn't ride comfortably in the groove, causing distortion and possibly excessive wear of the record. Another requirement was to design a pick-up with a fairly lightweight head to follow the grooves more delicately.

The giant Philips Company produced a lightweight pick-up in the early 1940s using a crystal head in lieu of a magnetic head. The crystal was actually Rochelle salt, which produced a piezo-electric effect (electric charge) when subjected to mechanical pressure such as the movement of a gramophone needle. This phenomenon had actually been discovered as far back as 1880, when Frenchmen Pierre and Jacques Curie noted the effect.

The disadvantages of the crystal pick-up were that it had to be delicately handled and was affected by heat, major reasons for its rapid decline in popularity when the new pick-up came on the market.

Refinements in the design of amplifiers, microphones and loudspeakers were also critical in the lead-up to high fidelity recording in the 1950s.

Instantaneous recording

From the beginnings of broadcasting, Australian station operators yearned for a method of making disc recordings that could be immediately broadcast, but it was not until about 1933 that technology made this system practical—yet far from perfect.

The British company Garrard, which concentrated mainly on the manufacture of electric turntables and record-changers, produced a recorder for home use. It consisted of a heavy pick-up which traversed a blank disc of aluminium by means of a feed-screw mounted under the turntable. There was no cutting process, the grooves being made by indentation by the pick-up, which carried a lump of lead to give it sufficient weight. The stylus had a knurled, rather than a sharp, point. A bamboo or thorn needle had to be used to play the record on a gramophone. I had one of these recorders in 1934. The sound was terrible so I was pleased to get rid of it, and so was my mother, who was slightly unhappy about me damaging her prize rose bushes when harvesting thorns to muck around with. Strangely, she wasn't impressed, either, when I declared it was in the cause of science.

A peep into the past: the pressing engagement of Logan McPherson

When I called to see Logan McPherson at his home at Camden Head on the New South Wales mid North Coast in 1987, he was going on 80 years of age ... but he didn't look it. Maybe it was due to the fact he kept himself in tip-top condition by shunning grog and maintaining a lithesome body by tripping the light fantastic at every opportunity.

Slim and slightly built, he must have had just the right figure to glide around the dance floor with gentle grace or, in contrast, kick up his heels with the Black Bottom or Charleston at the drop of a hat, being two of the popular tunes of the times ... the times being the Twenties and early Thirties.

They were the dancing years when most young people with a bit of 'go' in them were caught up with the craze. Logan was one of them.

Even during his advancing years he would do a foot-tap whenever a tune came on the radio which took his fancy. In fact, the day I called, he got so wrapped up in memories of his dancing days that when I came up with a few titles like 'Moonlight and Roses' he hummed the melodies. And when I tossed in 'Charmaine' and 'Carolina Moon' he just couldn't restrain himself. He was up and about doing a one-two-three around the billiard table. As I didn't have all that much time available, I had to bring him down to earth with a somewhat cruel question.

'What do you think of popular music of these days, Logan?'

'Music? It's not music. Just a noise,' he snorted. 'In the years from about 1925 to the war years, the accent was on melody and rhythm, making the music good for dancing.'

'I suppose you were one of those young bloods of the Twenties and Thirties who always turned up at the Saturday night hop?' I enquired.

'My word. In fact, most nights of the week—except Tuesdays and Fridays. They were dress nights. I didn't have a dinner jacket then. Couldn't afford one!'

'And your favourite haunts?'

'There were so many of them. Most Sydney suburbs had a dance hall in those days. Weekly dances were held in the Petersham Town Hall. Then there was the Rockdale Hall. Miss Allen's weekly dance in St George's Hall in Newtown was a beauty. There was a four-piece band, The Strollers. Of course, the Palais Royale at the Showground was tops. I remember the American band, The Californians, the first American band to come out here. They stayed for three years. The Jim Davidson band was the best for dancing, in my book. Then there was Frank Coglan's at the Trocadero in the late Thirties.'

'As a tripper of the light fantastic you must have had many pressing engagements on the dance floor, Logan!'

'I'll say!'

'What did you do for a crust?'

'A bit of everything. Jobs weren't easy to get and hard to hold once you turned 21. But I had a good run once I got a job in the record industry.'

'When was that?'

'That was in 1925. I worked on a record press at Brunswick Records.'

'So, you had another pressing engagement?'

'Yes, you could say that.'

'Hold it, Logan. There's a piece of history here. When you worked at Brunswick Records, you would have been one of the pioneers in this country in the manufacture of gramophone records.'

'That's right. The factory was owned by D. Davis and Company, and operated in leased premises in Junction Street, Surry Hills. Davis had two sons, Bert and Jack. They started manufacturing as soon as a franchise was obtained from Brunswick Records in the United States. The matrices were imported. We had five presses going flat out. I was on one of them. After the company had been operating a couple of years, the old man set up another factory to make cheap records under various labels. They sold for two shillings. This company was Clifford Industries and it was in Riley Street. That's in Sydney, of course. I worked at Clifford Industries until we all decided to join a union. I was made union delegate. Old Davis heard about it and called me into his office. He made it quite clear there was no room in the factory for the two of us. I took the hint and left. Fortunately the union got me a job at the Columbia Graphophone Company, which had just been set up at Homebush. That was in 1928. I worked there until the effects of the Great Depression of the Thirties caught up with us. From working around the clock, shifts were reduced to one a day.'

'Where was His Master's Voice in those days?'

'In a little building in Erskineville.'

'That must have been another interesting period of your life, particularly when Columbia began recording Australian singers and bands at Homebush?'

'Yes; I well remember Peter Dawson, the Australian baritone, and Gladys Moncrieff. But my biggest thrill was to meet Don Bradman. Columbia wanted him to record something about his cricket career, but he was more interested in recording a piano solo. They met him halfway but never released the recording. It was terrible!'

I must have struck the right chord with Logan McPherson. When I left him, he was gazing fondly at a pile of his 78s and humming a popular tune of the Twenties … or was it the Thirties?'

If 1925 was a significant year for Logan McPherson, being the year he got a job pressing out gramophone records, it was also a significant year for the record industry as a whole. In April 1925 the first commercial electric recordings were marketed in the United States. Less than two years later they were in music shops in Australia, producing a much superior tone in gramophones than the mechanically made records. The manufacture of electric amplifiers and an improvement in the design of loudspeakers followed.

Returning to the subject of instantaneous disc recording and playback, in 1932 researchers found a method of making records for immediate playback of a suitable standard for use by broadcasters. Using an aluminium disc as a base, a lacquer comprised of cellulous acetate was evenly applied to cover both sides of the disc. These blank discs were referred to as 'acetates'. Professional recordists were now able to replace the old wax-coated masters with acetates, thereby reducing costs, improving fidelity and allowing the performing artists to exit the studio immediately after cutting.

The Presto Recording Corporation of America was one of the first manufacturers to produce instantaneous recording/playback equipment for use in broadcast station studios. Soon most metropolitan stations and a few of the larger country stations in Australia were equipped with Prestos.

Fairchild, Neuman and Universal were three other manufacturers to make precision recording gear. Meanwhile, the Presto Corporation was producing a portable disc-recorder, used extensively by the Australian Broadcasting Commission to cover events during World War II.

By 1948 recording techniques used by manufacturers and broadcast stations in Australia had reached a high standard, not only at the original speed of 78 rpm but also at less than half that speed, 33 1/3 rpm, due mainly to the fine grain of the acetates which reduced the 'scratch level', the finer cut of the highly polished durable stylus and the employment of equalisation during the cutting process.

Equalisation provided a gradual emphasis of the higher frequencies as the cutter moved toward the centre of the master, frequencies which otherwise would have suffered from the slower speed and from the inability of the stylus to settle comfortably in the now compressed groove.

Incidentally, Berliner's original flat discs played from inside to out both or this reason and for he fact the tip of the playing stylus (needle) would more than likely be worn by the time it was called on to faithfully follow the compressed grooves.

Nipper, the dog that became a howling success

In the year 1900 a little fox terrier dog who answered to the name Nipper made his first appearance on the label of a gramophone record. Since then, the painting of the little dog by the London artist Francis Barraud

(1856–1924) has become one of the most famous trademarks in history, not so much because of its artistic quality, but because of the appealing image of the dog listening to his master's voice. In actual fact, Nipper was not listening to the voice of the artist—as many of us have been led to believe—but to the voice of his brother Mark, the dog's owner.

Mark Barraud was a well-known theatrical set designer. Much of his time in his latter years was spent behind stage at Prince's Theatre in Bristol designing stage settings, with his dog Nipper at his side.

After his brother's death, Francis Barraud took charge of Nipper. One day as he was playing an Edison-Bell phonograph with Mark's voice on the cylinder, he noticed Nipper's alertness to the sound of his former master's voice, and the idea of the painting was conceived.

After submitting it to the Royal Academy and having it rejected, Barraud offered the painting to the London office of the Edison-Bell Phonograph Company. Unimpressed, the company turned down the offer. As far as the company was concerned, 'dogs just don't listen to phonographs'.

On the advice of a friend, Barraud changed the colour of the horn from black to brass, masked over the phonograph and replaced it with a flat-disc playing machine produced by an Edison-Bell rival, the Gramophone Company, then located in Maiden Lane off the Strand in London, and took the painting there.

His timing was perfect, as the cylindrical recording method was just on the verge of giving way to Berliner's flat-disc method. Manager of the Gramophone Company, William Barry Owen, offered Barraud £50 for the painting and £50 for the copyright, a figure large enough to appeal to the artist.

Asked what he was going to call the painting, Barraud replied, 'His Master's Voice.' Less than one year later, in January 1900, the label His Master's Voice, commonly known as HMV, was born. Before long the fortunes of the Gramophone Company changed for the better, and in 1931 it merged with the Columbia Graphophone Company to become EMI.

The original painting now hangs in the boardroom of EMI at Hayes in Middlesex. A miniature copy was painted in the early 1920s for Queen Mary's doll's house.

Nipper died a few years after he had become famous, and was laid to rest beneath a mulberry tree in Kingston-on-Thames, not far from the well-known store of Bentalls in Surrey. Once a year, so the story goes, someone would make a pilgrimage to his grave and leave behind a posy of flowers in a jar of water. Whether the visitor was Francis Barraud or a representative of the grateful Gramophone Company—or just a dog lover—was never known. However, it seems significant that the visits ceased about the time of the artist's death.

Although Mark and Francis Barraud and the friendly little terrier are long gone, Nipper will long be remembered.

Recorded shows

Using 16-inch discs revolving at 33 1/3 rpm, up to fifteen minutes of programming could now be recorded, with four 15-minute discs (transcriptions) required for an hour-long show. *Australia's Amateur Hour* was typical of the many shows recorded when radio broadcasting was at its peak of popularity. The programme would be landlined to the AWA recording room from the town in which it originated. The masters were then sent, initially, to the EMI studios at Homebush for processing, later to AWA's own plant.

The Australian Record Company was one of several companies set up to record and process soap operas and most other shows hitting the airwaves. In the 1950s ARC added standard 78s to its repertoire and produced its own labels, including Pacific and Rodeo.

In 1948, when I was in the employ of 2UW Sydney, I developed a sideline in the form of Paramount Recorded Productions. I built my own 16-inch disc recording equipment, capable of recording both 78 and 33 1/3 rpm transcriptions.

I was living in Epping at the time, in what was then a very, very quiet and reserved neighbourhood. At least, it was until I came on the scene. I converted the one and only garage into a studio and control room and soundproofed it as best I could. As my efforts didn't do much to suppress what was going on inside, I wasn't all that surprised when several neighbours came knocking at my door demanding I get rid of the 'noise', as they had the cheek to call my productions.

I used to record pianist Leo White from his performances on a Sydney ABC station to add to his personal collection. If I recall correctly, Leo was a member of the European group the Weintraubs, when they toured Australia, after which he decided to settle here. I also recorded a newly formed jazz band for publicity purposes. I well remember the poor blighters carting their instruments, including a double bass, by train to Epping station and then humping them to my place.

One of my other enterprises was to set up my recording equipment in a Parramatta department store at Christmas time for the express purpose of recording Christmas greetings on 6 inch acetates.

The store was Murray Bros. I provided suitable cardboard envelopes decorated with Christmas Bells, ready to post overseas or wherever. Murray's kindly allotted me an alcove in the showroom to do my stuff. This novelty idea took on and I soon had citizens and their kids milling around my recording set-up, anxious to send loving greetings to their relatives or friends in their own voices!

After recording a hundred or so over a few days, I was confronted with a slight problem. The acetate coating on the base aluminium discs was not of good quality. To my horror, I discovered that when my recordings were subjected to warm weather in transit, the acetate was inclined to peel off, rendering the records slightly unplayable.

As a result, some customers didn't take too kindly to Paramount Recorded Productions, and came looking for me. Some visited me to say their piece, while others just vented their spleen on the phone, firmly suggested where I should shove my 6-inch discs—not exactly in accordance with the Christmas spirit, I thought. They didn't find my explanation very 'appealing', so to speak. Under the circumstances, and in the interests of peace and goodwill, I decided not to do it again next Christmas.

At that point, strongly encouraged by my wife, I decided to accept an offer to move to the bush to manage station 2KM Kempsey, notwithstanding the knowledge that the 'Big One'—the 1949 flood— had destroyed part of Kempsey and more than likely washed the studio and transmitter out to sea.

Strangely, my rather standoffish neighbours suddenly warmed to me when they heard the news of my pending departure, and made a point of calling on us to congratulate me on my appointment and to wish us well— and when would we be leaving? 'We'll certainly miss you and your studio,' they chorused.

Long-play and micro-groove

Experimentation in recording and playing a narrow-width groove was initiated by Thomas Edison in 1927. Although a long-play recording resulted, the breaking-down of the groove walls mitigated against commercial production.

A few years later, in 1932, Radio Corporation of America produced a long-play record at 33 1/3 rpm, but it didn't take on. It was not until after the war years, in 1948, that Columbia Records in the United States began marketing long-play micro-groove records. Made of vinylite, they were almost unbreakable. A year later, the opposition record company, RCA, introduced the 7-inch 45 rpm. These developments resulted in a wonderful improvement in fidelity but created a big problem for broadcasters and the public, as turntables now had to provide three speeds—78, 33 1/3 and 45 rpm. To make the situation even more complex, about this time the stereophonic technology of using a method of recording vertically and laterally in the one groove had advanced to the point where commercial production had become practicable.

Magnetic recording

The technique of recording sound magnetically had its genesis in 1898, in work by the Danish scientist Valdemar Poulsen, but it was not widely used until the end of World War II. German engineers had dramatically improved the technology during the war years.

The principle of the magnetic recorder and other systems of electro-magnetic induction and the creation of an electro-motive force came from the basic discoveries of the English physicist Michael Faraday (1791–1867). Although his genius opened the door for the study and adoption of electricity in all forms, he is almost forgotten in the annals of science nowadays.

When I was in London a few years ago, I was informed that the laboratory in which he made many of his experiments and discoveries, including what is known as the Faraday Effect, was open to the public. Furthermore, it was in easy walking distance from Berkeley Square, where I spent several hours straining my ears to catch a trill from Vera Lynn's nightingales. (They had apparently decamped by the time I got there.) I very much regret I didn't take the opportunity to make that visit.

Returning to magnetic recording. Poulsen's system employed first a steel wire, and later a steel tape, and the machine was called a Telegraphon.

In 1930 French film producer Louis Blattner designed a long-play steel tape-recorder christened the Blattnerphone, based on the patents of the German engineer Dr Kurt Stille. Although unsuitable for recording music because of its high degree of distortion, it was suitable for voice broadcast, and was used extensively by the BBC and ABC in the early years of the war.

Shortly after war's end, magnetised wire recorders of reasonable quality appeared on the market. Here in Australia a locally manufactured portable recorder by Pyrox found wide acceptance with broadcast stations and the public by 1949.

Meanwhile research involving magnetised tape covered with an iron oxide compound as a substitute for magnetised wire was well advanced. The German company BASF was one of the leaders in this field. The combination of a highly polished plastic tape base and an improved granular ferric compound, a speed of up to 15 inches per second, and a closer gap between the recording head and the tape brought about the tape recorder we have today. Apart from providing easy splicing and editing, the tape recorder produced a wider dynamic range than gramophone records. That is to say, it allowed a greater contrast between pianissimo and fortissimo.

As the development of the tape recorder proceeded apace, further attention was also given to stereophony, improvements being achieved by the use of additional microphones, separate channels and more tracks.

Optical recording

This method of recording was introduced in the United States in the late 1920s. It used the photo-electric cell to provide sound-on-film as an urgent replacement for the cumbersome sound-on-disc of the early Talkies. This system also had a limited application for broadcast station use. Pioneered by Fred Miller in the United States in 1931 and improved by the Philips Company in Holland, the machine was known as the Philips-Miller. It was used in Australia by the ABC and a few commercial stations, but soon gave way to magnetic recording. The Philips-Miller, unlike sound-on-film, used a combination of a mechanical and optical process, using a very small cutter to engrave a sound track on a gelatinous coated film. The result was produced optically.

The year 1960 saw the introduction of light amplification by simulated emission of radiation, 'laser' for short, ushering in the ultimate method of recording by optical means. This method, using a thin—very thin—beam of light, led to the development of the Compac disc and associated technologies, aided and abetted by the development of the transistor.

By now—in my mind—the romance of recording sound had disappeared. Today's jumps in technology are simply accepted without thought, leaving the mind unruffled—unless something goes wrong.

When a crystal set was the cat's whiskers

These days there aren't many chaps around to talk about their boyhood in the 1920s, when listening to the wireless on their crystal set was just the cat's whiskers.

I know of one boy who loved to plonk on a pair of headphones and snuggle under his bedclothes at night, especially Saturday night, gently set the cat's whisker on the crystal and then slide the thingummybob along the top of the coil fastened to a wooden base alongside the crystal detector until he found his favourite station, stiffening in anticipation as the broadcast he revered was about to commence. It was a description of the Saturday night motorbike races from South Brisbane Speedway, where his idol, Charlie Spinks, would be revving up his Indian—or was it his Douglas?—ready to lead the field.

Actually the boy could hear the thunderous sounds of a dozen or so speed bikes in action more clearly than he could hear the voice of the commentator, as his home in the suburb of Toowong was just across the river and a bit down from the speedway. So it was double excitement—an excitement that had to be contained, however, as the slightest movement in bed would cause the cat's whisker to jump off the perfect spot on the crystal for good reception.

Reception came from a piece of wire attached to the iron mattress of the iron bed the boy occupied on the verandah of his home, serving as the aerial. Another wire, poked through a hole in the verandah floor and fastened to a lead pipe stuck in the ground under the house, was the essential earth wire. The little wireless receiver sat on top of the boy's eiderdown, just below his chin.

The boy was me.

Incidentally, my bed was on the verandah and not in a bedroom as the result of an edict from our family doctor, who told my mother—after he had cured me of double pneumonia that left me with a valve in my heart that wasn't opening or closing at the right time, or something— that if she wanted her boy to live to be a man, he must always sleep on the verandah, never in a closed room.

As you may have gathered, I survived long enough to write these tales.

Crystal sets were used in the pre-valve days. Being of simple design, they were mostly made by home hobbyists, although they could be purchased in radio shops, complete or in kit form. Magazines such as *Wireless Weekly* provided much advice on their construction and operation.

Basically the set consisted of a crystal detector which served to rectify the signal coming from the wireless station by eliminating the radio frequency (RF) component, retaining the audio frequency (AF) component to energise a pair of headphones. The closer to the station the stronger the sound coming from the headphones, naturally. There was no amplification available to vary the audio strength. Usually an outside aerial was needed for satisfactory reception.

A tuned circuit made up of a coil and tuning condenser or an adjustable coil was used to select the station. The crystal detector comprised a lump of crystal with a fine alloy wire contact shaped in the form of a light spring, which looked like a cat's whisker. Several varieties of manufactured or naturally occurring crystal were used. The first was manganese oxide, used as far back as 1906. Zinc oxide and lead sulphide (galena) were commonly used in the 1920s, with galena being the most popular. Great care had to be taken to obtain the best possible vibration-free contact by the cat's whisker.

The beauty of the crystal set was that no batteries or electricity were required. If the set was operating virtually in the shadow of the wireless station, more than likely there would have been enough volume to drive a horn or cone loudspeaker, certainly enough to fill a room.

Housed in a highly polished wooden box, the crystal set, along with the gramophone, was a proud possession in many Australian homes in the 1920s.

The next step in the development of wireless receiving sets came with Lee de Forest's invention of the triode vacuum tube (thermionic valve). By 1925 crystal sets were on sale in Australia with an added component, an amplifier, which initially consisted of one valve. The filament was lit by an A battery and the high tension to operate the plate of the valve was provided by a B battery. Then came the power pack, which plugged into the 240-volt power supply, but had to be separated from the receiver to reduce the hum level, a bugbear in early receivers and amplifiers.

Toward the end of the 1920s tuned radio frequency (TRF) sets were being produced, which eliminated the crystal detector. TRF employed several RF stages to strengthen the signal coming in from the wireless station, and an audio stage to provide sufficient power to drive a loudspeaker. There was one big problem with the TRF set—a matter of stability. At its most sensitive tuning point it would be on the verge of oscillating, breaking into a howl. The knack was to tune it slightly back from the howl. Improvements in the design of valves did a lot to reduce this problem.

By this time another element, a cathode, had been introduced along with the triode, allowing for alternating current mains operation. Another introduced element gave the valve more amplification as a pentode. The manufacture and supply of valves was now big business.

In 1933 AWA set up a valve factory at their Ashfield works for large-scale production. In 1936 the Dutch Philips Company established a valve factory at Hendon in South Australia. Standard Telephones and Cables (STC) followed suit in 1939, manufacturing valves initially for military and PMG use. The factory was at Liverpool in New South Wales.

The next receiving set to come on stream was the superheterodyne, developed by US scientist and millionaire Major Armstrong, who also brought us frequency modulation (FM). The superheterodyne provided stability and sensitivity. This new form of reception was quickly adopted by the industry, giving good reason for an explosion in the sales of receivers from 1930 onwards, with many new brands coming on the market. Pioneer company AWA was well to the fore, with its Radiola; Astor, Eclipse, Stromberg-Carlson and Philips were a few of the many other manufacturers producing domestic superhets in the 1930s. The cabinet was now an essential part of the superhet, giving much employment to cabinet makers.

Quick to seize on the sales potential from cabinet appearance was a Brisbane man of the name of Kelly. Kelly was a victim of the Great Depression, and was living in a boarding house in the suburb of Auchenflower when he decided to set up a radio factory. Notwithstanding the fact he had little money available, the owner of the boarding house allowed him to use the laundry under the house on a temporary basis to make his radio sets until he got himself established.

Not being a radio engineer or even close to being one, Kelly hired an engineer from 'down south'. The engineer was Jim Grant, a clever radio man. Between them they established the Music Masters Radio Company. The only other company manufacturing radio sets in Brisbane at the time was Crammond Radio at North Quay.

The radio sets, containing from four to eight valves, were named after the 'music masters', the great composers of yesteryear. The 4-valve set, the smallest, was called the Chopin. Mendelssohn, Mozart, Beethoven and Liszt also posthumously lent their names. The largest set, the 8-valve Beethoven, was the ultimate in reception, sound and appearance. The cabinets, made of beautiful Queensland timbers and veneers, were a joy to behold—especially the Beethoven. Owning this 8-valver was a status symbol for many Brisbanites in the 1930s.

Within a few months of starting up Music Masters, Kelly obtained larger manufacturing premises in a warehouse in the Willbridge & Sinclair building in Elizabeth Street, alongside St Stephen's Cathedral in the heart of the city. By then staff numbers had grown to ten. Working for Music Masters was my first job after I left school. Three chaps were employed as assemblers and three as wirers. I was one of the wirers, a job which involved putting the set together under the chassis. We never followed circuit diagrams. We were expected to carry them in our heads. Producing each set was really a labour of love and a proud achievement, which we turned into a work of art. The top of each steel chassis carrying the components was sprayed a silver colour and the under-chassis a pale blue. The wiring was laid out in what we called a 'clothes line', because of the elevated bus-bars to which the resistors and condensers were uniformly attached by soldered joints.

There were several reasons for concentrating on the underside appearance of the sets. One was that the best-looking set of the month would be displayed in the window of the newly established showroom in Adelaide Street and earn the lucky wirer a bonus. At least, that is what we were promised.

Managing Director Kelly had two sons. One of them, Theo, rose to a high rank in the retail field, earning him a knighthood. As Managing Director of Woolworths his business acumen had a lot to do with setting that company on the path to the prosperity it enjoys today as a leading food retailer.

After a year and a bit with Music Masters I moved into the broadcasting business as a junior technician with 4BH Brisbane.

The lingering ghost of Mr Edison

When John L. Smith started collecting early 'talking machines', he had no idea that the ghost of Thomas Edison would linger with him for the rest of his life. Not that he minded the presence of the spectre of the inventor of the phonograph as it created just the right aura for a museum he established in Port Macquarie in the 1980s, which is where I got to know him. Port Macquarie has become the home of many active and retired members of the radio industry, a unique concentration of historical knowledge and expertise, and the logical place for John to set up his museum.

Life was busy for John in the 1960s. He was a foreman with Westfield Constructions in Sydney, and he had a much-loved collection of 450 birds which he carted about to every bird show around town. Then there was his music, which kept him out playing with a band most nights of the week. That is, until he had a heart attack on Christmas Day 1967.

John started collecting and repairing musical machines in 1945, and over the years accumulated a unique assembly of almost every type, every brand of sound-reproducing device dating back more than a hundred years to when the first machine was produced by Edison. It was fitting that he should call his exhibition 'Century of Sound', a name that he later extended to the Mobile Music Museum which he took around country shows and schools for 20 years, lecturing on the history of sound. He won the prestigious Museum of the Year Merit Award, presented by the Museums Association of Australia, in both 1982 and 1983,

It was a wonder John didn't drive his wife crazy with his passion for gathering about him every conceivable type of record player, and in later years radio sets, juke boxes and musical instruments. It reached the stage that the collection in a huge garage in their Sydney suburban home was overflowing into the lounge room. With more than thirteen tons of collectibles, this was no longer just a hobby. It led to their purchasing a cottage in Port Macquarie and setting up the museum.

Having introduced the Smiths, it's time for a word picture of this exhibition of a lifetime of collecting, walking through the corridors of a century of sound. We start with a Swiss music box which goes back to 1860, in perfect condition and producing a delightful tinkle of 20 tunes. Nearby is another musical device, a Polyphon, which makes music from a rotating steel disc, while over in a corner of the room is a German Leipzig piano, well over a hundred years old.

Moving along, we come to a group of Edison phonographs of various sizes, all lovingly restored and in perfect working order. A few turns of a handle and the piping voice of Enrico Caruso leaps out through a huge brass horn. Another machine, a turn of the handle, and Harry Lauder works his heart out with 'I Love a Lassie'.

In the same group stands a magnificent machine, John's favourite. It is an Edison Diamond Disc Phonograph. The cabinet, nearly two metres wide, is a work of art and the machine inside it produces the closest approach to 'true' sound of the Twenties. Several examples of the diamond disc method of recording and reproduction, or hill-and-dale, are on display.

Also in John's collection are a number of portable gramophones (British manufacturers preferred the word 'gramophone' to the American 'phonograph'). By the late Twenties the British company, His Master's Voice, shared dominance of the world market with Edison's Victor Talking Machine Company. By then portable machines were a must for picnickers, and a more fluid population of travellers, as the motorcar became more widely used. Among a collection of more than 3000 records John has gathered an example of almost every recording company of the day.

But fleeting was our fascination with these new gadgets. By the time of the short-wave broadcasts of Test matches, which popularised wireless as a home entertainment in the 1930s, the 'old gramophone' was starting to take a back seat, relegated to a spare room or the verandah. The display of cabinet work among the large collection of vintage sets is a reminder of craftsmen who took pride in their work as the wireless became not only an important part of daily life but a beautiful piece of furniture in the home. John has also put together a fascinating collection of the paraphernalia of musical and wireless accessories, and testing equipment used in the construction and maintenance of these machines.

I hear the Century of Sound Museum closed in the late 1990s. I devoutly hope the collection is kept together for posterity, as it is one of the best I have seen outside a major museum.

Episode 18

'Don't bump the mike!'

That was the first piece of advice given to cadet announcers in the early 1930s. The second was: 'Don't blast the mike—or I'll have your hide!'

Such forthright comments from a studio manager—emphasised with finger pointing—would be sufficient to put a little tremolo into any young announcer's first utterance, but it was better for the young 'un to know where he stood, or sat, from the outset—which had to be the correct distance from the microphone, mouth at the same level and speaking with a fair volume, but not loud enough to blast the diaphragm of this instrument—the key to fame or disdain.

You may recall mention in an earlier Episode of my first professional association with the microphone as a short-term actor in a play, one night at 4BH Brisbane. It was a night I prefer to forget, so I won't mention it again.

The first microphones used in wireless telephony employed carbon granules as the main ingredient. By connecting the microphone in series with the transmitting aerial and earth, speaking into the unit was sufficient to vary the transmitted current, creating a variation in power output by modulation.

The problem was the two electrodes in the microphone carrying the current through the granules got rather hot, and on most occasions water had to be used to cool them. A rather messy operation!

Shortly after the end of World War I, the US company Western Electric designed a double-button microphone especially for broadcasting. This unit consisted of two carbon buttons with a metal diaphragm separating them. Acting in a push-pull fashion when sound impinged on the diaphragm, a variation in voltage at the buttons already carrying a current occurred. Its predecessor was the single-button species. Nowadays these microphones only have a place in museums.

Then came the condenser microphone. As its name implies, it consists of a condenser or capacitor with one fixed plate and an opposite plate which moves when hit by sound. In doing so, the distance between the plates varies, creating a change in voltage across the capacitor.

When the condenser microphone became available in the mid-1920s, it was widely used by A Class stations and some commercial stations, mainly because it not only eliminated some of the problems associated with carbon-granule types—including hum, blasting and granular noise level—but also lowered the level of distortion and provided a much higher frequency range. Furthermore, the speaker or artist's distance from this unit was less critical than with the carbon type, which if one got within six centimetres was subject to distortion and/or blasting. (If the speaker simply had to get up close, the technique with that type was to talk across the diaphragm and not into it.)

There was one disadvantage to the condenser microphone in the early days. The output was so low a pre-amplifier was necessary, and it had to be positioned to connect directly with the microphone. Initially A and B batteries were used to operate the pre-amp, which was generally it a one-valve unit. The microphone and pre-amp were housed in a wooden box. This type of microphone was used extensively by the BBC and the ABC for many years. It was not suitable for outside broadcasts.

By the mid-1930s the condenser microphone had disappeared from most studios. However, the wheel of microphone development has gone full circle and it has regained its popularity in studios in Australia, due to the advent of the transistor, FM and solid-state technology, which today make it an ideal microphone for studio broadcasting and recording work. Suitable for interviews on radio and television is the clip-on mike, which contains a miniature pre-amp with a built-in UHF transmitter. It is a wireless-microphone, which has eliminated the need for trailing mike cords. Most importantly, it is unobtrusive.

In the progression toward better microphone technology in the 1930s, the moving coil and ribbon (velocity) species were developed in the United States. Robust and capable of covering a wide frequency range, the moving coil became the most suitable type for both outside broadcasts and studio work, including orchestral and vocal performances. The versatility of this microphone has a place in present-day broadcasting and public-address use. It operates on the same principle—but in reverse—as the moving-coil dynamic loudspeaker.

Replacing the moving coil with a metal strip, but using the same principle, produced the ribbon microphone, the principle being a variation in the magnetic flux between the poles of a magnet caused by a movement of the coil or metal strip (the ribbon) by sound impingement, thus generating a voltage. Ideal for studio interviews because of its two-way characteristic and also for broadcasting plays and orchestral performances because of its two 'dead' sides—handy for eliminating unwanted sounds—the ribbon mike is still used nowadays in various forms. It was greatly used by film-makers.

Next in line was the crystal microphone. Using Rochelle salt as the crystal, this type operated on the piezo-electric principle. That is, sound waves impinging on the crystal cause it to distort and in so doing to generate a voltage. Like the moving coil and ribbon species, it generates its own voltage, as distinct from the carbon-granule types which need a polarising voltage to operate.

Two models of crystal mike were produced, a diaphragm type and an open cell type. The former consists of a small metal rod attached to the centre of the diaphragm, with the other end of the rod sitting on the crystal. Sound hitting the diaphragm causes the rod to vibrate and activate the crystal. The open-cell type consists of several connected crystals standing in a frame covered by a grille.

The earlier crystal mikes suffered from temperature variations and humidity affecting their performance. The crystal microphone was in popular use just before and after World War II but had a weakness, in picking up hum interference if the leads were not completely screened. Furthermore it was not robust enough for outside work.

Reverting back to the years of the carbon-granule types, by 1932 the Reisz microphone was in wide use. Developed by the German scientist Dr E. Reisz, it was quickly adopted by the BBC through the Marconi Company and by Australian stations, both national and commercial.

This microphone consisted of a block of some heavy material, preferably marble, measuring about 10 x 7.5 cm. A cavity about 7.5 cm, to a depth of a little less than 10 mm, was carved into one face of the block. Two carbon electrodes were sunk flush into the back of the cavity and connected to terminals at the rear of the block. The face of the cavity was covered by a thin material, usually split mica, making a chamber. Highly polished carbon granules were poured into the chamber through a hole in the top of the block. The better class of Reisz used gold-plated electrodes, not only for good conductivity but also to ensure the carbon particles wouldn't bunch up against the electrodes in humid conditions, rather than lying loosely in the chamber waiting to be moved around by voices or instruments.

Although marble was preferable, both because of its appearance and because it was heavy enough to be inert, thereby reducing the possibility of introducing resonance, a heavy block of wood would suffice. The beauty about this kind of mike was it could be made in one's own workshop. Many broadcast station engineers made them for studio work and limited outside broadcasts. I made my own while still a teenager.

I had thoughts of getting a local stonemason to cut a marble block for me and carve out the grooves, but I had to back off because of the cost. Knowing that's what I wanted, a friend of mine, a bit of a villain, turned up at my place one day with a block of marble which, strangely enough, was almost of the right dimensions. He wanted 15 shillings for it.

It looked to me as if he might have picked it up at the local cemetery or perhaps broken off a bit of headstone, or prised it out from an ornamental grave. When I mentioned my suspicions he hotly denied them. By now convinced he *had* purloined it, I upbraided him and made it clear I didn't want anything to do with him.

'You ought to be ashamed of yourself for stooping so low!' I opined. 'And then to have the nerve to try and sell it to me. That's disgusting! I'll give you five bob for it.'

He wouldn't accept my generous offer and went on his way mumbling something or other about friendship.

Determined to make the mike, I got hold of a nice block of mahogany from the local sawmill, did the gouging out myself and then polished the wood to a mirror shine. Rather than use mica for the diaphragm I decided to use a more sensitive material, rubber, the ideal type coming from a condom (or French letter, as it was called in those days).

Lacking the courage to go in to the local pharmacy to purchase said article in the name of science, reluctantly I asked my villainous friend to buy one for me, which he willingly agreed to do … at a price! I paid him double the going price and went on with the making of my Reisz. It worked perfectly into the amplifier of the public address system I had just completed in time for my first assignment, which was the opening of our church bazaar.

This was to be the curtain-raiser for a project under the title of 'Be a Brick and Buy a Brick'. The object was to invite parishioners and others to each pay the cost of purchasing one brick which would go toward the cost of the restoration of our old church. The very popular Queensland Governor, Sir Leslie Wilson, agreed to perform the official opening of the bazaar and launch the campaign.

It was a very proud occasion for me. My very own home-made

microphone, my very own home-made amplifier, a freshly painted baffle board with loudspeaker, carrying my name in golden letters on a black background. My public-address system was willing and ready to beef out a huge 10 watts of power.

There was one little weakness about a French letter. When exposed to moisture, such as from a speaker with a tendency to splutter, the highly stretched rubber was inclined to split if not replaced before reaching its use-by date.

As I stood alongside the dais, Sir Leslie fronted up to the microphone to say his piece and receive due ovation. Unfortunately he got a bit too close to my lovely mike. No sooner had he got his first word out, when Catastrophe! Catastrophe! The diaphragm split asunder, causing my lovely carbon granules to spew down the front of the mike—which by now was dead. Very dead!

After a moment of shocked surprise, the King's representative, with typical British aplomb, continued with his speech into the dead mike, at the end of which he was greatly applauded, especially by those sitting close enough to could hear every word without the need of amplification.

For his part, the Rector, with a sort of fixed smile of gratitude, thanked the honoured guest and also me for providing my services gratis. By this time I had slunk out of sight, wondering where I could get another French letter in a hurry. I have often wondered if the church organising committee got enough bricks to undertake the restoration.

I happened to pass by this church not long ago during a brief visit to Brisbane. It looked to me to be just the same as it was when I was a callow youth. But then, that was a long, long time ago, well back in the last century when King George V was our reigning monarch. Maybe this old house of worship is now due for another restoration. I wonder how many good old 'bricks' still living thereabouts would be willing and able to make a contribution?

Episode 19

The long and short of Drake-Richmond

Hardly known in Australia then or now, and certainly unsung, Harold Drake-Richmond made an outstanding contribution to the advancement of wireless technology in this country on behalf of his mentor, Guglielmo Marconi—during the 1920s and 30s in particular.

A brilliant engineer with the Marconi Company in England, Drake-Richmond was sent out to Australia in 1926 to select a suitable site for setting up a powerful short-wave station for communication with London, and to supervise the installation of the equipment. This was the outcome of a recently signed agreement between the Australian Government, AWA and the Marconi Company.

But that was not the long and the short of it, as Harold Drake-Richmond ('Drake') told me when I first met him in 1946. At the time I was Chief Engineer of the South Burnett Broadcasting Company. Station 4SB operated on a much higher power than other country stations in Queensland because of the large area it was designed to cover. Although generating 2000 watts, I was not satisfied that we were getting the maximum efficiency from the antenna system, so I requested the designers, AWA, to send up one of their antenna experts to investigate and hopefully find a means of improving the system.

The system consisted of a Marconi flat-top T-array hung between two steel masts. Whereas the down lead would normally be connected to the coupling box and the box connected by transmission line to the transmitter in the nearby building, this particular design ended in what we called a 'fish tail'—being a loop at the end of the down lead, held aloft by two 3 metre high steel poles, and then connected to the coupling box. I was convinced this fish tail wasn't doing any good for us.

When the AWA engineer duly arrived at the transmitting station near the township of Wooroolin by taxi from the nearest railway station, I was most surprised, indeed almost aghast, to observe he was an elderly gent with not a wisp of hair on his head and about to greet me with a wide toothless grin. Quite frankly, he looked as if he'd come from an era long before wireless was wireless. I couldn't imagine him finding the cure for what was a rather complex problem, but as soon as he assembled his test instruments and got down to business I had to concede he knew his stuff.

By the end of the day he had mostly solved the problem. I was happy, he was happy—enough to make us firm friends. As we had sleeping quarters and other facilities at the station I offered him overnight accommodation, which he gratefully accepted. As there was still some daylight we sat down near the coupling box for an hour or so, to enjoy the sunshine left to us, the beautiful scenery which took in the peanut country spread around us, and to have a bit of a natter.

Drake told me his trip to Australia organised by the Marconi Company was arranged for two purposes—to set up the short-wave station and to get him out of the hair of the Chief Engineer of the Marconi Company.

Although held in high esteem by his employer, particularly for his inventiveness, which led to several patents under his name, the fact that he was a bit of a gadabout with a penchant for fast cars, and the ladies who went with them, didn't go down too well with the puritanical Chief Engineer, nor with Marconi. Drake's favourite car was a Bugatti in which he was often seen tearing along at a breakneck speed of up to 130 kilometres an hour, on both race-tracks and public highways.

One of his innovations was the use of a phasing resistor to give 180-degree reversal in the early direction-finding loops. Others were mainly concerned with methods of Morse code keying for high speed transmission.

He mentioned how he worked out one particular modification, which came to him on an occasion when he was entertaining a lady in a rather elegant restaurant in France. Before it slipped out of his mind, and being in high spirits at the time, he drew the circuit for his proposal on the snow-white tablecloth, using a black crayon he had with him. He whisked the cloth off the table and marched out of the restaurant with his lovely guest in tow, followed by an angry, explosive manager, and despatched it to London, with instructions that it be hand-delivered to the Marconi Company.

They didn't click

Harold Drake-Richmond and AWA Managing Director Ernest Fisk met in the London office of the Marconi Company at the time details were being finalised for the company to establish the first short-wave station in Australia. Fisk had approval to sign a contract on behalf of the Australian Government. Drake-Richmond was to carry out the terms of the contract on behalf of the Marconi Company.

Drake and Fisk just didn't click from their first meeting. The fact they travelled on the same ship did nothing to draw them closer. Rather, they kept their distance all the way. It was this frigidity that was to keep Drake on the AWA fence for the rest of his career. As he told me, he was never invited into the inner circle.

As soon as the ship berthed in Melbourne, Drake had a quick look around and made a mental note of what appeared to be a suitable site for the station, at Rockbank. However, when he arrived in Sydney, it was soon made clear to him that the AWA engineers favoured a location near Sydney, not far from Penrith, and a 'suitable site' was already under consideration. When Drake saw the Blue Mountains and the possible barrier they could impose to long-distance transmission, he made his mind up that Rockbank was the place. No matter how much the AWA engineers endeavoured to persuade him in favour of Sydney he wouldn't budge, a situation that didn't exactly endear him to Fisk. Finally it was decided to let Marconi settle the issue, so a cable was despatched to London. The reply came back that the Marconi Company had every confidence in Mr Drake-Richmond. AWA had to settle for Rockbank.

When Drake departed for Australia, his charter was to install a 20-kilowatt high-speed telegraphic short-wave station. At the time, Marconi scientist C. S. Franklin was working on an experimental beam array. Before Drake's arrival in Australia, advice had been received that Franklin's beam array was now a practical reality, so the system about to be installed in Australia must now encompass the beam method. Drake had not been involved with experiments in directional transmission and knew little about the beam system. Nevertheless, working from a series of cables sent from London, he was able to peg out the exact position for each 76 metre supporting steel tower, arranged to carry the antenna array pointed in the direction of London. It was decided to make Rockbank the receiving station and Ballan, near Ballarat, the transmitting station. To appease Fisk, it seemed, Ballan was later renamed Fiskville.

By harnessing the signal into a narrow directional path (beam), the strength of the signal at the receiving station was considerably stronger than from the non-directional method, equivalent to an increase of 90 times the transmitted power. The fact that it followed two paths around the globe was even more beneficial. One path was referred to as the long haul, the other as the short haul. The best haul for good communication was selected according to the time of day and ionospheric predictions.

Short waves over long distances

The use of short waves (HF) for long-distance communication was a complete departure from the long and medium waves used throughout the world since the inception of wireless. Indeed, Marconi's original proposal to the British Government to circle the British Empire by a series of wireless telegraphy stations involved the use of long waves. However, Marconi and Franklin had continued to research short-wave phenomena, much of this research being carried out on Marconi's yacht *Elettra*.

They soon discovered that short waves offered communication over longer distances, though the signal strength behaviour was more erratic. The other advantage was that the equipment required was less cumbersome, and was only a fraction of the cost of the equipment for operating long waves. Marconi announced the success of the short-wave experiments with a certain amount of bravado because it flew in the face of his long-wave commitments.

Further research revealed the behaviour pattern of short waves was influenced by the position of the sun and that the choice of frequencies was most critical. It was postulated that long-distance communication by short waves was due to a bouncing process, that the signal left he earth at a tangent instead of hugging it as long waves did, and was reflected back to earth by a layer of ionised gases surrounding the globe, taking off again in a kangaroo fashion.

This theory proved to be correct though it was found that the process was more of a refraction (bending back) than reflection. It was also found there are two ionised layers—well apart—whose influence greatly depends on the choice of frequencies being transmitted and the position of the sun. The layer nearest the earth was named the Kennelly-Heaviside layer after its discoverers, the second the Appleton layer, after its discoverer.

Then the news broke about the success of Franklin's experiments in concentrating transmitted energy into a narrow beam, giving greater amplification to the signal. And on 6 April 1927 the first public overseas wireless service, known as the Beam Service, was inaugurated between Australia and England, allowing messages to be transmitted with the speed of light, initially at an average of 150 words a minute.

Official opening

The Beam Service was officially opened at the Australian end by the Governor-General, Lord Stonehaven, transmitting a message to King George V which read: 'On behalf of the people of Australia, I desire to convey to your Majesty on the occasion of the opening of this new station, an expression of loyalty to your throne and person.'

The Governor-General's official message was followed by others, including one from Prime Minister Stanley Bruce: 'It must be a source of deep pride to every member of our race that we should be associated in the provision of the longest and most important direct telegraphic service in the world. We in the Antipodes realise, perhaps even more than the people of Britain, the significance of this great event.'

Harold Drake-Richmond stood well in the background at the official function while VIPs and others less involved in the project held the limelight.

The first paid public message transmitted from Australia was from a passenger on board the *Niagara*, two days out of Sydney. The message was received at the AWA marine coastal station at La Perouse in Sydney, sent to the Beam Service operating room in Melbourne and transmitted from there to England.

In June 1928 a similar service was established between Australia and Montreal in Canada, for which additional equipment was installed at Rockbank and Fiskville. Linked with the existing Canada–England circuit, it provided an alternative transmission route to England. On 30 April 1930 the Beam System was used for the inauguration of the radio-telephone service between Australia and England.

Picturegrams

On 9 September 1929 a picturegram service between Sydney and Melbourne was opened; this was mainly for the benefit of newspapers. The picturegram was transmitted along telephone lines, but considerable thought was being given to transmitting pictures by radio, as wireless was now called. By 1932 the picturegram service was being landlined to all capital cities. I saw a receiving set in operation in 1931, installed in my photographer father's darkroom in the old Daily Mail building in Queen Street, Brisbane. Two years later picturegrams were being transmitted across the Atlantic Ocean by radio. In 1934 the longest radio-picturegram service in the world was opened between London and Melbourne, conveyed by the Beam Service. Now Australian newspapers could publish photographs of overseas events just a few hours after they occurred.

The first overseas photograph received in Australia was of Australian pilot C. J. ('Jimmy') Melrose beside his plane at Mildenhall Aerodrome in England, preparing his kit for the start of the England–Australia Centenary Air Race. This picturegram appeared in Australian morning newspapers on 17 October 1934. On the same day an image of a dramatic event in European history was sent by picturegram to Australia, clearly showing the assassination in Marseilles of King Alexander of Yugoslavia. Radio picturegrams, referred to technically as 'facsimiles', were now an integral part of newspaper publishing in Australia.

The Great Depression

Looking back over the years it seems almost incomprehensible that these innovations in the use of radio were all achieved at the time of the Great Depression, which troughed in the years 1929–30 but continued well into the 1930s.

Although it was to be some years before television became a reality and a public utility, it too was more than a dream during the Depression. As I mentioned in an earlier Episode, experiments in television were under way in Brisbane, as also in other states at the time.

Government revenue from telegrams by land and air, and income from the telephone service, was badly affected during the Depression, yet scientists, engineers and planners managed to push ahead, their inventiveness providing improved services in the mediums of telegraphy, telephony and the transmission of images, all of which were to make a major contribution to Australia's war effort during the conflict which lay ahead.

Living in Brisbane during this period it was obvious to me that for many the Depression remained a fact right up to the start of World War II. I recall many a school leaver with a reasonable education had difficulty in finding any employment other than clerical work. Not until they joined the services did they have coins to jingle in their pockets.

After the war, of course, we entered an affluent society.

The Laughing Jackass and international broadcasting

It was appropriate that the Laughing Jackass, better known as the Kookaburra, that cheerful-sounding denizen of Australia, should herald the beginning of the country's international short-wave broadcasting service. On 27 September 1927, just a few months after the launching of the Beam Wireless Service, the laugh of the kookaburra, followed by a programme of music and the identifying call sign VK2ME, was transmitted from the AWA Centre at the outer Sydney suburb of Pennant Hills, operating on an experimental licence. VK2ME's programme's were the curtain-raiser to the Empire Broadcasting Service, inaugurated by the British Broadcasting Corporation in 1932.

VK2ME's initial programme, which came from the studio of 2FC in Farmer & Company's building in Sydney, included a number of well-known Australian artists, pianists Lindley Evans, Frank Hutchens and Alexander Sverjensky among them, and soprano Strella Wilson. Prime Minister Stanley Bruce sent a goodwill message to Britain landlined from his home at Frankston in Victoria. Then the New South Wales Governor, Sir Dudley de Chair, spoke from Sydney.

The most outstanding short-wave broadcast from VK2ME was transmitted in 1930. On this occasion, members of Admiral Byrd's expedition in Antarctica were able to hear sections of the sound track of Maurice Chevalier's film *The Love Parade*, landlined to the studio from the projection box of Sydney's Prince Edward Theatre.

One of the first announcers on VK2ME was Percy Farmer. Another was a colleague of mine, Phillip Geeves. A long-time staffer of AWA, mostly with 2CH, Phillip spent some years until his death in 1983 as AWA's archivist. His interests included writing a newspaper column on the history of Sydney. He was also a member of the Royal Australian Historical Society, his activity in this field earning him a gong—an OAM.

Regular international short-wave broadcasting began in December 1930 from AWA's experimental station VK3ME, located at Braybrook in Victoria, which had been operating on an intermittent basis for a few years. AWA operated another experimental station, VK6ME, near Perth in Western Australia, but VK2ME remained its most powerful station.

In 1934 the National Broadcasting Service was extended to provide stations on the short-wave band to carry ABC broadcasts to Australians living in remote areas of the continent, using the call sign VK3LR. The transmitter was located at Lyndhurst in Victoria. An increase in power saw the call sign change to VLR. In 1938 another short-wave station, VLW

Perth, was added to the network, to enable remote listeners in Western Australia and the Northern Territory to enjoy ABC programmes.

The BBC had launched its Empire Broadcasting Service on 19 December 1932 from its transmitter at Daventry, with a Christmas message to the British Empire from the reigning monarch, King George V.

Britain was not the first country to providing 'empire' broadcasts, however. On 1 March 1927 station PCJJ, owned and operated by the giant Philips Company in Holland, transmitted a programme on the short-wave band to the Dutch East Indies (now Indonesia), from its works in Holland. It consisted mainly of music from gramophone records. In June that year Queen Wilhelmina made her first broadcast to the Dutch dominions.

AWA experimental short-wave stations continued to provide Australia with an international broadcast service until shortly after the outbreak of World War II in September 1939, when the Federal Government cancelled its experimental licences for reasons of security.

Following Cabinet approval in October 1939, an overseas short-wave service recommenced on 20 December that year, under the banner of 'Australia Calling' and controlled by the Department of Information, using the existing transmitters at Lyndhurst and Pennant Hills. In April 1940, a transmitter at Perth focusing on South Africa was added to the chain. Due to the comparatively low power of these three transmitters, interference and atmospheric problems, this service made little impact overseas. The answer was higher power output and a more suitable central location.

In May 1944 the first of three powerful stations installed near the Victorian town of Shepparton began transmitting on a power output of 50 kW; the second, a 100 kW unit, was brought into service at the end of the war in August 1945. The third, with a power of 100 kW, commenced transmission early in 1946. By now this international service, known as Radio Australia, was covering most countries of the world.

The Shepparton establishment was gradually enlarged over the peaceful years with more powerful transmitters. Transmitters were also installed on the Cox Peninsula in the Northern Territory near Darwin, and at Carnarvon in Western Australia. The purpose of the Cox Peninsula transmitting complex was to boost the signal to target areas of South-East Asia, where the reception was not strong or clear enough from Shepparton. The Cox Peninsula set-up was both a receiving and transmitting station.

Sadly, on 24 December 1974, Cyclone Tracy damaged the Cox Peninsula transmitter building and almost wiped out the aerial transmission system. It was not for another ten years that this complex was brought back into service at a cost of almost $10 million. In June 1997 the Federal Coalition Government decided to close the Cox Peninsula complex on the grounds that it was no longer needed for the Radio Australia broadcasts—but in 1999, when the crisis in East Timor erupted, the Government found it did not have an avenue for broadcasting into the area, and had to rent a transmitter in Taiwan.

Several countries expressed interest in leasing the Cox Peninsula building and transmission equipment to strengthen their image in Asia, but it was not until the year 2000 that a deal was struck with the Coalition Federal Government—not by a foreign government, but a religious organisation which saw this as a wonderful opportunity to spread the Christian gospel.

Episode 20

Pedal wireless and the mission of John Flynn

At the time that Beam Wireless and marine services were getting into gear at the end of the 1920s, an Adelaide engineer named Alfred Traeger was experimenting with a method of providing a ready power source for small telegraphic transmitters. The outcome of his experiments—known as pedal wireless—was to revolutionise communication and improve the lives of the people of outback Australia.

Traeger was a protegé of the Reverend John Flynn (better known as Flynn of the Inland), whose main ambition in life was to provide spiritual comfort and medical services to people living in remote areas of the continent. With untiring zeal but little money at his command, Flynn initiated the launching of the Australian Inland Mission with the blessing of the Presbyterian Church, the first tangible move to improve the life of Inlanders.

This led to the establishment of the Flying Doctor Service and, in later years, the Radio Sunday School and the School of the Air, facilities still being provided through a series of base stations, though satellite radio and the Internet are progressively replacing the earlier technology. Flynn's was a vision of great enormity that became a reality of equal proportions— but it would never have been realised were it not for the development of a practical system of wireless communication.

Conscious of a pressing need to keep Inlanders in touch with civilisation, Flynn's first move was to set up a portable transmitter to pass messages across the arid distances of the Outback. The transmitter was installed in his old Dodge car, the power source being the car's generator.

At the time the only wireless links with the Outback were through two government-operated stations, one at Wave Hill in the Northern Territory and the other at Camooweal in Queensland. These stations had a limited range and their use was restricted to transmitting government messages and telegrams.

The story of installing these stations and getting them to function is well worth telling.

AWA provided the equipment and sent two engineers to carry out the installation. They were Sid Trim and Murray Johnson (mentioned in earlier Episodes). The equipment and the engineers arrived in Townsville by ship, and the gear was sent by rail to Dajarra, the station nearest their destination. Sid went on to Wave Hill to do the installation there and Murray to Camooweal. I recall Murray telling me about the many obstacles he encountered.

With the object of collecting the equipment at Dajarra and taking it to Camooweal, he purchased a second-hand Model T Ford, a 'Tin Lizzie'. The track was so rough Lizzie lost her four mudguards. Undaunted, Murray pressed on, managing to pick up another four, and went on his way again until Lizzie broke her radius rod, causing her to run off the road and slam into a tree. This resulted in a bent front suspension.

Using a branch from a tree, Murray mended the radius rod and travelled on for several hundred kilometres until he ran out of road … er, track. A compass he was carrying kept him going in the right direction from that point!

After completing the installation at Camooweal, Murray was sent on to Brunette Downs in the Northern Territory, where he was to endeavour to get a transmitter operating. It hadn't functioned since it was installed two years previously. He soon found the problem—a burnt-out condenser. The only snag was he didn't have a replacement with him so, once again, necessity became the mother of invention. Using a piece of glass taken from a newly arrived window pane, and metal taken from a kerosene tin, he fashioned a condenser of about the right capacity. That night he was in communication with Sydney, by Morse code, of course. The year was 1925.

To return to the Reverend Flynn and *his* problems …

Flynn's ambition to use wireless to inform and provide a 'mantle of safety' stemmed largely from the effects of the influenza epidemic which followed World War I. Worldwide, some 21 million people died, more than the number killed during the war. In Australia, close to a third of the population was infected, half of the deaths occurring in New South Wales. But it was originally the death of a young stockman in the remote settlement of Halls Creek in Western Australia in 1917 that spurred Flynn's efforts.

The stockman, Jimmy Darcy, was badly injured when he fell from his horse as he was endeavouring to divert a cattle stampede heading in his direction. Jimmy's mates carried him to the nearby homestead at Ruby Plains, thence on the long trek to Halls Creek. The postmaster at Halls Creek, Fred Tuckett, had a smattering of first aid and was often called upon to mend broken bones and treat and bandage wounds, which gave him quite a reputation in this doctor-less district, so it was to the postmaster they went. As there was no doctor available within 830 kilometres, the postmaster sent a Morse code message by the local telegraph office and landline to a Doctor Holland, some 4000 kilometres away in Perth. From the information he received, Dr Holland diagnosed the patient's condition as a ruptured bladder, and instructed Tuckett to operate immediately if the young man's life were to be saved.

Denied the benefits of surgical instruments and chloroform, Tuckett performed the operation following step-by-step Morse code instructions from Dr Holland. The operation was successful but, sadly, the much-weakened patient died hours later from the effects of malaria, a disease which had plagued him for some years.

The idea of using an aerial ambulance to quickly treat sick and injured Outback people was first put to John Flynn by a young man with medical ambitions, Lieutenant Clifford Peel of the Australian Flying Corps. While on active service he had suggested the notion in a letter to Flynn, but before he received a reply was shot down and killed in a reconnaissance mission over France. However, the seed was sown, and led to the Flying Doctor Service taking to the air on 17 May 1928.

Operating on a temporary licence from the PMG's Department, Flynn established the first Australian Inland Mission (AIM) wireless station, 8AB at Alice Springs, which was used initially to make contact with field station 8AD at Hermannsburg Mission, some 140 kilometres away, in a back room of Adelaide House, which adjoins the magnificent Flynn Memorial Church. I had the pleasure of visiting the old base many years ago. I do hope it is still there and available for public view.

In the early years of wireless communication Morse code telegraphy provided the only reliable method, as greater distances could be reached and with better clarity than telephony. 8AB wasn't the answer, however, as there was still no satisfactory method of taking wireless communication into Outback homes. Alfred Traeger, who had accompanied Flynn on several trips, quickly realised that the only way to establish personal communication was through a reliable generating source that could operate a small transmitter and receiver. He developed a generator which could be satisfactorily operated by foot power to provide the necessary voltages. Pedal wireless was born!

From funds mainly supplied by the AIM, pedal wireless transmitter-receiver units were installed in many station properties and police stations throughout the Inland. A base station was set up at Cloncurry in 1929. This was to become the headquarters of the Flying Doctor Service.

The beauty of pedal wireless was that operators' hands were free to write down messages as they pedalled away. The big disadvantage of any system in use at the time was that communication had to be by Morse code, which had to be taught to the users of the equipment. But this problem was quickly overcome after Traeger converted typewriter keys to carry dots and dashes. For example, the letter A became a dot and dash (dit dah), B a dash and three dots (dah dit dit dit), and so on.

With more transmitter power and a suitable choice of frequencies for day and night operation, Traeger's pedal wireless graduated to radio-telephony. Thus the spoken word became the link with all that happened in the Outback.

After World War II the pedal generator was replaced with a vibrator to supply the high-tension voltage to operate the equipment. By 1962, the AIM had set up 1500 outposts through thirteen base stations across the inland states.

The Dry Continent was now covered with words!

I first saw Traeger's little pedal wireless unit when still at school. At my Presbyterian-Methodist school the Reverend John Flynn spoke of his Outback mission and produced the set for inspection at an Assembly.

Today, as I pen this narrative many, many years later, the Royal Flying Doctor Service—as it is now rightly titled—still provides a vital facility for Australians living in remote districts, through a link called Outback Radio. As a matter of fact at this moment I am tuned to the RFDS station VJN Cairns from my home near Herberton in Far North Queensland, expecting a call on the same frequency from my son-in-law Timothy Daniel.

Tim is jointly leading an expedition across the continent from Allora on Queensland's Darling Downs to Port Essington on the Coburg Peninsula east of Darwin, tracing the epic 5000 kilometre exploration of Dr Ludwig Leichhardt in 1844–45. The expedition was arranged by Leichhardt's great-great-great-grand niece and nephew, Carrie and Ben Williamson, of Kentucky in the United States. As the party is traversing a great deal of uninhabited country, Tim has me on Watch.

The world's first flying doctor

When the Flying Doctor Service began in 1928, the first official Flying Doctor was an eminent Macquarie Street specialist, Dr Kenyon St Vincent Welch. 'The first of the kind' was how Dr Welch described this new service to a reporter of the *Brisbane Courier.*

However, there was a flying doctor operating in the Outback some six years before the FDS was formed. The doctor's daughter, Marjorie, told me the story of this extraordinary, but little-known man, a few months before she died in 1984. This—in part—was the story I published in that year:

On a very, very hot day on the 27th December 1922 a middle aged medical man donned a leather helmet and goggles and climbed somewhat gingerly into the passenger cockpit of an Avro Dyak aeroplane standing in a paddock alongside a shed at Longreach in Central Western Queensland.

Firmly clutching his black medical bag, the doctor crouched forward in readiness for the blast of air as a mechanic swung the propeller after getting the thumbs up from the pilot. As soon as the engine, the fuselage and the two wings came to terms with each other, the mechanic pulled the chocks away.

It was now time for the pilot to let the Avro know who was boss of the situation as he trundled the machine on its frail undercarriage toward the end of the paddock that had yet to be called an aerodrome. The pilot turned the machine around, gave it full throttle and seconds later the Avro Dyak was reaching for the sky.

As soon as he had obtained a safe altitude of a few hundred feet, he turned the machine's nose in the direction of Winton and throttled back to a cruising speed of 65 miles an hour. Meanwhile his passenger was relaxing—as best he could—whilst taking in the view below him. Fortunately he wasn't cramped as this particular machine could carry two passengers in the one cockpit. A little more than two hours later, the Avro landed at Winton after what was considered an uneventful trip, save a few heat-caused air pockets, bent on giving the pilot and his passenger a few bumps.

While the pilot remained with his machine to prepare it for the return journey the following day, the doctor was whisked off by car to the township, where he was to perform an emergency operation.

The Avro completed the round trip in a total of 4 hours 10 minutes flying time.

Filling in his log book after the flight, the pilot wrote alongside his usual entry, 'for operation', and in the passenger column, the name of the passenger as he heard it pronounced, 'Dr Meechoh'. In such simple terms this pioneer pilot had recorded a unique historical event in civil aviation—the use of an aeroplane for medical service. Thus his passenger, Dr Archibald Hope Michod, became the world's first flying doctor.

The pilot was Thomas Quarles Back, an Englishman who saw service with the Royal Flying Corps over France in the first Great War. Barely out of his teens, he had come out to Australia and worked as a jackeroo in western New South Wales. Illness, caused by too much exposure to the sun, forced his return to England. He was there when the war broke out. After being demobbed, once again he came out to this country, this time to look for a property to purchase in Queensland. While he was looking the country over, he heard that a fledgling aerial service was looking for a pilot. He applied and got the job to become the second pilot for the newly formed Queensland and Northern Territory Aerial Service, which was to become better known as QANTAS (now Qantas).

The Avro Dyak he flew on that mercy mission was one of two aeroplanes operated by Qantas. The other was a wartime BE2E, which was also put to use in flying Dr Michod to urgent medical cases, usually piloted by the manager, Hudson Fysh. Like pilot Thomas Back, Dr Hope Michod was an Englishman to his bootstraps, but as much an Australian as any pioneer of the outback.

About the turn of the century Dr Michod had left a lucrative medical practice in London to seek a drier climate for the sake of his health. He couldn't have found an area drier than Tambo in south-western Queensland, where he was appointed medical officer of the local hospital. Here he met and married Alice Hamilton of Tambo Station. Shortly after their marriage, the couple moved to Roma where Hope Michod established a medical practice. In 1906, at the age of 34, he accepted an appointment as medical officer at the Longreach Hospital in central western Queensland.

When the Michods arrived in this desolate town, the district was just recovering from the Black Drought of 1905, which had caused an enormous amount of devastation. Money was scarce and there was little sign of progress, yet the indomitable spirit of the people so impressed the doctor that he and his family were to spend the next 20 years in the town. He was as determined as the long-time residents to make good.

Even the state of the hospital didn't discourage him. Consisting of a few buildings constructed of timber, the institution was lacking in most facilities required to fully function. The daily patient average was eighteen.

The staff comprised just a matron and a trained nurse. There was no overnight accommodation provided for the staff, other than a bed on the verandah. There was no operating theatre. Operations were performed in the dispensary, using a horsehair couch as an operating table.

Two days before the Michods arrived in town, Hospital Hill was visited by a cyclone which shifted the roof of the convalescent ward and flattened several outhouses. That, briefly, was the scene the morning Dr Michod arrived to inspect his new headquarters. One of the first things he set about doing to improve the lot of medical cases was to ask the hospital committee to provide an operating theatre. Its members were astounded at such a request, and made it clear to the new arrival that there was no money in kitty for such a facility. Undaunted, the good doctor organised a raffle with a gold watch as the prize. The outcome was an amount of £100, to which the Government added another £100. The operating theatre was on its way.

Dr Michod's devotion to the welfare of the community, and to the advancement of the town of Longreach, was typical of the stoicism of the people of the West in their endeavours to carve out a livelihood under what were fairly primitive conditions. In 1913 he resigned from his post at the General Hospital and helped to set up a private hospital, funded by the local community. This hospital was burnt to the ground in 1919, and rebuilt a year later.

By this time the Michods were deeply involved in local affairs, so it was a foregone conclusion that when a local grazier, Fergus McMaster, and two wartime aviators, Hudson Fysh and Paul McGinness, were trying to set up an aviation company in the district, Dr Michod would be associated with the venture. He was an early director of the company, and occupied the seat of chairman while the foundation chairman, McMaster, concentrated on his property in the years 1923 to 1926.

Less than two years after the formation of the Queensland and Northern Territory Aerial Services, this great humanitarian, whose devotion to the West went far beyond his Hippocratic oath, was frequently in the air on his way to an urgent medical case hundreds of miles from Longreach.

In 1926 the time had come for the doctor and his family to move on. He resigned from the Qantas board and set up a specialist practice in Brisbane, retaining his link with the aviation industry as president of the Queensland Aero Club.

Ever since aviation went to outback Queensland, there had been much talk about using the aeroplane to provide prompt medical attention to settlers living far from habitation. But it was not until May 1928, six years after Dr Michod made his historic flight of mercy, that the Reverend John Flynn's scheme got off the ground. Several books have been written and many newspaper articles published about the Flying Doctor Service, but there has been little credit given to the world's first flying doctor. A Brisbane newspaper in 1960 did make brief mention of the pioneering service, but confused the name. Reporting the discovery of the fuselage, propeller and wheels of a wartime BE2E in a garage in Brisbane, the newspaper said it was the same model used by the first flying doctor. The paper called him 'Hope McLeod', probably confusing Michod with a Major McLeod who served on the Qantas board for a short duration but was not a medical man.

I had the pleasure of meeting one of the late Dr Michod's sons, Bill, while he was visiting the home of his sister Margery in Port Macquarie. Bill served with distinction in the Royal Australian Air Force during World War II. Margery, looking much younger than her years, held many pleasant memories of her girlhood days at Longreach in the 1920s, including that first day her father took to the air as a flying doctor.

During this visit another story about Dr Michod surfaced. It concerned a pair of hinges. Around 1935 Dr Michod, who was then practising in Brisbane, received a parcel in the post. It contained a pair of hinges, which looked brand spanking new. There was no covering letter to identify the sender. After pondering the contents of the parcel for a few minutes, Dr Michod suddenly recalled an incident which took place about 1920, when a pair of hinges came in very handy. He had been called to a township out of Longreach after a man was badly injured. Both hips had been badly crushed. The possibility of the man walking, let alone living, seemed at first very remote. There was only one thing for it, an operation—on the spot. The spot happened to be an hotel. The doctor prepared a makeshift operating table, then called the hotel yardman and instructed him to remove a pair of hinges from a box mounted in his sulky. The box was used to house raincoats and gumboots for use on rainy days, the sulky being without cover. By inserting the hinges into the injured man's flesh against his hip bones, after cleaning them as best he could, he managed to keep his patient together. Before long, the man was getting around again. In his will the man had included a codicil that on his death the hinges were to be removed from his body and sent to Doctor Michod as a gesture of appreciation; a message from a man whose life he had saved so many years ago.

Episode 21

The Buccaneer of the Airwaves

Here in Australia in the 1930s we had a few buccaneers of the air, unlicensed amateur wireless operators, but we called them pirates. In England, as recently as the 1960s, one man was headlined by the press as the Buccaneer of the Airwaves. His name was Allan Crawford, and he was my brother-in-law.

Allan was born and raised in New South Wales city of Newcastle. I first met him at the Crawford family home in the suburb of Merewether when I was courting his sister Jean, soon to be my wife. It was during the war years. I had just completed aircrew training on Catalinas at nearby Rathmines and was about to depart for the South-West Pacific. Allan was then a callow youth employed by BHP as a sub-accountant. A rather serious-looking chap wearing heavy spectacles, he appeared a typical clerical type to me, probably deskbound for the rest of the war. But I was wrong. Three years later he was flying bombers over Germany. When the war ended, Allan elected to take his discharge in England to enable him to study music at the famous Guildhall.

When he was in London he happened to meet Ralph Peer, principal of the US Southern Music Publishing Company. Peer was about to set up an office in Sydney and offered Allan the job of manager, impressing on him the fact that he would have to operate on a shoestring budget, at least for the first year. Allan accepted. The year was 1948. With just £1,500 to support the first year of operation, he awarded himself a salary of a mere £4 a week, which provided for modest accommodation in a garret at Kings Cross, an occasional pie with tomato sauce at Harry's Café de Wheels down in Woolloomooloo, and the odd sandwich or two during the week. He spent most weekends with Jean and me at our Epping home, where he was assured of a couple of substantial meals.

His office occupied a very small area in the basement of an insurance building in George Street. Purloining the services of his father and myself—we happened to be a pair of wood-butchers on the side—counters were made, partitions erected and some second-hand doors fitted. I built and installed record-playing equipment, Jean provided some carpeting. Finally, a battered old piano, once the pride of Allan's grandmother, was wheeled into position.

The Southern Music Publishing Company was now officially in business in Australia. The timing was absolutely perfect. *Australia's Amateur Hour* and various other radio shows had discovered some worthwhile talent, but they had nowhere to go. Southern Music was quick to sign up budding composers and artists. The problem was to break the grip long-established publishers had on the music and record industry to get enough air time for Southern publications. This hurdle was soon put aside by persuading the head of Australian Record Company, Dudley Fegan, to take his company into the production of gramophone records. At the time, the only company of substance producing records in Australia was EMI at Homebush in Sydney. This company controlled the HMV, Parlophone, Columbia, Regal-Zonophone, Decca and RCA Victor labels.

Australian Record Company engineers had no experience in making 78 rpm records, as production had been restricted to recording and pressing soap operas and radio shows on 16-inch transcriptions for the radio broadcasting industry. After a few months of experimental work, goaded on by Allan Crawford, the Rodeo and Pacific labels were born. The deal was that a good percentage of releases would carry at least one Southern Music publication.

Frank Ifield, Tim McNamara, and also Reg Lindsay, if I recall correctly, were some of the many talented young performers who owe their start in show biz to Southern and its livewire manager. After two successful years, Allan moved his company into more prestigious premises in the National Building in Pitt Street, Sydney, and months later to a suite in a Margaret Street building. In the mid-1950s he went overseas on a business trip— much to our relief. A hell of a nice chap, but difficult in many ways. While he was in London the manager there died and Allan landed his job, which went smoothly until Ralph Peer, passed away. His widow clashed with Allan—end of story.

Some months later he set up his own publishing and record company in England, carrying four labels—Crossbow, Canon, Sabre and Carnival. He established record shops in the West End of London and a talent agency with four well-known pop groups under signature. But the BBC wouldn't have a bar of him or his music. The three hours a day given to 'needle time' were completely dominated by England's established music publishers, who were determined to keep Allan away from the broadcasting scene. That's when he made up his mind to go his own way to get exposure for his music and his artists by setting up a radio station in international waters where he could not be touched by the broadcast authorities.

He phoned me from London, told me his plans and his intention to purchase an old freighter in Holland and anchor it in the English Channel. 'I can get it for a song,' he declared.

'That should be music to your ears, Allan,' I said, playing a weak pun.

He asked me how he should go about setting up the station, so I gave him a few clues about the equipment needed and so forth.

The almost derelict 800 ton ship cost Allan £75,000. A few days after the deal he phoned me again from his London office (in Mayfair, by the way), to tell me he had acquired the services of a retired BBC engineer and would soon be on the air as Radio Caroline. At the time the only commercial radio station servicing Britain was Radio Luxembourg, operating from Europe. Within six months Radio Caroline had established an audience of several million with a fair swag of advertising to keep things humming along.

The Advertising Institute stood in the wings for a couple of months, then, when the coast was clear, lifted their embargo and placed orders on behalf of hordes of advertisers, including Unilever and the Ford Motor Company. Radio Caroline was now steering a course toward a fortune for Allan, until things went wrong. Another pirate station, Radio Atlanta, came on the air, splitting the market at the same time as a bit of skullduggery occurred within his own enterprise, ending up in a court case. Allan's fortune went down the drain. He was soon down to his uppers, trying to make a crust selling insurance in London.

About this time Australia's commercial radio stations were having a bit of a battle with the major record manufacturers, who were demanding a fee for the privilege of playing their records on air. Through their industry association, the Federation of Australian Commercial Broadcasters, the stations refused to pay this imposition, pointing out to the manufacturers that they were enjoying free exposure for their products. The Australian Broadcasting Commission was already paying the fee, however, which gave the record manufacturers some ammunition.

Although the demand was withdrawn, the warning was there. A couple of networks got together and formed their own record company, M7 Records. I got in touch with Allan. After negotiations with representatives of M7 he was appointed to operate the new company in Sydney. He produced some terrific stuff, including contemporary rock music, but it was a little ahead of its time. M7 could not afford to keep him, so he went back to London to peddle insurance policies; this led him into the brokerage business.

But Allan couldn't get pirate radio out of his blood, out of his mind. The next thing, I got a phone call asking my opinion of the feasibility of setting up a powerful radio station to beam into England from Spain. He told me he had the financial backing and was almost ready to go.

'Forget it!' I said, a little unkindly. 'You'll do your dough.' This was at the time commercial radio was about to get the government nod in Britain. Allen dropped the idea.

A couple of months later, yet another phone call. 'Gawd! Wonder what it is this time?' I said to myself as I picked up the telephone. He wanted me to book him and his partner into a posh hotel in Sydney and engage a livewire public relations firm to handle media interviews.

'Blimey! I'm living in the bush these days, Allan. I've been out of touch with that stuff for years,' I responded as politely as I could.

However, I relented and got in touch with someone to book them into a suitable hotel and engage a PR firm. Allen's partner was Tirath Khemlani, and they hoped to finalise a proposed loan to the Whitlam Federal Government. The proposition fell through, so the two of them were soon on their way back to London.

A few days before Allan's departure, I went with him to Newcastle to see his mother. On the train we discussed the recently held competition to find a new national anthem, which was a bit of a fizzer. Allan told me he had just composed an anthem, and was in no doubt it would be accepted. I stared at him.

'Tell you what, I'll sing it for you and the others in the carriage, right now. I'll just stand at the entrance to this toilet to get a nice echo behind my voice.'

'You can't do that,' I declared. 'That's the Ladies.'

'Ah, they won't mind. It's all in the cause of art.' On that note, he launched into our 'new' national anthem. I just sat there wincing.

After he had bellowed out the last verse, he was greeted with applause from his captive audience, either in appreciation of his vocal efforts— and the song—or the fact it was now all over. The only fellow passenger not looking happy was a lady waiting for him to remove himself from the entrance to his echo chamber.

Months later I received a phone call from my sister-in-law Marjory in Sydney to tell me Allan had just written another musical play, about the fifth he had composed in the last 20 years.

'This is it!' he'd told her. 'This one will make my fortune. We'll launch it in London, then go across to New York, after which maybe Sydney. By the way, Marj, would you have Bern's telephone number handy? I seem to have mislaid it.'

That was about sixteen years ago, if I recall correctly. Although I had kept in touch with Allan through my daughter Jane's frequent visits to London when she was studying at Stockholm University, I had not seen him since he brought Khemlani out to Australia. Since then Allen had become afflicted with diabetes, which confined him to a wheelchair and a rather lonely life, with but a few close industry friends and occasional visits from the British crew of the bomber he captained during the war years to cheer him up. One leg was amputated, then less than twelve months later, the other. By this time, he had lost most of his sight and was having renal problems.

We knew he was in hospital and feeling very despondent when Jane and I arrived in England in 1996. Allan was expecting us and—from what I was later told—was very excited about us getting together again, after all those years. Excitement also came from the news he had just been accepted into a nursing home in Wales, which provided 24-hour nursing service. It was a good day for Allan and for me. Far from being down in the dumps as I was led to believe, he appeared to be on top of the world.

'I've just written another musical. This is a beauty! I've put two songs down with about five to go,' he said, brimming over with enthusiasm.

'What about your lack of eyesight, Allan, and will you have a piano available at the nursing home?' I queried.

'Don't need a piano. All I need is for someone to copy down the notes of the songs and the score. I'm carrying them in my head.'

That really stunned me. I sat silently in front of my dedicated brother-in-law for a few minutes while he continued with the same fervour, the same supreme confidence in his ability, that he had exuded in the 1950s when he was in good health. Here he was, sans legs, sans sight, bubbling over with the good things he was planning for the years ahead.

Sadly, I later received a call from Allan at his nursing home in Wales, letting me know that an Englishman to whom he had introduced us, who declared he would do all he could to ease Allan's plight, had eased him out of about £20,000 by forging his signature and was now on the run. How low can one get?

In December 1999, Allan Crawford, this very talented man, who bore his illness and disability with fortitude and dignity, left us suddenly as the result of a bout of pneumonia. Before he died he dictated his life story on tape. I'm sure his autobiography will be a bestseller.

Episode 22

'Good morning … is the billy boiling?'

You're not likely to hear this call over the airwaves on the civil aircraft radio channels nowadays, but back in the early Thirties for those in the know it was both a message of good cheer and an indication that all was well. Also— that someone 'up there' was dying for a cuppa!

Mateship between the crews of commercial aircraft flying the Outback routes of Australia and communication outposts along the way prevailed during the early days of aviation, when the calm and collected voice of the radio operator at the ground station meant as much to the pilot and crew as sophisticated navigation aids do to the armchair aviators of today. In those days the personal touch was the thing, in matters of air safety.

The aircraft would probably be a two-man operated De Havilland biplane or a Douglas DC-2 monoplane, about to make a landing at some remote town of western Queensland or New South Wales. The ground operator and his equipment would usually be located in a hut alongside the aerodrome.

As soon as the aircraft had come to a standstill outside the terminal building—more than likely just a shed—and the passengers been disgorged, the pilot and crew (in the case of the DC-2) would head for the hut and a chat and, of course, a quick cup of tea. If the aircraft happened to be carrying a hostess, she would probably take along a few left-over biscuits, a rare treat for a radio operator living far from real civilisation. Minutes later, the aircraft would be up, up and away, heading for another western town or home base.

The operator of this lonely outpost was one of a band of highly skilled communicators employed by the Department of Civil Aviation in a string of radio stations to make both voice and Morse code contact with aircraft and to provide direction-finding facilities, where available, to guide the pilot to a safe landing. This network, established in the early 1930s, was known as Aeradio, an air safety organisation which provided meritorious service during the fledgling period of commercial aviation, and also during World War II.

The contribution made to the war effort by Aeradio's civilian radio operators, particularly after hostilities moved into the South Pacific, has never been headlined or justly recognised. Air-to-ground radio communication in Australia had its genesis back in the 1920s, following successful experiments in Europe and America.

Experimental work in this country was carried out by the RAAF. In 1928 AWA installed a transmitter-receiver in Kingsford Smith's tri-motor *Southern Cross* which operated on the long-wave band at a frequency of 500 kilohertz (600 metres).

It was a most cumbersome unit, powered by a generator and a bank of lead-acid cells. By the time Kingsford Smith and Ulm had formed their own airline, Australian National Airways (ANA) on 1 January 1930, more efficient, more compact equipment was being manufactured by AWA. The airline began a Melbourne–Sydney service on 1 June that year, using Avro-Ten three-engine aircraft, and on 19 January 1931 a Melbourne–Hobart service, also using Avro-Tens. The Great Depression forced the company to suspend its operations, the last flight being on 26 June 1931. ANA's aircraft were given names similar to the *Southern Cross*—the *Southern Sky, Southern Moon, Southern Cloud* and *Southern Sun.*

AWA was engaged to supply the radio equipment in the four airliners. A prototype of the company's latest development was installed in the *Southern Cloud,* to be tested on the Sydney–Melbourne run to determine whether it was practicable to carry radio suitable to communicate with ground stations during the flight. The engineer in charge of the project was my old friend, Murray Johnson.

Years later he told me about it:

We fitted a suitable receiver in the *Southern Cloud* and I was to carry out the test on the next flight to Melbourne. Fortunately I was taken ill and could not join what proved to be a fateful flight. In a severe storm the *Southern Cloud* was lost in the Southern Alps and was not found for 25 years. I carried out tests on the *Southern Star* about two weeks later but the tests were unsuccessful due to interference from the aircraft ignition system.

Soon afterwards ANA ceased operations, to be reborn in 1936 by Holyman's Airways and shipping interests.

Shortly after the establishment of the Civil Aviation Board in April 1936, AWA was contracted to set up and install the equipment in the network of Aeradio stations across country, backed by the company's knowledge of air-to-ground communication gained since 1928. Some of this experience came from a joint operation with the RAAF in 1934, operating a mobile station at Charleville in Queensland to provide contact with aircraft in the London–Melbourne Centenary Air Race, as well as providing direction-finding facilities. The first competitors to make contact were the Dutchmen Parmentier and Moll, flying a Douglas DC-2. After making contact with Charleville, they steered a southerly course toward Melbourne, but became lost. The RAAF Charleville station played a big part in guiding them to an emergency landing at Albury.

The groundwork had now been done for the setting up of a network of direction-finding (DF) and air-to-ground traffic stations, in the interest of air safety. Hence Aeradio. By 1938 some twelve stations were operating, including one at Kempsey, which also provided a radio beacon using the very latest Lorenz system. If my memory serves me correctly, the Lorenz approach beacon operated on 33.8 megacycles (now megahertz). Strategically located halfway between Brisbane and Sydney, the Kempsey station continued until well after the end of World War II. By the time war broke out, 34 stations had been installed, including one at Lord Howe Island.

As the war progressed, the shortage of staff and long hours placed an enormous strain on operators, who were now concerned not only with the safety of commercial aircraft but also with that of RAAF planes flying in their vicinity.

The first DF system used was the Bellini Tosi. The equipment was manufactured in the AWA works at Ashfield in Sydney to a Marconi Company design, initially for use in ships. The first installation for aviation use was at the Essendon airport in Melbourne. Then came the German Lorenz system.

Before DF was introduced, it was customary when visibility was poor, with cloud blanketing an aerodrome, for the radio operator at the Aeradio station to take a microphone on a long lead to the tarmac so he could talk the aircraft down. After determining the plane's position from the direction of the sound, the operator would direct the pilot to a break in the cloud (if there was one), enabling him to gradually reduce height with safety. Well, that was the idea!

By 1944 there were 54 stations functioning on mainland Australia and on a number of islands in the South Pacific. Some stations within the war zone were operated by AWA under contract, some by RAAF personnel. In fact, although strict silence was the order of the day—except in an emergency—the RAAF's own stations worked in parallel with much of the communication work of Aeradio. One such station was at Milne Bay.

This radio station was 'in the heart of it' during the landing by the Japanese and the battle with the Australian defenders in August–September 1942. A friend of mine, the late Peter Alexander of the New South Wales town of Port Macquarie, was one of the RAAF operators at the station who managed to maintain vital communication during what was a very sticky situation with the invaders at the door. The Australian victory of the Battle of Milne Bay and the American victory of the Battle of Midway undoubtedly marked the turning back of the Japanese invasion of the South Pacific.

When the war ended, the Aeradio network continued to expand until there were some 62 stations in operation. By 1953 much of the responsibility for the part of the network outside the mainland had been taken over by the Overseas Telecommunication Commission (OTC), established by the Commonwealth Government in 1946. By this time, almost all the DF equipment and transmitter-receivers were seriously outdated, and the demise of Aeradio had become inevitable.

Today the only visible evidence of a network that guided so many aviators to a safe landing, saving many lives in war and in peace, is the odd decaying hut seen at a few airfields out west, and alongside it, maybe a couple of rusted towers, once used to carry the antenna system.

Mentioning this sparked memories of an incident which occurred in those early, heady days of commercial and RAAF flying. Read on!

The day I made a bloomer

In those days not all aircraft had a fixed antenna. When long-distance communication with the ground station was essential, the wire used for receiving, about 30 metres long, was wound on a drum located within the machine alongside the radio operator and fed out through a tube under the fuselage. Attached to the end of the wire was a cylindrical lump of lead. The lead weight prevented the wire from being wrapped around the fuselage in the slipstream.

When the drum of wire was fully wound out the antenna would trail at about 45 degrees. Winding out the antenna as soon as the aircraft obtained sufficient height and winding it in again before the aircraft landed was no problem. That is, providing the operator didn't forget to do just that! Many an operator was carpeted for that little oversight.

I well remember one occasion when I was the radio operator on an Avro Anson during the war. 'Aggie Ansons', we called them. We had just completed a lengthy navigation exercise and, justifiably, I was feeling a bit weary. Lo and behold if I didn't forget to wind in the antenna before landing. I woke up to the oversight just as the plane passed over a few houses at the end of the aerodrome, seconds before the pilot approached the end of the strip.

I wound the drum furiously in the hope of getting the antenna in before losing most of the wire on someone's back fence or washing line.

As soon as the Aggie came to a halt, I jumped out to make a check—and nearly had a micky when I observed a pair of lady's bloomers jammed in the chute. My first fear was that they might have been on the lady at the time the piece of lead struck her and that her body was lying somewhere out in the ditch at the end of the drome. My second fear—a lesser one—was that the garment had been plucked from the lady's clothesline when we sailed over her back yard as we came in to land. For the life of me I didn't know which way to turn.

If I reported the little mishap I knew I was a goner. If I said nothing, I'd just have to sweat it out until the Orderly Officer or the Commanding Officer came hunting for me should a complaint be lodged. The one thing in my favour was that I had managed to extricate the bloomers and put them under my flying suit without being observed.

In the end, I decided to do the brave thing. I slipped away and buried the evidence in the ditch at the end of the drome which, I found out later, happened to be alongside the back fence of the owner of the bloomers.

I did hear on the grapevine that a somewhat irate woman had paid an unscheduled visit to the Commanding Officer, demanding the return of her bloomers instantly on account of a social engagement she was committed to that night. Otherwise, she wanted compensation in the shape of a new pair. Anxious to placate a neighbour, the CO explained that they could have been plucked off her clothesline by a sudden upward draught or by a 'twister', the result of the abnormal weather conditions prevailing over town and district at the time—or so the story goes.

As for me, I was more than pleased to receive a signal from Air Board two days later, posting me to a flying-boat course at Rathmines. What a lovely change, I thought. At least I won't have to worry about winding the antenna in and out any more.

A Christmas message

Radio, wireless as I still prefer to call it, was not the only means of air-to-ground communication. Morse code by means of an Aldis lamp was the alternative. Navy signalmen were experts in its use, but the crews of commercial and RAAF planes found it rather cumbersome to operate and not all that easy to read from any distance—say 2,000 feet. Maintaining eight words a minute was considered a fair speed, as long as the aircraft didn't run out of fuel—as time dragged on when trying to get the message across.

Fortunately, during the two and a bit years I spent in Catalina flying boats over the South Pacific, I was only called on a few times to use the Aldis lamp. I recall one occasion when one of our Catalinas was on a reconnaissance mission well north of New Guinea and came across a formidable-looking cruiser travelling at full speed—it seemed—in the direction of Port Moresby.

Before sending a warning signal to Moresby, the skipper decided to challenge the cruiser to identify herself. Was it a friendly ship of the Royal Australian Navy or the US Navy, or was it the enemy? It was left to the radio operator to clear the air, by flashing the challenge and demanding the code, using the Aldis lamp. Every member of the crew was on tenterhooks awaiting the response. From their vulnerable height of 2,000 feet the airmen could clearly see a large group of naval ratings gathered around two menacing anti-aircraft guns at the stern of the vessel, poised to strike, or so it looked from their point of view.

The reply, swift and to the point, was 'Piss off!', thereby identifying the cruiser as a friendly ship of the Royal Australian Navy!

I forgot to mention the date was 25 December. When the Catalina returned to base the local RAN representative curtly informed the skipper and crew that by special permission of the Captain, some of the off-duty ratings had been gathered at the stern of His Majesty's Australian Ship to celebrate Christmas Day in a truly Christian fashion—with a keg of beer to be followed by Christmas carols rendered by the ship's choral group—when the Catalina interrupted the proceedings. Furthermore, the vessel was a corvette, not a cruiser, as any dumbcluck should know. Well, that was the story passed on to me.

In case you are jumping to conclusions, dear reader, I was not the operator with the Aldis lamp. Cross my Harte!

A step in the right direction

Mentioning flying boats, the RAAF flew two types in the early days of the war, the Catalina and the Sunderland. Twenty Squadron, out of Port Moresby initially, was provided with Catalinas. Ten Squadron was equipped with Sunderlands. When war broke out, RAAF crews were undertaking a familiarisation course in England before flying them out to Australia for coastal surveillance.

At the request of the British Government, 10 Squadron operated out of British bases to the end of the war. Meanwhile, the civilian version of the Sunderland, the Short Empire Boats owned and operated by Qantas were seconded to the RAAF to serve in 11 Squadron out of Port Moresby.

One of the 11 Squadron skippers had a love affair with land-based aircraft and wasn't all that thrilled at being transferred to flying boats. As far as he was concerned, they weren't in the race with land-based planes, which he just couldn't get out of his mind. On one occasion this skipper was ordered to fly his Short Empire Boat from Noumea (New Caledonia) to Sydney to pick up a clutch of VIPs and return them to the South Pacific.

As soon as the coastline was sighted, he asked the radio operator to call up the Aeradio VZSY at Mascot to request a clearance for landing. The signal was promptly acknowledged and landing permission given. As he was making the approach for the Mascot strip, and was just a few feet from touching down, one of the crew went up to him.

'Excuse me, skipper. Do you mind if I mention something?'

'No. But make it quick, I'm about to touch down.'

'I thought I should mention, sir, that this is a flying boat, not a land plane,' said the devoted crewman.

'Ooops!' was the quick response.

Just in time the skipper pulled up the nose of the flying boat, gained speed and flew over Mascot and headed for Rose Bay. He asked the radio operator to call Aeradio VZSD, located alongside the Qantas Rose Bay base, to request clearance for alighting on the Harbour. This was given. Coming into Rose Bay the pilot made a copybook job of touching down and taxiing up to the buoy for tethering.

The crashboat set out from the Qantas base to pick up the crew. The skipper collected his log book and maps and, as he walked by the crewman, acknowledged his timely help.

'Thank you, Sergeant Smith,' he said. 'If you hadn't reminded me, I would have made a complete ass of myself.'

Then he opened the exit door and stepped out into Sydney Harbour.

Episode 23

Music ... the universal language

In the early Twenties families and friends loved to group around the piano or pianola to give forth with a melodic 'Home Sweet Home' or a ribald 'Mademoiselle from Armentieres', among other popular tunes of the time, but from the time the Salonola became the prize possession in the drawing room broadcast music gradually pervaded our lifestyle.

The gramophone, the radio and the 'talking pictures' provided ample creative stimulus for the tunesmiths of the Thirties to pluck out a song for just about every occasion. Since then television, the miniature radio, the tape recorder and, more recently, the video cassette, have soothed and assailed our ears in turn, in the building-up of an industry in Australia that appears to be on a never-ending upward climb.

For young people in particular, the transistor alongside at the beach, or drooping from a shoulder as they stroll through a shopping mall, earphones firmly clamped to their heads, or maybe next to their pillows, has become their communicating link with the big, wide, wonderful world of showbiz and an escape from reality. Nowadays there's hardly a home without some sort of a device to reproduce music, and every star-rated motel or hotel has music piped through the system.

Factories use music because time-and-motion people told executives they'll be able to squeeze a little more sweat out of their workers if they give them something to hum to. Construction workers wouldn't feel at home on the job without a boom-box blaring 20 metres away, even though the noise emanating therefrom is likely to be less melodious than the sounds made by the tools of their calling.

Over in the bails, Strawberry and her mates have had their favourite tunes on tap ever since English scientists proved beyond doubt that milk production goes up whenever there's a song in the air in the dairy.

Starvation diet

Music … music … music! It's the most accessible audible sensation to tickle our fancy, yet so few listeners or users of it are aware that it doesn't all come freely. Somewhere, sometime along the line someone has to pay to give composers a just reward for the sweat of their brows—to save them from the pauper's grave.

Not all composers are Rogers and Hammersteins. In fact, less than one per cent of the composers in the world today are making a substantial living from their musical creations. If it weren't for the fact that most countries have legislated to give composers a right to collect money for the use of their property, many would probably end up starving in a garret, just like the composers and artists of yore.

Good Queen Anne

Although the application of copyright to music, books and other forms of intellectual property is relatively new in this country, the legal right goes back nearly 500 years in British history to the fifteenth century, following the invention of the printing press. As more printing presses came into use in England, King Richard III issued a Royal Decree in 1483 granting a right, in the form of a licence, to printers, and thus the first copyright was created.

Authors weren't spared a thought, but this situation was soon to change. They stopped sending their works to the printers, so before long there was nothing to print—and it wasn't the printers alone who felt the pinch. So did King Richard. His purpose in licensing the printers had been to provide another source for filling up the royal coffers.

During the following hundred years or so, the licensing system was also used as a convenient form of censorship to prevent the spread of any literature antagonistic to the Crown. Until 1642 the Crown, through the notorious Star Chamber, continued to regulate the number of printing presses in use and the material they produced.

It was not until the eighteenth century that the sole right for printing and publishing a book was vested in the author. It came about through an Act of Parliament in 1709, during the reign of Queen Anne. Various other Acts of Parliament passed in the eighteenth and nineteenth centuries extended copyright protection to cover other means of creative property, such as engraving, sculpturing and photography, but composers of music had to wait until 1833 for clear recognition of the sole ownership of their works.

Before this recognition, it was virtually impossible for a composer to earn a living from writing music. Even after copyright protection of sorts was given, most of the early composers obtained their income not from the music they wrote, but from performances.

Rossini (1792–1868) earned £7,500 in five months from fees he received for playing in private concerts, an exceptional amount in those days. Earlier, Mozart and Beethoven depended on the favours bestowed on them by patrons or by recitals to earn a living. Beethoven died in abject poverty for lack of copyright protection, and so did Mozart. And in the field of literature, Shakespeare didn't earn a brass razoo in royalties from the performance of his plays. He earned his living as an actor-manager, not as a playwright.

In spite of a number of Acts of Parliament passed in successive years, the statutes still held many weaknesses; so much so that music composers and writers were still without sufficient to enable them to earn an income commensurate with the degree of their creativity.

Copyright Act

The most significant move was made in 1911 when the first British *Copyright Act*, which included the right of the composer to control the performance of his works, was passed. However, granting a composer this right was of little benefit without also establishing a means of enforcing it and a system of collecting payments from public performances of his music. This need led to the formation of a society to act as an agent for all composers in Britain by collecting performance fees. It was called the Performing Right Society (PRS).

Britain was not the first country to form such a society. That privilege went to France. Here in Australia, after the passing of copyright legislation in 1912, the Australian Performing Right Association (APRA) was formed in 1926 to act as attorney for composers who were willing to assign their rights over to the association.

The association gradually grew in strength after becoming affiliated with similar collecting organisations throughout the world, and more Australian composers came to light, but it was radio broadcasting that gave the greatest fillip to the activities of APRA and encouragement to composers throughout the world and on the local scene.

APRA is a non-profitmaking organisation acting for song writers and music publishers (who, in turn also act for composers and their own interests). The royalties collected from public performances are passed on to composer members of the association in Australia and composer members of overseas affiliated societies, less a small amount, about 12.5 per cent, to cover the cost of administration. Under this scheme composers don't have to lift a finger to collect their dues. Payment is made annually in December.

This arrangement has led to an extraordinary network of affiliates shunting royalties around the world. For example, whenever Neil Diamond's songs are played on air or sung in a hotel lounge or in a club, he gets a little rake-off. And as Slim Dusty sang 'Waltzing Matilda' at the Opening Ceremony of the Sydney 2000 Olympic Games, the coffers of an American publishing company, which owns the rights to the song, were being filled to the tune of A$20,000.

It would be virtually impossible to check on each performance, so the sale of records, the number of air plays (gauged from returns sent to APRA by radio stations every couple of months) and the number of live performances is used as a popularity barometer, from which Diamond, for example, gets so many points for his allotment when the collective amount is dished out.

Close to the mark

Although not fully accurate, this form of assessment is pretty close to the mark. As APRA controls the performance of copyright music in this country, authority must first be obtained from this association before the music can be publicly performed.

Radio and television stations are given an unrestricted licence to broadcast music, and in return provide APRA with a small percentage of their gross revenue, in the case of commercial stations about 2 per cent. Cinemas must also be licensed before the music on the sound track of a film is played. The amount of their fee is governed by the number of screenings and seating capacity. Halls where copyright music is performed must also be licensed unless the person hiring the hall has an arrangement to seek a special licence.

Clubs and hotels, also a big thing in the entertainment field, are another source of revenue for the composer. And it comes from several directions—through live performances on stage, through piped music,

Bert Button.

An announcer hard at work making another battery.

A group of radio veterans still young at heart in 1993; the lady third from left, front row, is Mary Hahn; first on left, front row, is Patricia Riggs, at one time editor of the *Macleay Argus*. (Harte Family Collection)

James Dibble, ABC Television, with the effervescent Robyn Butler and
Penelope Evans. (Harte Family Collection)

Thomas Alva Edison.

Pianist Isador Goodman, who
played Liszt's Piano Concerto
No. 1 at the inaugural ABC
concert on 1 July 1932. He
repeated the performance on
ABC Radio for the 50th
Anniversary programme on 4
July 1982. (ABC Archives)

A variety of music boxes and a Pathé disc. (John L. Smith Collection)

Looking for His Master's Voice.

The earliest known photo of an Australian radio broadcast, taken at the 2FC studio built by AWA on the roof of Farmer's Department Store in the centre of Sydney. (AWA Archives)

On 8 April 1927 the Beam Wireless Service between Britain and Australia was officially opened. Pictured watching T. M. Johnson receive and send the first messages are, left to right, Senator J. D. Mullen, W. T. Appleton, H. O. Richmond, Mrs S. M. Bruce, Sir William Vicars, Lord Stonehaven, AWA Chief Engineer A. S. McDonald, Prime Minister Rt Hon. S. M. Bruce, AWA Managing Director Ernest Fisk and Sir George Allard. (AWA Archives)

Ballan transmitting station about 1928.

The first picturegram received in Australia, showing Australian pilot
C. J. (Jimmy) Melrose beside his plane at Mildenhall Aerodrome at the start
of the England–Australia Centenary Air Race, 16 October 1934. (AWA
Archives)

The first official photograph transmitted over the Sydney–Melbourne picturegram service, on 9 September 1929. (AWA Archives)

The Marconi Company and AWA were experimenting with global transmission of television signals as early as 1932. AWA's London manager, Alan Longstaff, is seated before a 30-line mechanical scanner (black box with aperture) and a photo-electric cell pick-up, slung from the top brackets. (AWA Archives)

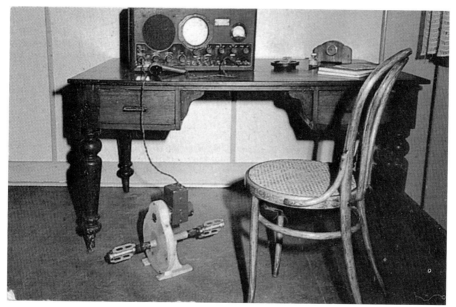

A pedal wireless similar to Alfred Traeger's invention.

A cycle-powered radio at AWA staff quarters in Rabaul, New Guinea, in 1930. Ted Bishton is the radio operator. Note the AWA logo on the laplap.

A24-10, one of the most enduring Catalinas of the Pacific War, crashed several times, yet saw the war out and was sold to a private syndicate in 1947

F/Lt. L B. (Bernard) Harte 23086 … a proud RAAF Catalina WAG

Catalina reunion at Albany, Western Australia, with John Hamilton, second from left, with three of his rescuers—Jim Cowan (navigator), Duncan Ridley and Bernard Harte. (Naureen Taylor)

through the playing of television sets not devoted solely to sport, through juke-boxes and radio sets tuned to programmes that include music.

APRA has a team of representatives in the field, quietly observing that no infringements of copyright take place. Sometimes arguments arise on what really constitutes a public performance. Any performance outside the family circle, except for demonstration purposes, is legally a public performance. Music piped into a restaurant at a motel constitutes a public performance, but the same music piped into the individual rooms does not, simply because the motel room is a home-away-from-home for the guest. There it is accepted as a private performance.

APRA and kindred organisations are concerned with only one thing, the performance of copyright music, and copyright extends to as long as 50 years after the death of a composer. There are, of course, many works not subject to copyright as they are in the public domain (the music of the great masters, for example). However, after the date of expiry, it is possible to re-copyright a piece of music, providing the original composition has been varied to 'an acceptable amount'. The same applies to books.

There are other avenues of income for the composer. There is the sale of music, the main breadwinner of early years, but generally representing less than 5 per cent of a composer's income. There is also the sale of records, cassettes and discs, from which the composer gets about 5 per cent of the retail price.

Mechanical right

So much for performing rights in Australia. There are other rights vested under the *Copyright Act* of 1968, one of which concerns the use of 'contrivances' that reproduce music—tapes, cassettes, discs and so forth. This right is given to the manufacturer of these devices, which is displayed on the record label and is known as the mechanical right.

The manufacturer holds a licence from the music publisher (acting for the composer) in the first place. You will notice the publisher's mark on the label. Once the manufacturer has made a record, they have created a property for which they hold the sole rights to its use. The label stipulates that the reproduction has been sold for private, not public use. For public use a licence from an organisation representing record manufacturers, the Australian Phonographic Performance Company, must first be obtained. Commercial radio stations don't pay a fee for the right to play records controlled by the company, on the grounds that air play provides the publicity to make record sales. The ABC, however, does pay a licence fee.

Record manufacturers are not very happy with the deal with commercial stations and have brought the issue to tribunals on several occasions. Although to date they have not exercised their right, the sword still hangs precariously over the heads of broadcasters.

Broadcasters, radio and television operators also possess a copyright, but it is one that is not enforced. It concerns the control of programmes. The taping of a sound broadcast or sound-and-vision broadcast and replaying it constitutes an infringement of copyright, even in the home, unless prior permission has been given. The broadcasters, just like the manufacturers of records, discs or cassettes, have created a property which, in the eyes of the law, they are entitled to control. German authorities have got around the enforcement of this copyright in the home by placing a surcharge on the retail price of audio and video tapes.

Pirates

Making unauthorised copies of original tapes and discs for sale has become a big headache for record manufacturers. Here in Australia this costs cost the industry something like $50 million annually, but the noose on these illegal operators has been tightening in recent years, now with the full cooperation of major Asian countries, long the main sources of illegal reproduction. Burgeoning Internet penetration and the availability of CD burners on the retail market have raised further issues of control.

By now I've probably hopelessly confused you about the restrictions placed on the public use of that 'wonderful noise' and the use of the gadgets that reproduce the stuff, so I'd best call a halt in this story of music. However, no matter how we use it—publicly or privately—I think we all agree that music is now a universal language which needs no words to reach the heart and speak the mind. And it doesn't end with mortals—so they say.

A touch of tinnitus

I don't know why crocodiles should prey so much on my mind these days, but whenever I get caught up in a dream a croc is always the predominant character. The dream always comes to an abrupt end just as I am making a last minute bid to extract my leg before his or her snapping jaws come together in technicolour. Why crocs, when there were so many pleasant humans and situations in the passing parade of my life more worthy of a replay?

My negative attitude toward these creatures began with a near encounter with a couple of them back in 1941, during the war years. I was in the Air Force at the time, based temporarily on the island of Gavutu in the Solomon Islands, operating on reconnaissance missions over the South Pacific to Santa Cruz and such places, mainly on the lookout for German raiders.

On one particular day, during a break from flying duties, one of the crew suggested we obtain a couple of canoes from the local staff at the base and visit a village upstream on the island across the way. With great excitement, we set out next morning, and arrived at our destination about two hours and a lot of paddling later.

The chief and his entourage came down to the water's edge to greet us, but not before he had secreted all the women of the village in a compound well away from our prying young eyes. With a mixture of sign language and the odd word or two we had picked up of the local dialect, we managed to swap felicitations, bringing a wide grin to the chief's face that immediately disappeared as we reboarded our frail craft to return to base. We should have realised that we were supposed to have proffered trinkets and other things like a couple of hatchets.

We were heading home at a leisurely pace along the watery path through the steaming jungle when I happened to turn my head in the direction of a large rock jutting out from the embankment. And there, staring me straight in the eyes, just a few feet away, was a huge crocodile. It was a mammoth thing. Naturally enough, my heart missed a beat or three before I managed to regain sufficient composure to croak out to my mates what I had just seen.

There wasn't a word in reply. Everyone was frozen stiff, no doubt hoping, as I was, that the croc would just let us drift by. We had no desire to hurt a hair of its head, or whatever it had on its scalp!

Not daring to look behind, we went quietly on our way and were about 500 metres away and just about recovered from the ordeal when we saw another monster slide into the river (which incidentally was only about 10 metres in width), and cut across our bows. It also left us to go on our way while not a word was spoken in fear or jest—especially not in jest.

A couple of weeks after that incident, which became a cause of great hilarity in the mess, I heard that one of our men was lost when he fell overboard. I had no doubt about where he ended up.

The next time I got close to crocs was during a trip to Timor on a rescue job. On the way over, it was necessary to stop over in Darwin, which had just had a pounding from the Japanese. I was assigned to stay on board our flying boat to keep an eye on things after we had parked it up a creek, off Anson Bay.

Aware of the big tides they have in those parts—about 7 metres—I allowed plenty of slack in the anchor. Nevertheless, I was uncomfortably surprised next morning to find the flying boat almost 'high and dry' in oozing mud. Around me were a couple of stickybeaking crocs. It was not exactly the time to rejoice about the fine weather we were having by doing a bit of sunning on the mainplane.

And so we come to 1982 and the story I've been trying to get around to telling you.

I was deeply involved in a dream with a heap of crocs and it looked as if there was no way I was going to extricate myself from a sticky situation. I was just about to lift my leg, at least with the hope of delaying their taste of me, when I felt a tug on the same leg and a bump. It was too late! I was a goner.

At that instant I awakened to find my wife beside me, wide awake. Certainly a more welcome sight than those crocs. It was she who had pulled me out of the jam, just in the nick of time, by giving me a real-life bump, and when that didn't work, tugging my leg. As she said, 'I had to do something to stop you thrashing about.'

She rolled over and went back to sleep while I was left wide awake because of a singing noise that had just started up. I tried to drown it out with the pillow but it persisted. I switched from crocs to sheep and tried to count them, but that didn't work. There was only one thing for it. I gave my wife a gentle bump and a slight tug.

'Can you hear that noise—like singing telephone wires?' I asked her.

'What noise?' was the tart reply.

By now I decided I must be going crazy, that I was well and truly a candidate for the giggle factory—and then the penny dropped.

I suddenly remembered an article I had read years ago about foreign noises. I gave my wife another gentle tug and told her not to worry about me, that I was quite sane and I had it all solved.

'Tell you about it later,' I said.

'That a promise?'

'That's a promise.'

'I can hardly wait.'

Next morning at the breakfast table, I tried, with the limited knowledge I had on the subject at my disposal, to explain the symptoms I had during the night. I had a touch of tinnitus. It's a condition of the auditory nerve, referred to in the dictionary as 'a ringing or similar sensation of sound in the ears, due to a disease of the auditory nerve'.

The condition can be brought on by an ear infection, anaemia, a brain tumour resting against the auditory nerve, the use of too many drugs, especially antibiotics, and too-lengthy exposure to excessive noise. There are other causes which could best be explained by a medical man. Of them all, the biggest villain is noise, not only by creating the condition of tinnitus but also in causing premature deafness.

Before I dwell a little on the subject of annoying noises, come with me on a journey through a typical ear hole to find out what goes on behind the scenes. That big flap glued to your head is, of course, the means of trapping sound and channelling it through a tunnel to the tympanic membrane, better known as the eardrum. Behind the drum reside ossicles which amplify the vibrations of the eardrum and drive them like a piston into the cochlea, a fluid-filled chamber shaped like a snail shell. Inside this shell are thousands of hairs standing out like teeth on a comb. It is these hairs, only about 5 microns in diameter, which hold the key to sound perception. They vibrate in sympathy with the movement in the fluid caused by variations in hydraulic pressure and in so doing convey through the auditory nerve to the brain the tone or pitch of the sound through electrical impulses.

If some of these hairs happen to get bent, flattened or ripped out, which is quite possible in response to excessive noise or illness or drugs, then the ear becomes insensitive to certain frequencies or pitch or tone, and partial deafness occurs. That's when the interior sound sometimes steps in, like the singing telephone wires I mentioned to my wife.

So that was the sound I heard or, more correctly, the sound I didn't hear, if you follow my meaning. The condition of tinnitus is likely to be manifest in people over 40 years of age, because from there on our hearing of the higher frequencies gradually diminishes. In such cases, the range of audibility, which extends to 15,000 hertz when one is brand new, has probably dropped to 10,000 (which is still pretty high, certainly enough to pick up most sounds). As the years progress, the high notes continue to fade.

The victim may not be aware of failing hearing until such time as he finds difficulty in sorting our individual sounds from a collection of voices and other noise-making machines like musical instruments. Most times he'll blame it on poor acoustics, not realising that he is getting a bit hard of hearing. For me in radio, good hearing was vital.

We have to accept that the ear just cannot accommodate itself to the excessive ear-bashing that is now part of our way of life. It's only in recent years that a noise-suffering society has rebelled enough to stimulate the interests of government to accept that noise can have a great influence on the efficiency of the work force and its peace of mind. The effect of excessive noise in the form of deafness and neurosis is now accepted as a disability.

Before the last war, the pneumatic road-drill or jackhammer was about the loudest continual sound to assail our ears. In those days their operators were not issued with ear muffs, so they were often the first victims. Then came the war. Before it ended, many members of air crews were suffering from partial deafness. I also found that excessive noise made me very irritable.

Since the war we have been subjected to much more excessive noise, from such sources as the perpetrators of popular music, who need the backing of many, many watts to get their message across. Before the amplified electric guitar came along, 40 watts of sound was sufficient to fill an average size dance hall. Now it seems 200 watts or more are needed. Even today's cinemas project sound far above the level of comfort. In our everyday activities we find we are surrounded by excessive noise. The highest up the sound ladder is the jet engine, which is about 140 decibels. Any lengthy exposure close in would mean irreparable damage to hearing.

Noise is measured in decibels—a decibel being one-tenth of a bel. It is not a measure of power but the relative intensity of the sound above a zero level, taken to be the faintest sound the average ear can detect. I remember accompanying my sister to a sort of country music lounge in a hotel on the Gold Coast, where our ears were assailed by magnified music. We tried several times to converse after shifting our chairs closer, but had to give up and watch while our ears continued to be pounded. After a quarter of an hour or so we could not endure the noise any longer and stepped outside.

The music we had been subjected to would have had a sound intensity level of about 115 decibels. Another 15 and we would have been on the threshold of pain. I put the singing noise that had kept me awake down to this confrontation, which had probably temporarily flattened a few hairs.

At this point in my explanation my concentration was interrupted by a whistling noise coming from the transistor, which was sitting up on the fridge a few metres away.

'Switch the damn thing off, love. It's playing up again. It's being doing that for days, breaking into that whistle,' I said.

'What whistle? I can't hear a whistle. Seems normal to me,' was her polite reply. 'Maybe you've got another touch of tinnitus.'

The music makers

During the Twenties and early Thirties, music was the main ingredient in broadcast station programming. Here in Australia, until the Gramophone Company (HMV) and Columbia Graphophone Company merged and got into full swing pressing matrices from Britain and the United States, and in 1931 initiating the recording of Australian artists at the Homebush factory in Sydney, all gramophone records—with the exception of the Brunswick label produced by Davis & Co.—were imported.

The Gramophone Company's first factory, at Erskineville in Sydney, was opened in 1926 by the Premier of New South Wales, Jack Lang. This British-owned firm was active in Australia as far back as 1900, when its first sales representative, P. H. Bohanna, arrived in Sydney with some 100,000 records to set up a sales office. Unfortunately business was so slow that in 1905 he was instructed to close the office, and the established merchants Hoffnung & Company of Sydney and Brisbane were appointed sole agents. I well remember the company's warehouse in Brisbane, mainly because I used to go there occasionally to try and wangle records from them at wholesale prices.

In the early days of recording at Homebush, the sound of locomotives speeding along the nearby railway tracks caused a few hold-ups. I was told Peter Dawson occasionally waxed a little angry when the Brisbane Express intruded on the recording of the 'Floral Dance' and the other ear-catching songs that made him famous. A few years later, George Edwards—who used to record *Dad and Dave* and *Inspector Scott* there—suffered a few hold-ups in production for the same reason. Improved studio insulation largely eliminated this problem.

The big bands

From the 1920s to the end of World War II, big bands dominated the ballrooms and recording studios—this period covered the Jazz era, the Swing era, even the Jitterbug era, all umbrellas of popular music of the times, giving plenty of scope for the use of string instruments to provide the sweet sounds from the pen of such composers as Berlin, Romberg, Gershwin and Kern.

As most of this music originated in the United States, naturally enough a large percentage of the big bands were American. The Paul Whiteman Orchestra was one of them. Whiteman was referred to as the 'King of Jazz', after his orchestra was featured in a film of that name, a handle that raised the ire of many other jazzmen. Nevertheless, Whiteman certainly set the scene and the pace for other band leaders to follow. Indeed, some of his top musicians were sufficiently enthused by his success to form their own groups. The Dorsey Brothers were two of his players who went their own way. Bing Crosby, one of Whiteman's Rhythm Boys, also went on to a successful solo career. Whiteman's biggest opposition came from Fred Waring's Pennsylvanians, another big band embellished with a vocal group, the Glee Club.

As soon as blowing hard into a horn to make a recording by mechanical means was replaced by the microphone, electric amplifier and electric cutting head, the recording industry boomed—that is, until the arrival of the Great Depression, which caused great unemployment in the industry.

Strangely, at the same time the British recording industry was on the up, providing scope for such big bands as those of Ambrose, Jack Hylton, Lew Stone and Ray Noble, and giving good reason for British bands to dominate the airwaves in this country well into the 1930s. The popularity of the Ray Noble Orchestra was undoubtedly due to its resident vocalist Al Bowlly, whose life ended in a London air raid during World War II. Who could ever forget Bowlly's renditions of 'The Very Thought of You', 'Goodnight Sweetheart' and 'Love is the Sweetest Thing', all composed by Noble.

Harry Roy's band and his pianists Ivor Moreton and Dave Kaye, Billy Cotton and his band and Jack Payne's band also had plenty of air play in the Australia of the 1930s. Harry Roy visited Australia when he was part of his brother Sid's band. After his much-publicised marriage to the daughter of the White Rajah of Sarawak, his recording of 'Sarawak' was a popular request.

Ah! Those were the days!

From orchestra leader to back stalls

I don't know about you, but whenever I get absorbed in good music, my emotions are stirred and my imagination runs riot. Such was the case one night, sometime during the 1980s, when I went along to the Port Macquarie RSL Club to hear the Melbourne Philharmonic Orchestra.

I was delighted to hear so many of the tunes that had been popular pieces for record collectors in the mid 1930s. As I sat in the front row, lapping up every note, my thoughts flew back to those days when I was but a callow youth anxious to build up my record collection. A better quality record was then being produced, with a much greater dynamic range than the recordings of a few years earlier. In fact, we thought the sound was remarkable—just the cat's whiskers. When you compare those recordings with the very latest, however, you've got to laugh. But in those days the tremendous sound of the Philadelphia Symphony Orchestra's versions of Liszt's 'Hungarian Rhapsody No. 2', Sibelius's 'Dance of the Imps in the Hall of the Mountain Kings' and 'Finlandia' used to send me into rhapsodies.

After I collected enough records, I decided that I was going to be a symphony orchestra leader—just like Eugene Ormandy, the popular leader of the day. The fact that I happened to be tone deaf and couldn't play a note of music didn't seem to be any barrier to achieving this ambition.

The bull fiddler

Before I had a chance to make a complete ass of myself, I switched my affections to the more popular music of the day and began another record collection. Before long, I had most of Harry Roy's records, a heap of Joe Daniels' Hot Shots, and all I could lay my hands on of Django Rheinhardt and the Hot Quintet of France.

Now well and truly caught up in popular music, and established as an 'authority' of some note because of my collection, I decided I would go into training to become a band leader. Walter Mitty had nothing on me. In hindsight, I must have been a bit of an odd bod. Instead of going home at night to dream of pretty girls, I used to dream of musicians and their instruments. In one dream I was playing a double bass in a dance band in Brisbane, the spotlight shining on my nimble fingers as I plucked away to my Harte's content.

As a matter of fact, after that particular dream I became so taken with the double bass—or bull fiddle—that I decided it was the instrument that would allow me to work my way up to band leadership. So I bought one. Then I joined the Queensland Swing Club, a collection of mainly professional musicians who used to meet in the home of one of the members every Sunday night for a jam session.

Although yet to qualify as a musician (I still couldn't play a note), I soon became a very popular addition to the club on account of the fact that I used to take along my amplifier with loudspeaker and microphone— a rare set-up in those days. As I didn't have a motorcar, I made the trip to club meetings by tram—two trams actually—Sunday after Sunday.

Fortunately, because it was Sunday the trams weren't too crowded, which was just as well. It took me about two minutes to shove the bull fiddle and all the amplifier gear aboard and the same length of time to get it off, by which time the bell-clanging by the impatient tram-driver was becoming a little embarrassing.

The baritone

After a couple of months of carting all the gear backwards and forwards, with not a soul interested in teaching me how to play the bull fiddle, I decided I wouldn't pursue my ambition to be the world's greatest band leader; instead, I would prepare myself to be the world's greatest baritone.

By this time I was worshipping Lawrence Tibbett. As far as I was concerned he was the greatest man on earth. When I heard he was about to make a tour of Australia, I was so excited I had nothing else on my mind—except how to get rid of that flamin' bull fiddle.

At the time Tibbett reached our shores, I had collected about every record he had made and knew the words of most of his songs and was wishing him good health, at the same time hoping that if his demise should occur within the next year or so I would be ready to fill his shoes. His most impressive record in my book was 'De Glory Road', on 12-inch HMV. On the other side was 'Edward Opus One Number One'. They were both dramatic works sung with all the feeling befitting such sad stories.

From what I remember, 'Edward' was the story of a gent up in Scotland who had just found out his daddy was dead by reason of the fact that he had been poisoned. Edward blamed his three brothers for the job and demonstrated his feeling on the matter by cutting off their heads, which didn't make him all that popular with his mum, who was watching the little episode in the kitchen. As he was wiping his sword on the kitchen towel, the penny dropped. It was his mother who had poisoned his beloved daddy. With no time left to apologise to his brothers, he ran his sword through his mother's gizzard—the end of a charming little tale.

'De Glory Road' was about a Negro who had a dream that he had snuffed it and was lying on his bier when he got a call from the Lord to go to Heaven. The Lord came along and invited him to jump on the back of his steed and off they went—up, up and away. Halfway up, the Negro looked back and saw Satan on the back of his horse, Sin, riding at full gallop, intent on dragging him below into the hot stuff. He called to the Lord to help him, just as Satan was breathing down the back of his neck. The Lord responded by putting his steed into top gear and they sailed into Heaven just in the nick of time.

When Tibbett appeared on the stage of Her Majesty's Theatre in Brisbane, every seat was filled, and those who couldn't be accommodated in comfort were satisfied to sit in the aisles. I was there, of course, right up the back in the cheap seats, and was all a-flutter waiting for my big moment. I was about to ask him to sing those two songs I just mentioned.

Ovation after ovation followed each number and each encore until the great man came to 'request time'. I got to my feet so quickly that I almost went through the ceiling and yelled out at the top of my voice my first request, 'De Glory Road!' He couldn't catch the title, so a rather uncouth gent a couple of rows in front of me passed it on. 'He wants "The Glory Bloody Road",' he yelled. Like I said, I was in the cheap seats.

Tibbett got the message, smiled and then sang the song while I stood to attention with eyes closed, capturing every note, every utterance. I was as if a zombie, until a couple of people told me to sit down.

The crooner

By the time Tibbett sailed for home I had lost my ambition to take his place when the time came. I couldn't spare a thought for him, as I was already in training to become the world's greatest crooner. I'd fallen under the spell of Russ Colombo and then his successor, Bing Crosby. Well, I never got around to be acclaimed the world's greatest crooner—probably because my voice was a little flat on it.

Undaunted, after trying myself out in the bathroom a couple of times I resolved to give it a go, but they wouldn't even give me a chance to try out when I was doing a few jobs for the Black Cats Orchestra in downtown Brisbane. The only time they let me near the microphone was before the show—and that was only to find out if it was working.

After killing off another career in midstream, I went on to do other things that kept me busy for the next year or two as I added record after record to my collection. To tell you the truth, I can't remember what they were, it was so long ago.

All I can remember is that I made it to the top in the end—even if it was only in my dreams.

Episode 24

The brass pounders

Born in the nineteenth century, the brass pounders were recognised as a breed of their own—considered a little on the mad side by those bewildered by their noisy activities and who lacked confidence in their achievements. Yet down through the years, well into the twentieth century these mad hatters were to become the key men of communication through their manipulation of the Morse code key.

Before I take another step in narrating the accomplishments of the brass pounders, come back with me through the corridor of history to when it all began.

We open the 'Book of Time' in the year 1837, when two English scientists, Charles Wheatstone and William Cooke, gave a successful public exhibition of their electric telegraph set. This was a system of deflecting magnetic needles at the receiving end of wire connections. The deflected needles pointed to letters of the alphabet marked on a chart. The first commercial acceptance of electric telegraphy occurred in 1839 after the operators of the Great Western Railway invited Wheatstone and Cooke to install their system in the Paddington and West Drawton railway stations—a distance of 30 kilometres—and link them by wire.

The success of this new method of communication, replacing the traditional visual semaphore system, heralded the start of a race of scientific development in communication. Described as 'the Perfect Invention' at the time, electric telegraphy certainly brought the world to the threshold of the ultimate in technology, facsimile reproduction of sight and sound.

'What hath God wrought!'

This rather ominous phrase from Deuteronomy was used by Samuel Morse tapping out the signalling code of his own making in the inauguration of the electric telegraph line between Washington and Baltimore in 1844. The new technology was shortly brought to the Australian colonies by a disciple of Professor Morse, the Canadian Samuel McGowan. In 1854 McGowan completed Australia's first electric telegraph line between Melbourne and Williamstown, a distance of 20 kilometres.

Apart from devising a signalling code, Morse developed a method of using a single wire with an earth return to complete the circuit, which dramatically cut installation costs. By now electric telegraphy was spreading throughout the world like wildfire. Fired by the ambition of linking the continents, experimenters were trying out underwater cables to convey Morse code messages, but finding suitable insulation to prevent the ingress of salt water into the cable was a big problem.

Necessity being the mother of invention, scientists discovered that a tree, fairly common in Malaysia, yielded a juicy sticky substance which soon hardened on exposure to the atmosphere and remained impervious to attack by salt water. The substance, called gutta-percha, was the forerunner of the resin plastics we know today.

The English Gutta Percha Company was formed to manufacture underwater cables, consisting of a single copper wire coated with the substance. In the year 1851 the first cable was laid between England and France. By 1870, Britain had almost girdled the globe by electric telegraphy, using overland and undersea links which ended in Dutch-controlled Java, leaving a gap of a little over 2500 kilometres to be bridged between Java and Australia. (Forty years later, Marconi cherished the same global ambition for wireless.) In November 1871 a cable was laid from Palmerston (the name originally given to Darwin) to Batavia to complete the link, an operation that was completed in less than two weeks.

The laying of the cable and the setting-up of cable stations was undertaken by the British-Australian Telegraph Company, conditional on the South Australian Government constructing a telegraph line between Port Augusta in south Australia and Palmerston and completing it in time to coincide with the establishment of a cable station at Palmerston. (The Northern Territory was then part of the colony of South Australia.)

Numerous delays—occasioned by local Aborigines resentful of intrusion, difficult terrain, illness and shortage of equipment—put construction of the overland telegraph line behind schedule. Under the leadership of South Australian Postmaster-General Charles Todd, this project became one of the greatest epics of human endurance in the history of Australia. When the line was completed in August 1872 the world was then linked by Morse code to every capital city in Australia.

A hand-operated key, made of solid brass with steel contacts, was used to transmit messages from point to point. The telegraphists who operated them became very skilful, being able to send and receive messages at speeds of up to 25 words a minute over landline and through wireless waves. They were affectionately referred to as 'brass pounders'.

The manually operated Morse code key is now a museum piece, and overseas telegraphic communication is by high-speed automatic transmission. Overland and at sea, the Morse code system has been replaced by the teleprinter and telephone, and on the air the wireless operator is now a thing of the past. But the blood of the early brass pounders continued to flow through the veins of a diminishing population of left-over mad hatters, well after the end of World War II.

In a crowd you probably wouldn't know them for what they are—or were—from a bar of soap, but if you saw them in groups you would probably settle for the fact that they seem a little different from the ordinary, enough to put them down in your mind as odd bods. Perhaps it because of was the way they perpetually cocked one ear while they spoke, as if in anticipation of catching a faraway sound, or because of the slight twitch on the face that came from years of straining the same ear.

These people who once pounded the brass were exclusive enough to form their own association, the Morsecodians. They were the telegraphists who used to send your confidential messages by Morse code or decode your telegram into copperplate handwriting and have it delivered to your home.

Remember those days when the customer came first; when a uniformed telegram boy—just out of short pants—would wobble his way along your street with a little black bag slung over his shoulder? Remember how often you stood on your verandah and watched him, wondering, heart in mouth, if he were heading for your place?

No doubt it would race through your mind that if he was bringing a telegram of bad news you hoped to God he'd not stop outside your place. Should he be carrying good news meant for you, maybe it was worth a slice of that freshly baked sponge cake sitting on the windowsill to cool. After a message of good cheer had been safely delivered, he'd hop on his bike and pedal his way back to the post office, whistling as he went.

Could you ever forget those anxious moments during the war years, when you observed the telegram boy unsmilingly making his way toward you? That dreadful moment of trepidation that the sealed envelope he was about to hand you might spell out the death of a loved one, or inform you he was missing, believed killed.

You knew the handwritten telegram would exude no emotion. There would be no words to provide solace. Just the stark message received at your little post office from someone of importance, far away.

No time to dwell

Traffic speed and the fact they were sworn to secrecy left the operators at each end of the telegraph line with no time to dwell on the texts of the messages of pathos, humour, commerce, tragedy, accomplishments and silliness that passed endlessly through their Morse code keys.

Nowadays the Morsecodians prefer to reflect on the more romantic aspects of the service, and on the part they played in getting the message through under all conditions along the longest telegraph line in the world, and by wireless.

Understandably, ears became less sensitive with age. Many postmasters in the bush got into the habit of keeping an empty tobacco tin close by the key. By placing it on the sounder, the clicks of dots and dashes were given some amplification, strong enough to call the postmaster's attention when he was serving customers at the counter.

It was in 1960—when teleprinters had replaced the Morse key in post offices—that brass pounders of this kind decided to form the fraternal of Morsecodians in each state of the Commonwealth. To perpetuate their skills as brass pounders, whenever these Morsecodians held a function, which maybe included a guest speaker, no spoken words were necessary as communication was by Morse code!

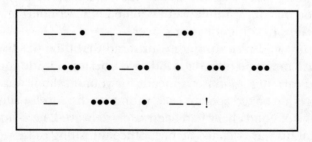

Ted Bishton was one of those telegram delivery boys. Born in Sydney in 1898, he began his career as a telegraph messenger at the Sydney GPO for the princely wage of fifteen shillings a week—less amounts deducted under Section 46 of the *Public Services Act.* According to his memoirs—handed to me recently—he seldom managed to draw a full pay:

> There were a couple of pimps employed by the Post Office to keep an eye on the behaviour of messengers. For instance, if you happened to be caught looking in a shop window, or walking along the street talking to other messengers, or watching a couple of newspaper boys fighting, or maybe watching any of those big ships leaving for overseas with all the bright coloured streamers blowing in the wind, you would suddenly feel a gentle tap on the shoulder and you knew instinctively who it was. You could be sure that when you returned to the GPO there would be a Section 46 waiting for you. These misdemeanours generally cost one shilling, two shillings or half a crown.

After his transfer to the Newtown Post Office, Ted Bishton learnt Morse code and a smattering of telegraphy. This was enough to spur him on to undertake a course in wireless operating (after working hours) with AWA. Before he could complete the course, World War I arrived and he immediately volunteered for service in the Army. After duties in India, Mesopotamia and the Persian Gulf, he was invalided home and resumed his job at the Newtown Post Office. Keen on going to sea as a wireless telegraphist, he completed the course with AWA and immediately obtained an appointment as a wireless operator in the coastal and island service. Although the war had ended by this time, coastal wireless stations remained under the control of the Navy until 1922, so Ted Bishton was enlisted in the Royal Australian Navy with the rank of Petty Officer and then sent to Rabaul, capital of the island of New Britain. A few weeks later, he was despatched to the nearby wireless station at Bitapaka, established by the Germans. A week later he was transferred to Manus Island.

When the Navy gave up control, AWA was reappointed to operate the coastal and island network, thus Ted became an AWA brass pounder. In this capacity he served at numerous settlements in Papua-New Guinea, the Solomon Islands and New Ireland, in fact, wherever there was a wireless station in the Mandated Territory. Ted was living with his wife at Kavieng on New Ireland when World War II arrived on his doorstep.

Very few Australians, even today, are aware of the tremendous havoc wrought on Allied shipping by German raiders and Japanese submarines in Australian waters, especially at the beginning of the war. Of the 86 merchant and naval ships attacked around our coast, the heaviest concentration was between Brisbane and Melbourne, where 40 ships were attacked or chased; 26 of these were sunk, including the hospital ship *Centaur* on 14 May 1943 just off Moreton Island, Queensland with the loss of 268 persons. HMAS *Sydney* was sunk by the German raider *Kormoran* in November 1941 off the Western Australian coast; the whole crew of 645 was lost.

German raiders were especially active in waters to the north and north-east of Australia. One, the *Orion,* was sent to the South Pacific to look for Allied ships and lay mines, disguised as a Japanese freighter (prior to the entry by Japan into the war). She sank several British-registered freighters and laid a string of mines just off Auckland, New Zealand. Together with another raider, *Komet,* she sent several more ships to the bottom. One victim, the 17,000 ton liner *Rangitane,* was sunk 36 hours out of Auckland on 28 November 1940, bound for England with a large number of passengers and RAAF personnel on their way to Canada for aircrew training under the Empire Training Scheme. There were 303 survivors. The non-combatants were landed on New Ireland, and most of the Air Force and merchant marine personnel taken immediately to Germany aboard another supply ship. A few days later the two raiders caught five ships loading phosphate off Nauru Island and quickly despatched them.

Enter the Japanese

Strangely, there was an odd air of complacency in the islands in the weeks after Pearl Harbor, Hong Kong, Singapore and several Pacific islands had been attacked in early December 1941. Even though ample warning had been given for months that something was about to happen, with the presence of high-flying unidentified aircraft, on photographic missions no doubt, an unnatural influx of Japanese 'tourists' and aggressive German activities at sea, there was little real preparation for war, either by civilians or Government officialdom, apart from the evacuation of most of the women and children on the *Macdhui* to Port Moresby.

That 'something' came in January 1942, with air raids and attacks by Japanese warships out of the big naval base at Truk in the Caroline Islands (mandated to the Japanese by the League of Nations as a World War I prize). After enduring weeks of bombing raids on Rabaul, where Ted Bishton was now located, he was one of a group who managed to get away at the time of the enemy landing on 21 January. They co-opted the schooner *Leander* and headed for Port Moresby, calling first at Wide Bay, south-east of Rabaul, to pick up a few stragglers.

Their next port of call was Pal Mal Mal Plantation, and then Caturp Plantation. While at Caturp, another boat arrived carrying an RAAF pilot. Ted Bishton thinks it might have been Wing Commander Lerew, CO of 24 Squadron, which had been based at Rabaul. He had come down in a battle with Japanese fighters and been posted missing. Using an AWA teleradio set, an endeavour was made to contact Moresby to advise that 90 Air Force personnel were at Wide Bay needing assistance.

Unable to make contact, Ted managed to send a signal to Moresby from the transmitter on *Leander* advising the situation. The message got through, and a rescue plan was put in operation, using two Short Empire Flying Boats to fly the Air Force men to Samarai, a small island on the tip of Papua. From Samarai they would be taken by Catalinas to Port Moresby.

As a member of 20 Catalina Flying Boat Squadron, based at Port Moresby, I took part in this operation with Squadron Leader Dick Cohen as captain of our Cat. (Cohen, by the way, later changed his name to Kingsland, and as Sir Richard Kingsland is presently Patron of our Catalina Association.) The date of the commencement of this rescue operation was 23 January 1942 and completion was 28 January.

Referring to my log book, I noticed that between our trips from Samarai to Port Moresby on the second leg of this evacuation (a 15-hour flight), we managed to squeeze in a bomb attack on Japanese shipping gathered in Simpson Harbour, Rabaul. This would have been one of the first attacks made by our squadron on enemy-occupied Rabaul.

After this incident we kept up our onslaught on Rabaul, Buka Passage on Bougainville Island, Tulagi (capital of the Solomons) and Truk, as well as participating in rescue missions which took us to a lake in the highlands of Dutch New Guinea (now Irian Jaya), to Woodlark Island to pick up some American survivors from a downed B26 bomber, then enemy occupied Portuguese Timor (East Timor) to pull out thirteen sick and wounded Australian commandos. But that's another story that I'll tell you later.

As for the party aboard *Leander*, they arrived in Port Moresby on 30 January. Days later, former World War I veteran Petty Officer and later Chief Petty Officer, Ted Bishton RAN, was inducted into the Army to become a veteran of World War II.

The captain of one of the two Short Empire flying boats involved in the rescue mission from near Rabaul was Len Grey. This is his story.

As a youth Len developed a hankering for flying at the time he was employed as a radio serviceman at Chandlers in Brisbane. At the age of nineteen he obtained his commercial 'wings' and shortly after joined Qantas. It was Len's experience in radio and his ability with the Morse code key as an amateur brass pounder, as much as his flying qualifications, which landed him the appointment of second pilot, flying the latest airliner in the Qantas fleet, the DH86. These machines carried no radio operator, so Qantas relied on the pilot's knowledge of Morse code to maintain contact with bases along the international Australia–Singapore route.

When the switch was made from land-based aircraft to flying boats for this journey and the Qantas base moved from Brisbane to Rose Bay in Sydney Harbour in 1938, Len underwent a conversion course and was soon elevated to captain status.

In 1939 two Qantas Short Empire flying boats were seconded to the RAAF and in 1940 another two. These flying boats and a couple of left-over Walrus seaplanes comprised the nucleus of 11 Squadron, based in Port Moresby, soon to be augmented by Catalina flying boats. Now a member of 11 Squadron, Qantas Captain Len Grey became Flight Lieutenant Len Grey RAAF.

Days after Rabaul had fallen to the Japanese, the two former Qantas flying boats were assigned to the rescue mission mentioned earlier. Flying along the coastline of New Britain, Len Grey brought his machine down on the open sea, but as close as he could get to the rendezvous, some 30 kilometres south of Rabaul. It was just on nightfall. With barely enough power to get off the water with his heavy load, he flew down to Samarai to safely deliver his passengers, from where we took them on to Moresby. Bringing the cumbersome flying boat down on the treacherous waters of Samarai in the dead of night called for the highest pilot skill. For this operation he was awarded the Air Force Cross.

After the war, Qantas Empire Airways resumed its passenger service to Singapore, using Short Hythe and later Sandringham flying boats. In 1947, the wheel of Qantas overseas aviation had gone full circle. The slow-moving flying boats, those stately Ships of the Air, bowed out, to be replaced by land-based Lockheed Constellations.

With the opportunity to now spend more time at home, Len Grey resumed his interest in his amateur radio station as a brass pounder. In later years he converted his transmitter to voice operation. He left us some years ago.

Goodbye, Mrs Mac

This is the story of a brass pounder of a different kind—Mrs Florence McKenzie.

In the 'Q' language of amateur wireless operators, QRT signals 'signing off—no further messages'. And that is just what Mrs Mac did at the age of 90, leaving us after almost a full lifetime association with amateur radio or, more correctly, amateur wireless.

Florence Violet McKenzie, OBE, ASTC, Patron of the ex-Women's Royal Australian Navy Association (WRANS), was the first woman in Australia to obtain an amateur wireless operator's licence. A tinkerer from way back, Florence operated station VK2FV for many years and was affectionately known throughout this worldwide fraternity as Mrs Mac. Florence was also one of the first women, if not the first, to obtain a diploma in electrical engineering. In 1930 she formed the Electrical Association for Women (Aust.), over which she presided for some years.

Along with her interest in electrical engineering and time spent as a brass pounder in her transmitter shack, Florence managed to find time to pursue another hobby, the study of denizens of the deep. For some time she conducted an hour-long weekly radio programme on the ABC about the sea and its inhabitants.

As soon as World War II loomed up on the horizon, Florence set about putting her skill with the Morse code key and her knowledge of communications to good account by founding a school to teach Morse code and signalling procedures to young men and women wanting to join the Armed Forces. Her training put these people, mostly aspiring telegraphists or signallers, in a wonderful position by the time they were called up to commence official training. Most of her students were women looking for a means to break down the barriers to get into the male-dominated Services.

With this in mind, Florence McKenzie formed the Women's Emergency Signalling Corps (WESC) and then wrote to the Minister for the Navy, asking him to give her girls a go. Taken aback at first by such audacity, the Minister sent an officer out to look over her establishment and observe her training methods.

The officer returned a favourable report, and in 1941 the first group of fourteen young women was recruited into the WRANS. All told, Mrs Mac taught more than 12,000 men and women during the war years. In 1950 she was awarded an OBE by a grateful government.

Following a long illness which kept her away from the public eye, Mrs

Mac suffered a stroke in 1976 but four years later managed to muster enough strength to attend a quiet service in the Navy Mariners' Church in Sydney. Sitting in a wheelchair and looking very frail, this dear lady observed the unveiling of a plaque to commemorate her work during the war years. Through this tablet the late Mrs Mac will be long remembered. But will Morse code be long remembered? I think not.

With the widespread use of two-way voice communication, Morse code gradually faded away, eventually to be replaced by the Global Marine Distress and Safety System (GMDSS), an automatic position-signalling method routed through satellites with built-in two-way radio. Should a ship be in trouble, an officer simply hits the distress button and the GMDSS message controller sends the call out to every vessel and land station equipped with the system. On 31 December 1999 the system of communication invented by the American painter Samuel Morse, which led to the development of telegraphy, gave its last dash for dots and dashes.

The coastwatchers

Operating during World War II in Australia's Mandated Territories of Papua-New Guinea, the British Solomon Islands and some mainland outposts, this uniquely Australian group of dedicated, self-reliant, mainly volunteer civilians, known as coastwatchers, willingly imperilled their safety in providing enormous assistance to the Allies—especially during the South Pacific conflict. Their assistance did much to hasten the end of the war.

The coastwatchers comprised mainly patrol officers, planters, government officials, civilian radio operators, gold prospectors and retired citizens who elected to stay behind during the Japanese onslaught and occupation of islands to the north, to provide vital information concerning enemy movements on land and sea and timely warnings of air raids through a radio reporting network. The coast watchers are the unsung heroes of the war in the South Pacific.

The coastwatchers' organisation had its genesis in 1919, shortly after the end of World War I. Conceived by Captain C. J. Clare of the Royal Australian Navy and adopted as a unit of Naval Intelligence, its purpose was to keep a weather-eye on shipping and, later, aircraft movements along the northern Australian coastline and Mandated Territories and to report any suspicious sightings in time of war. The personnel manning the organisation were volunteers drawn from the police service, PMG and some other government departments, using existing telephone or telegraph lines for communication. When World War II broke out more volunteers were recruited.

In the islands—where landline communications were almost non-existent—radio was the only means of contact. The responsibility for providing radio facilities fell on the shoulders of AWA, which already had a network of small stations operating on behalf of various government departments, with its Port Moresby and Rabaul base stations handling all radio traffic to Sydney.

Clearly, for the coastwatchers' network to function, portable radio transmitting-receiving sets were required. The answer was the Teleradio portable set, designed and manufactured by AWA. Well, not quite portable; certainly moveable. Consisting of a transmitter and receiver capable of handling both Morse code and voice, the set operated from batteries kept alive by a charger, which required a small petrol engine to function. The initial model, the 3B, could transmit on four crystal-controlled frequencies, each referred to as Frequency 'X'. Crystal control meant the need to tune dials for the correct wavelength was obviated. Trouble was, up to twelve carriers were needed to transport each 'portable' set between locations, sometimes in a great hurry. Before the development of the Teleradio, AWA had mainly used a pedal wireless transmitter-receiver, a modification of the device developed by Alfred Traeger.

Under the command of former RAN reservist, Lieutenant Commander Eric Feldt, the coastwatchers' network was rapidly expanded in numbers and reporting facilities, until by mid-1942 some 800 had been recruited, most of whom were provided with Teleradio sets. Many of these personnel were sourced from the RAN and from Army M and Z Special Units (highly trained insertion groups of three to five men, active throughout the Pacific Islands).

Initially a simple code known as Playfair was used in despatches, but it was soon replaced by an improved cipher, the Playfair Feldt Method. This system was in turn replaced by a code developed by the RAN.

The range of the Teleradio was up to 1000 kilometres for Morse code under favourable atmospheric conditions and locations, and about 650 kilometres for voice transmission. These were the ideals, but the tropical conditions of wartime portage and atmospherics often played havoc with ideals. Many transmissions were lost, some skipped to odd receival points, while others had to be relayed.

With the emphasis on portability, AWA produced a smaller unit, but the few that became available were almost as cumbersome. Eventually, with input from the RAAF, a more suitable transmitter-receiver was developed to replace the Teleradio.

The unseen army of the coastwatchers, many operating from deep within enemy held islands, some from precariously located hideaways, and more often than not on the move to escape detection by enemy troops, provided a vital service to Australian, US and British forces in the South Pacific, saving thousands of lives and enabling General Macarthur and the US Navy to push ahead the campaign to clear the path to the Philippines and ultimately Tokyo.

The greatest tribute to the importance of the coastwatchers was paid by the Commander of US Naval Forces in the South Pacific, Admiral William F. Halsley, when, referring to the successful outcome of the horrific battle for the Solomons, he said: 'The coastwatchers saved Guadalcanal and Guadalcanal saved the Pacific.'

Supreme Commander General Macarthur also paid tribute to these gallant men. One of them, Reginald Evans, figured in the rescue of US torpedo commander John Fitzgerald Kennedy, who had been posted missing after his torpedo boat was cut in two by a Japanese destroyer. Using his Teleradio, Evans reported the rescue of the man who went on to become President of the United States of America.

Many coastwatchers did not survive the war, some executed by the enemy, others succumbing to disease or malnutrition. Forty-two were killed and 58 captured.

The nurses and the thunderbox

The US Army and Navy operated an extensive communication set-up in the South-West Pacific, including several units based in New Guinea to work aircraft on bombing missions. That reminds me of an incident which took place at Finschaven just a few weeks after the area was recaptured from the Japanese.

It seems a party of Australian nursing sisters arrived at Finschaven in a C47 for a comfort stop. They were on their way down to Moresby and had been in the air for some time. Forewarned of the stopover, the Adjutant of the Army base had a six-holer erected on a rise, just a hundred metres or so from the strip. Naturally it was fenced off from prying eyes by a hessian screen. The Adjutant was justly proud of this edifice, constructed in record time by willing helpers.

No sooner had the C47 touched down than the nurses were out of the plane and on their way to the six-holer at a brisk but dignified pace. A minute or so later, one of the nurses came down the slope toward the watching Adjutant, terribly flustered, her face as red as beetroot.

'Is there something wrong?' asked the Adjutant, somewhat timidly.

'Yes, there sure is,' said the nurse. 'There's a bloody man down there!'

'Surely not,' replied the Adjutant. 'We've had a roll call and there's no one missing. There just can't be a man down there.'

Seconds later, another nurse arrived, in much the same distraught condition.

'She's right. There's a bloody man down there! I heard him with my own ears,' she said.

In no time at all each of the first contingent of six had reported the intruder to the Adjutant. Somewhat appalled—yet not abandoning his military stance—he sprang into action and had the path barricaded while he launched an investigation to solve the mystery.

Just over the rise, a small group of US Army signalmen had set up a temporary base and were quartered on the job. They watched the construction of the six-holer with a great deal of admiration, and decided to make their contribution to the war effort by installing a loudspeaker down the pit. Then they ran a lead back to an amplifier and microphone set up in their camp. As soon as they spotted a nurse disappearing behind the screen, they gave her 30 seconds or so and then a voice boomed out from underneath: 'Excuse me lady; would you mind moving over? I'm working down here.'

Episode 25

The Jesus Box

The Jesus Box arrived out of the blue—as it were—toward the end of 1941, a few weeks before the Japanese kicked off the war in the Pacific.

I was then an RAAF wireless operator/gunner of Port Moresby-based 20 Catalina Flying Boat Squadron. We were absolutely astounded when we first saw the Jesus Box sitting in a steel rack alongside the radio compartment in our Catalina A24-10. It had been installed when we were ashore for a few days while the regular 240-hour maintenance inspection was being carried out by ground staff.

After twiddling a few knobs and having a good gander at the cathode-ray screen and the blips displayed during a test run over Port Moresby, we happily decided the Jesus Box was just the cat's whiskers for our type of work—which involved long reconnaissance patrols over the South Pacific Ocean and scattered islands, searching for elusive German raiders and submarines and checking on the bona fides of any stray ships we came across. Now, with the Jesus Box we would be able to 'see' objects well beyond visual range during daylight and at night.

As we were to find out a few days later, the real name for this gadget was the Air Surface Vessel, or ASV, but we insisted on calling it the Jesus Box in the hope that Jesus would be on our side. In my case, He certainly was. I wouldn't be writing this narrative otherwise.

The blips I referred to on the cathode-ray screen were visible evidence of an object ahead, such as a ship. The ASV transmitted a minute signal which was reflected or echoed back to the ASV receiver. The time taken to receive the blip was a measure of the distance between the object and our Catalina in flight. This system of detection became better known in the following months as 'radar'. The word was coined by a US naval officer, Commander S. M. Tucker, following successful experiments which began as early as 1934 at the US Naval Research Laboratory. In the United Kingdom this phenomenon was known as RDF (radio direction finding), so named to disguise its real intent, but in 1943 'radar' was officially brought into the English language.

Although Germany was the first country to produce a practical radar system, the United Kingdom sprinted ahead with its development. Indeed, it played a big part in the air defence of Britain, contributing greatly to the success of the Battle of Britain in 1940. A member of the Air Defence Committee at the time, Professor P. M. Blacket said: 'Without radar, the Battle of Britain in 1940—a near thing at best—might have been lost, with incalculable historic consequences.'

Aircraft of RAF Squadrons 217 and 270 were the first to be equipped with ASV radar in September 1939, just a few weeks after the outbreak of the war.

In Australia, radar research began in 1939, at the request of the UK government. The first step was the formation of the Radio Physics Advisory Board comprising the Joint Chiefs of Staff, officials of the PMG's Department and chaired by Professor Madsen of Sydney University. The first object was to develop a detection system for the Army's coastal defence network. The next step was for the Federal Government to make the Radio Physics Board responsible for the development of radar for the Army, Navy and RAAF, and later for the US Forces in the South Pacific.

Wing Commander A. G. Pither of the RAAF supervised and 'fathered' the development of units for aircraft as well as setting up a strategic surveillance network of ground stations along the mainland coast and on Papua-New Guinea and northern islands. This warning system rapidly grew until there were some 142 ground stations functioning, and 500 RAAF aircraft carrying the system. At its peak of service, close on 6000 members of the RAAF and WAAAF (Women's Australian Auxiliary Air Force) were engaged in radar installation or operation. Sixty-five died— including one WAAAF—and thirteen were taken prisoner by the Japanese during their active service. Only nine of these POWs survived to return home, according to an article I read in the RAAF Association magazine *Wings*.

On 22 March 1999, overdue recognition of the outstanding war service of members of Radar Units on mainland Australia and in the South-West Pacific during World War II, was given by the unveiling of a plaque during a dedication ceremony in the Australian War Memorial in Canberra.

And now back to Catalina A24-10, our ASV and also a lovely new AWA-manufactured ATN/AR8 transmitter-receiver, recently installed, which meant goodbye to the outdated, inefficient units we had been using for air-to-air and air-to-base communications.

Our ATN/AR8 was one of the first off the production line. With all this new stuff aboard we were ready to face the oceans and enemy ahead. Well, almost ready. There was one little fly in the ointment—a matter of armament. When the first, second and third batches of Catalinas were ferried out from the factory in San Diego, the United States was not then at war, so the planes could not carry armament. They had to arrive as civilian aircraft.

All the RAAF could drum up to equip the new arrivals for combat use were Lewis guns, relics from World War I. Manufactured in Belgium in 1917, they didn't look menacing enough for engagement in World War II. The bullets were contained in a round magazine sitting atop the machine. When the gun was operated, No. 1, No. 2 and No. 3 stoppages, in that order, were the usual. In other words, press the trigger and the machine would jam up after one burst. That's if it got that far. Along with my fellow aircrew I had plenty of practice trying to get the bow gun to function. That was the wireless operator's responsibility. When not in use the gun had to be stowed in the bow compartment and kept protected from the spray during take-off by a transparent perspex dome, part of which had to be removed to prepare the thing for action stations. Trouble was, the section to be slid out to make way for the Lewis gun was held in a waterproof situation by a strip of neoprene (synthetic rubber). As a seal, neoprene was so perfect it was irremovable in the tropics, making it impossible to swing the machine gun into position without a major operation.

On one occasion, when we were leaving our target over Rabaul, I spent a quarter of an hour or so in the bow compartment trying to get the flamin' Lewis gun at the ready position, just in case a couple of Japanese Zeros happened by. Unsuccessful in my endeavours, I decided I'd just have to sit it out should we be attacked.

A few weeks after this little incident, our Lewis guns were replaced by Vickers GO (gas-operated) machine guns. Manufactured in the 1920s, they weren't quite so outdated! Finally, thanks to Pearl Harbor and America's entry into the war, new Cats arriving from the United States were equipped with the very latest Browning Point 5s. Compared with our museum pieces, the Browning made it a lovely war for us, in a manner of speaking.

One other little problem we had in the early days was the matter of parachutes. Before the Japanese came into the war we used to cruise at about 800 feet at the breakneck speed of 130 knots. When Rabaul and part of Papua-New Guinea fell to the enemy we were committed to flying at about 5,000 feet on bombing and inquisitive missions, which called for parachutes. When I went along to the RAAF store in Moresby to collect one, I discovered the few in storage were mildewed, so I concluded it would be much safer flying without the blasted things. However, we did have Mae Wests available to help keep us afloat if ever we went into the drink.

On 4 December 1941, we received instructions to fly to Brisbane to pick up an American of some substance, an adviser to the US Government, but we were not told his destination. Apparently he had been sent to Australia to confer with our defence chiefs about the threat in the Pacific. Our first stop was Port Vila, where we had an AOB (advanced operational base), then on to Fiji and Tahiti. With visions of cavorting with flower-bedecked beauties in Tahiti, we were all smiles when we took off from Suva. Less than an hour on our way, a signal came through to return to Fiji with our VIP. Pearl Harbor had just been attacked and the United States was at war.

Our disappointment was mollified somewhat when the gent handed each member of the crew a pound note in appreciation for services rendered. A few hours later he was being whisked back to Washington in an American bomber. The attack on Pearl Harbor had seemed to catch the Americans with their pants down, but what surprised me was the fact that about 300 American Marines had been encamped in Fiji and monitoring Japanese signal traffic for many months, reporting to the highest level in Washington.

Next day we flew north to Moresby and the drama heading our way.

The nerve centre

RAAF operations in the South-West Pacific and Timor Sea were directed and controlled from North-Eastern Headquarters at Townsville in North Queensland. The heart of all that happened was the Operations Room. Group Captain Bill ('Bull') Garing, formerly of England-based 10 Squadron, was officer in charge.

In 1995, to mark the 50th anniversary of the defeat of the Japanese and the end of World War II, Garing, now an Air Commodore (Rtd), revisited Townsville where he inspected the former Operations Room in the Commonwealth Building, now just a shell of its former active self.

Walking through the building evoked many, many memories of the war in the Pacific and the responsibility he held, as he mentioned to a reporter of the *Townsville Bulletin*. I also visited Townsville at the time and spent a few hours with the Air Commodore swapping memories.

The secret life of the eavesdroppers

The eavesdroppers were the crypto-analysts—code-breakers of the RAAF—who, as expected, lived strictly by their code during service in the war with Japan, and for months before hostilities began. This code prevented them from disclosing anything of their outstanding work as code-breakers until some 50 years after the end of the war, when one of them, Jack Bleakley, obtained approval from the Australian Defence Force to reveal their story. This he did, with the publication of the outstanding book *The Eavesdroppers: The Best-Kept Secret of World War Two*.

Having mentioned another clandestine organisation of the time, the coastwatchers and their courageous intelligence work, and the radar operators and wireless and direction-finding operators who maintained a communication service under sometimes adverse conditions in tropical jungles or isolated outposts, it would be fitting if I were to tell you something of this select group of RAAF and WAAAF personnel whose contribution toward the defeat of the enemy never reached headlines nor gained a mention. They were members of special Wireless Units (WUs), several of which moved from mainland Australia to Papua-New Guinea and islands north, in step with the American and Australian thrust to pave the way to the Philippines and, ultimately, Japan.

This secret service had its genesis in Melbourne in 1940 under the direction of Commander T. E. Nave of the Royal Australian Navy, who returned to Australia in 1939 armed with valuable knowledge of Japan's territorial ambitions gained during government representation in Tokyo and Hong Kong. The small committee he formed worked closely with the coastwatchers under the command of R. B. Long of Naval Intelligence in Melbourne.

In 1941 the Australian Defence Committee, now very conscious of Japan's preparations to spread its tentacles beyond its Mandated Territories, approved the further development of a code-breaking organisation to work on intercepted Japanese wireless transmissions. In the same year a course on intelligence interception was held in Melbourne for military and RAAF personnel who were already competent wireless operators. To keep up to date with Japan's intentions these operators had first to learn to interpret *Katakana*, the name given to the Japanese written and spoken language (referred to by Australian operators as 'Kana'). The work of interception was made a little easier because many of the Japanese transmissions were in plain language. Breaking the code used in other messages was the main application of the eavesdroppers.

The United States and British governments were well aware of Japan's intention to wage war in the Pacific Basin. What was not known was when. Parallel to the secret work of the RAAF, both US and British intelligence groups were amassing information on the progress of Japan's aggression in China and Manchuria and its activities in French Indo-China, handed to them on a plate in 1940 by the French Vichy government. Japan's main objective was to rid the Pacific and South-East Asia of Western influence.

The Americans sent their information to Washington, the British sent theirs to Singapore, and the Australian operators of Sigint (code name for Signal Intelligence) sent the information they gathered to a bureau in Melbourne. From Sigint's inception, secrecy was very much the order of the day. By 1943, Australian and American code-breakers, working in harmony under the overall command of General Douglas Macarthur, were able to report just about every move or anticipated move of the enemy at sea, on land and in the air.

As the war moved north of Papua-New Guinea, Sigint operators also moved north, as far as the Philippines. The outstanding work of these men and women was lauded by Macarthur and his staff. Following the capitulation of Japan, Macarthur's Chief of Intelligence, General Willoughby, stated that signal intelligence 'chopped two years off the war in the Pacific!'

The wireless air gunner

The RAAF was divided into two distinct categories, those engaged and trained under the banner of the Empire Air Training Scheme and those who joined and trained as members of the Citizens Air Force. Until the beginning of the war, aircrew personnel were members of the permanent Air Force. Once hostilities began, the permanent force was augmented by recruits from the Citizens Air Force.

There was then no such mustering as Wireless Air Gunner. Aircrew comprised Pilot, Observer or Wireless-Observer and Gunner—flying open-cockpit aeroplanes. When two-engine planes arrived in the shape of De Havilland Avro Ansons and Lockheed Hudsons, the Air Board had to provide appropriate crews, giving a higher status to navigation and wireless communication, which led to the establishment of No. 1 Air Observers School at Cootamundra.

The wireless operator was mustered as a W/T (Wireless Telegraphist) Operator. He wore an arm badge depicting a cluster of sparks, but had no aircrew status. He was a member of the ground staff, and paid an extra five shillings when engaged in flying duties. To differentiate between the W/T Operator employed in ground signal stations and one who flew, the latter was referred to as a W/T Op Air. Later, another category was created—Wireless Electrical Mechanic (WEM). WEMs were mainly engaged in servicing wireless equipment.

The training programme for W/T Operator followed the permanent Air Force syllabus. It was an intensive course lasting about six months, with lecturers from the 'old school'. The *Admiralty Handbook* (very much outdated) was used as the main book of instruction for trainees. The procedure used in the RAAF closely followed RAF training.

In 1940 the Empire Air Training Scheme (EATS) came into being, providing training facilities in Canada, Rhodesia and, if I recall correctly, South Africa, and later Australia. By this time the mustering of Wireless Air Gunner had been created, giving the W/Telegraphy Operator aircrew status.

On completion of training the WAG was given the rank of Sergeant. Later, after allocations had been provided, some were commissioned at the end of the course. The course in wireless and gunnery was not as extensive as the training undergone by members of the Citizens Air Force, yet sufficient to provide for a wireless operator's duties in flight. He was not expected to repair his equipment or trace faults, nor was he expected to reach the speed of sending and receiving messages imposed on CAF operators.

You could imagine the feelings of the W/T operators, after being thoroughly trained in most aspects of communication at the *alma mater* of the RAAF, Point Cook, when they were given no elevation beyond the lowly rank of Aircraftsman which they already held. Many of these W/T operators had offered their services to King and country within weeks of the outbreak of the war and were either on the Reserve List waiting to be called up or already in training when EATS was formed. (Point Cook was amalgamated with the staff colleges of the Army and Navy in March 2001and now operates as the Australian Defence College at Weston, Canberra.)

At the time war broke out, Australian-trained W/T operators formed part of the crew of Sunderland flying boats of 10 Squadron, which happened to be 'Johnny on the spot' after completing flying boat training in England.

When the Seaplane Training Flight was established at Rathmines in New South Wales, W/T operators were sent there to undergo aircrew training, gunnery and marine work. All operators had been carefully selected by RAAF Headquarters for their proficiency and knowledge of the equipment installed in the flying boats.

Before the close of 1941, both 11 Squadron and 20 Squadron were operating out of the main base at Port Moresby and newly established advanced operational bases (AOBs) at Rabaul (New Britain) and Kavieng (New Ireland), Gavutu (Solomon Islands), Noumea (New Caledonia) and Port Vila (New Hebrides). The fact that the Catalinas of these squadrons were often away from the main base for some time was another reason for the careful selection of aircrew, as maintenance at these remote spots had to be undertaken by the crew.

Now with the rank of Leading Aircraftsman, W/T operators were involved in search, rescue, patrol and bombing missions over the South Pacific, covering a huge area, with the responsibility of communication by wireless and Aldis lamp and, of course, plotting by the use of high-frequency direction-finding (HFDF) stations, as well as having gunnery and mooring duties. Initially two operators were carried. Later, sometimes three operators were posted to cover the long periods in the air—generally from 17 to 23 hours per flight.

During the first three months of the war against Japan many of these highly trained W/T operators were killed by enemy action or in crashes, or taken prisoner. By this time, most had become very disgruntled about the lack of recognition by the Air Board in granting aircrew status and appropriate rank. I was one of them. It was decided that one of us would seek a parade with a representative of RAAF Headquarters to state our case, drawing attention to this anomalous situation and to the fact that those who had joined up early in the war were being victimised in rank and status. If I remember rightly, we appointed my old friend Brian Buzzard to appear on our behalf when the officer visited Rathmines.

As a result, we were all elevated to the rank of Sergeant, on a par with a WAG, and some later went on to commissioned appointments. Sadly, Brian died a few years ago. His book *A Rascal and a Gentleman* makes fascinating reading about those days.

When I finished my operational tour in March 1943, I was sent to No.

3 Wireless Air Gunners School at Maryborough, Queensland, where I lectured on operational procedure and the necessary radio theory. After I was granted a commission, I undertook a Gunnery Leaders Course, and later RAAF Headquarters sent me to Laverton to undergo a staff course with a dozen or so General Duties officers. With my appointment of Staff Officer Radio Training, operating from Eastern Area Headquarters, I covered all squadrons between Queanbeyan in the south to Lowood in the north, where there was a Beaufort squadron. I mention this because at Lowood I was confronted with a big problem in assessing the proficiency of the WAGs in the squadron. I noted that most of them had been trained overseas and commissioned off course, but were lacking in combat experience.

After training in Rhodesia or Canada, they had been sent to the United Kingdom at a time where there was a surfeit of aircrew, as the European conflict was winding down. They were then sent to an Australian squadron without undergoing a conversion course to the local scene. Operators had to be familiar with ionospheric predictions for the time of the year when selecting the correct frequency to operate on. I noted one plane had been lost somewhere east of the Barrier Reef a month or so before my arrival and a Court of Inquiry had been held. After checking these WAGs, I wondered if the operator in the lost plane would have been using the correct frequency to communicate with base. It was just a thought, but it troubled me.

After a few days puzzling about the incident, I came to the conclusion that the overseas-trained WAGs lacked sufficient training to continue combat flying, and signalled a report to this effect to Headquarters. As a result, they were temporarily grounded. On the night of my arrival at Lowood they had been well disposed toward me in the officers' mess, but after my critical report, I was given the cold shoulder by all but one—the Adjutant—who gave me a pat on the back for my boldness.

As I said to him, 'They might hate my guts, but at least I believe I saved some lives!'

I didn't hear the outcome of my visit as a few months later I was at 11 Group SWP, in the same capacity, headquartered at Morotai. The day the Japanese decided to pack it in, I was at Tarakan in Borneo.

Going back in time like this leads me to recall a few incidents I was involved in as a WAG. Sit back while I tell you a few tales tall and true. But first …

The nuclear scare

In the 1960s doom talk about a possible nuclear attack on Sydney by a foreign power was rife, moving the Federal Government to do something about protecting its beloved taxpayers and others should the situation arise.

The government decided firstly to initiate a system of radio communication with the public in the event of an attack—assuming there would still be some listeners on deck. The plan included the construction of a transmitting station at Emu Plains, west of Sydney, at the base of the Blue Mountains. The transmitter was to be housed in a specially designed building, not underground as originally envisaged, but in a World War II-type air-raid shelter with thick concrete walls.

The transmitter would operate on the same frequency as ABC station 2FC Sydney, using the same call sign. The real 2FC, along with all other radio stations in Sydney, would be assumed to have been obliterated. The project was all very hush-hush at the time, no more than a handful of citizens having knowledge of it. It was a case of 'Mum's the word' to avoid possible public panic.

My predecessor as general manager of 2KM Kempsey and 2KA Katoomba, Alfred Paddison, a political lobbyist, with his mentor of many years, former New South Wales Premier Jack Lang, heard about the Government's intention. With the idea of turning the project into a revenue-earner for 2KA he phoned for my thoughts on the practicability of a proposal he had in mind. I gave the idea the green light, and so we put our proposition to the Broadcasting Control Board: if the Board were agreeable to our placing the 2KA transmitter in the new building and broadcasting to the Emu Plains–Penrith district as well as to the Blue Mountains, thus allowing us to reach a big listening population in western Sydney, we would maintain the 2FC emergency transmitter. We looked at this proposal as a national gesture. The Board thanked us for our kind gesture but turned us down. By this time, the nuclear cloud had blown over and the Federal Government was settling back to its orderly routine of governing.

Episode 26

Tales tall and true

I spent much of my RAAF flying career during World War II as a wireless operator/gunner in Catalina flying boats, mostly covering the South Pacific theatre from mid-1941 to 1943. Operating out of Port Moresby in Papua and recently established advanced operational bases in the islands, including the Solomons, we were involved in reconnaissance work to guard the shipping lanes from German surface and submarine predators.

A beer-bottle barrage and stealing into Timor

When Japan came into the war we turned our attention to evacuation and bombing missions on Rabaul, the tip of Bougainville Island and Guadalcanal in the Solomons. We did get as far north as the Caroline Islands on one occasion, to attack the giant Japanese naval base at Truk. It wasn't a successful operation as our bombs went astray when the weather closed in over the target—which was just as well, as we wouldn't have stood a chance in an air battle.

For the first three months or so of 1942, Catalina Squadrons 11 and 20 kept up a relentless programme of strikes against the Japanese, with no more than three Cats between us serviceable at the one time until we moved our operational base to Cairns at the end of April. The long hauls to targets would generally keep us in the air from 10 to 20 hours at a time.

We could carry up to twelve 250-pound bombs on these missions. One day we ran out of our usual 250-pounders and to fill the gap took along a couple of crates full of 20-pound fragmentation bombs. Each one had to be fused by hand, using a pair of pliers, and then thrown over the side à la World War I. This meant circling the target for about half an hour to get rid of them all, which could get unhealthy.

When the supply of 20-pounders was almost exhausted—and our 250-pounders still had not arrived—one crew decided to augment their small arsenal on the next trip with a couple of crates of empty beer bottles, kindly supplied by the Cairns Brewery. The noise generated in the throat of an empty bottle falling from a few thousand feet could be quite frightening to those below, even more frightening if a razor blade was stuck in the neck of the bottle—so we were told. But we didn't get around to testing that report.

Certainly we didn't anticipate killing many of the enemy with our beer-bottle barrage or decimating them with 20-pounders. Our main purpose was to keep them from getting any sleep at night, with the willing cooperation of the hordes of mosquitoes that inhabited the area under attack—Buka, on the tip of Bougainville Island. We counted on the Japanese being too exhausted at the break of dawn to give the scheduled flight of American bombers even a friendly wave as they dropped their clustes of 500-pounders.

Although bombing missions were our main activity in 1942–43, now and again we were diverted to rescue jobs—which weren't exactly all beer and skittles either.

The rescued and the rescuers

In April 1942, at the height of the conflict in the South-West Pacific, a US Army B-26 Marauder aircraft came to grief during aerial combat. Although the B-26 was badly damaged, the pilot managed to put his aircraft down in the Solomon Sea within sight of Kiriwina, a small island a few hundred kilometres off the north-eastern coast of Papua. The island is part of the Woodlark Islands group.

The aircraft floated for just a few minutes and then disappeared, leaving the few surviving crew members to swim to shore through a heavy sea. As this drama was taking place our RAAF Catalina out of Port Moresby-based 20 Squadron was winging its way from Tulagi in the Solomon Islands to enemy-held Rabaul to leave a calling card for ships in the harbour in the shape of twelve 250-pound bombs. Before we got very far on this mission, a faint message was received from Townsville Operations Room instructing us to alter course to look for possible survivors of the downed B-26 'somewhere out there'!

A few hours later the Americans were sighted and a rescue attempt was immediately under way. Setting a fully bomb-laden Catalina down in a heavy sea is a very difficult and dangerous operation. But skilful work by the captain, Flight Lieutenant Terry Duigan, and his crew, brought her down safely and she was soon waddling her way toward Kiriwina. As the Cat stood several hundred metres off the island, the survivors were ferried aboard by the ever-useful rubber duckie.

One of those to make it was crewman John Hamilton of Tennessee. In the late 1980s a grateful John, now retired as an engineer with the Bendix Corporation, came to Australia in an endeavour to locate any members of the crew of Catalina A24-21 who had survived the war and to thank each one of them personally for saving his life. Since that first visit, John has made the trip to Australia every two years to maintain the friendships he established and to attend national Catalina reunions. His latest visit was in 2001. As one of the crew of A24-21 I have maintained a close association with John, sustained in part by the magnificent Christmas cakes he sends me each December.

Commando rescue

One of our stickiest ops was on 18 August 1942 when we stole into enemy-occupied Portuguese Timor (now East Timor) to pick up thirteen sick and wounded Australian Commandos. The rendezvous was a thin strip of beach near the Dutch Timor border, which meant putting the Catalina down on the open sea and then standing off the beach about 100 metres. To avoid being washed onto the beach, we took along a few extra drogues and an auxiliary anchor, plus a long length of rope which we took ashore, fastening one end to a tree, the other to our Cat. The rope was to be our lifeline.

From dusk to 3.30 next morning, two of us kept up a shuttle service with rubber duckies, pulling ourselves along the line, carrying one passenger at a time to the Cat, then returning to the beach with supplies wrapped in waterproof groundsheets. The supplies—radio equipment, ammo and food—were for the rest of the Commandos working their way south through the jungle.

I found getting onto the beach was a bit dicey. Nearing the shore the swell would get hold of my duckie and dump it upside down in the surf, intent on sucking it and its contents back to sea. At the right moment the Commando would hop in and grab everything he could lay hands on—including me. Minutes later, I would be on my way again with another passenger, dodging the giant floating Cat as it swung restlessly at anchor.

We had been instructed to be airborne before dawn to avoid the coastal sweep the Japanese flew every morning, using a flight of Zeros. Trouble was, we could only get one engine to function—we were sitting ducks.

Luckily the Zeros didn't materialise that morning, so we were free to try and coax the dead engine back to life. After about an hour bouncing about in the sea, we found the fault—a burnt-out solenoid in the starter motor. We were now committed to a hand start, using a crank handle—like the one we used in the old days to start the family car, though this one had a rod about 1.2 metres long.

We had only taken a skeleton crew on this operation, for obvious reasons, so it fell to me to wind up the huge motor. Noticing my struggles, the officer in charge of the Army contingent climbed up on the mainplane to lend a hand while the sick and wounded remained entombed in the stifling hot, flightless Cat. After 30 minutes or so winding away with me, the officer went back to placate his men, who were now restless and very concerned about the delay.

Meanwhile the skipper, Gil Thurston, stood on top of the pilot's cabin, wringing his hands but still maintaining a sense of humour. 'Bernie,' he said with a grin, 'this is the unhappiest day of my life!'

'Gawd! That's not very uplifting when I'm trying to start this bloody donk,' I retorted.

Thursty's declaration was enough to spur me on to greater effort. The engine also got the message and sprang into life after a few more turns of the crank. I just had time to extract the handle from the bowels of the engine before Thursty revved her up. Then I was nearly blown into the sea. Fortunately I managed to grab a small handle, set into the mainplane for the use of maintenance men, and held on like grim death as I eased my way down into the blister compartment, helped along by someone grabbing my feet. By this time Thursty was taxiing our beloved Cat for a quick take-off.

Precisely 3 hours and 50 minutes later we touched down in Darwin Harbour with thirteen very relieved Commandos. I wonder what happened to them and their officer as the war progressed?

Skipper Gil Thurston transferred to Qantas in 1945 after a meritorious career in the RAAF, not only in the Pacific but also in the European theatre, flying Sunderlands. Sadly he died in Singapore after becoming ill as captain of a plane on the Sydney–London run.

War is a lottery. A few months after that rescue mission the RAAF decided our crew all needed a bit of a break from operations. My posting was the first to come through and I was on my way home to my beloved on 8 March 1943. The others were expecting their posting the next day.

On that afternoon the Squadron Commanding Officer, Wing Commander Frank Chapman, got a scratch crew together for a mission over Buka at the tip of Bougainville in the Solomon Islands. The flight engineer on that skeleton crew, Jack Dewhurst, with whom I flew on every operation from mid-1941 until 1 March 1943, was caught by the Japanese the very night I was winging south, during an attack on the Japanese base at Buka, on the northern tip of Bougainville in the Solomons.

On that mission the Cat was loaded with a new type of incendiary, which accidentally caught alight about halfway to the target. The flying boat, now in flames, was put down on the sea with outstanding skill and all the crew taken off—by the Japanese. Jack was taken ashore near Gasmata in southern New Britain and decapitated, along with the rest of the crew. Their remains lie in Bitapaka War Memorial Cemetery, Rabaul.

The luck of the draw

On 7 October 1944 I made a return trip to Timor as a supernumerary Gunnery Leader in a Mitchell B-25 out of Darwin, to attack enemy barges and a gun emplacement on shore. One of our three aircraft was shot down and went into the sea. We returned to base unscathed. As soon as we got back to base, I was informed I had stepped into the wrong aircraft due to a mix-up on the manifest. I should have been on the one shot down, which carried my friend Bernie Weisneski. Luck—once again— had been on my side, though not for my mates.

The remains of the crew were never recovered but they are remembered by an inscription on a sepulchre in the Adelaide River War Cemetery, Northern Territory.

The Cat with the broken back

Many of our missions involved the bombing of Rabaul. I have vivid memories associated with the place, although I've never actually been there. When the Japanese took Rabaul, we took part in evacuating RAAF personnel from New Britain, which was carried out in two legs—from the beach at the back of Rabaul by Sunderland flying boats to Samarai (at the southern tip of Papua), then from Samarai to Port Moresby by Catalinas. I was involved in the second leg. The Sunderlands—Qantas-owned—were seconded to the RAAF.

Occasionally, after we had dropped a load on Rabaul and Japanese shipping, we would scoot for home, flying over the mouth of one of the two volcanoes in the harbour. Matupi was still smouldering from the time of its gigantic explosion in 1937. Its companion volcano was Vulcan. We had heard stories that the Japanese were reluctant to chase their unwelcome visitors across a volcano as they had some spiritual thing about it. Actually, I think that story was a furphy.

At the time of these operations, the hull of our flying boats would be coated with grease, to give some protection from the elements and possibly provide less water resistance during take-off. One day at Moresby, when our Cat had been slipped for a 240-hour inspection, I wandered onto the scene and was aghast to see the thin duralumin hull was pitted with thousands of white holes. Then the penny dropped.

The combination of the metal hull, the minute carbon particles from the smoking volcano that had impregnated the grease, and the salt water created tiny but perfect voltaic cells. In other words, the hull had been attacked through a process of electrolysis. This would eventually have turned it into a sieve! We promptly abandoned the flight path over the volcano. Maybe the Japanese already knew.

Another reason for Rabaul being forever deeply imprinted in my mind is that the remains of so many of my comrades lie in the Rabaul cemetery.

At Port Vila, on one occasion around this time, we had a slight mishap when taking off in the open sea with a full load of bombs and fuel. The bombs were destined for Rabaul. With a heavy sea running and an all-up maximum weight, Cat A24-10 just couldn't get enough speed to remain airborne. After kangarooing half a dozen times she fell from about 35 metres, hitting the waves with such force she broke her back. The impact ripped the hull open.

While we were treading water, skipper Charles Thompson skilfully manoeuvred the Cat into the port and shallow water, jettisoning bombs and fuel along the way. Next day, a French boat-builder arrived and declared he would soon put our plane back together. Starting with a long length of 3 x 4 inch oregon, which he laid on the bottom ledge of the bulkhead doors, he secured a series of struts. When he completed the job, he had actually constructed the framework of the hull of an upturned boat with the length of oregon as the keel.

While he was hard at work, we were busy patching the torn hull with hessian soaked in bitumen. Apprehensive about the tail assembly remaining with us, the skipper took us on a test flip. Lo and behold, nothing came apart, so we fuelled-up our lovely old Cat and flew her to

Australia on a 15-hour journey. It wasn't exactly a comfortable trip as the struts prevented us from sitting down. About two hours out of Vila we ran into a *guba* (Papuan for 'fierce tropical storm') which slowed us down somewhat and tossed the old Cat about a bit. Apart from losing much of the paintwork, everything remained intact.

Being a WAG wasn't exactly a case of living in the lap of luxury.

The Gutless Wonder

Back at Port Vila a few weeks later, one of our crew, let's call him 'Smith', wasn't feeling the best due to a spot of dysentery, which had been nagging him for some time. As a result he'd lost a fair bit of weight. He was getting weaker day by day, yet he still had enough strength for his daily ablutions. As there was no water laid on at our base, we used makeshift arrangements. To shower, we would fill a bucket to the brim with water and then haul it aloft to a beam by a rope and pulley arrangement. At the right moment, using another length of rope, the contents would be tipped over.

The fact that Smith, now without any spare flesh and in a weakened state, still managed to make the haul earned him the admiration of fellow crewmen. They affectionately bestowed on him the title of the 'Gutless Wonder', a title which stayed with him to the war's end.

One night, when his malady was into the third week, Smith had an urgent urge to go just as we happened to arrive over our target, which was shipping in Simpson Harbour, Rabaul. The toot in the Catalina stood in the centre of the catwalk, between the blisters which housed the port and starboard machine guns. Both blisters were wide open, enabling the gunners to have their guns at the ready in case a Zero happened to come our way.

Smith must have found it as cold as charity sitting there with a bare bot with a cold draft roaring in through the opened blisters at about 5,000 feet. To make the situation even more uncomfortable, the skipper sent the Cat into a deep dive twice, or maybe thrice, and followed up with a few sharp turns.

After each manoeuvre Smith was tossed off the toot, but each time regained his seat and composure. Nevertheless, it must have been off-putting.

'Gawd, that was close!' screamed the starboard gunner. 'I thought he must have had us in his sights.'

'What do you mean?' Smith inquired politely.

'Bloody hell! Didn't you know we had a Zero on our tail?' yelled the port gunner. 'And you were just sitting there, you silly bugger.'

Within an hour of our return to main base, the CO had Smith on the mat.

'I'm blowed if I know what to do with you, Smith,' he said. 'I don't know whether to put you on a charge of cowardice for walking away from your radio desk at a vital moment and at the same time neglecting to man the bow turret gun when your plane was attacked, or on the other hand, to recommend you for a bravery award for sitting it out, calmly and unperturbed until it was all over … Look, will you settle for a week's leave to get over that business! And stop backing off while I'm talking to you.'

'Sorry, sir,' spoke Smith. 'It's just that I have to go again.'

'Right,' replied the CO. 'If you can still hear me, for God's sake pop in and see the MO on your way out!'

By this time Smith was already knocking on the door of the medical section, well out of earshot.

Well, that's the story as I know it. I do know Smith finished the war with few signs of wear and tear. After all, who should know better?

Pygmy 'tails'

The date was 10 January 1943. Our mission was to evacuate a group of missionaries who had escaped from Java after the Japanese invasion and somehow made their way to Dutch New Guinea (now Irian Jaya).

To reach Wessel Mere, a lake 5,000 feet up in the highlands, we staged through Merauke on the south coast, facing the Arafura Sea. Merauke would have to have been one of the most uninviting places we had ever come across. The bay on which we touched down, the mouth of the Merauke River, was covered by a yellow, smelly scum with no signs of a current to take it out to sea. There was an oppressive stillness about the place, with the whole area infested with mosquitoes. Yet the RAAF considered Merauke strategic enough to have set up a radio base. The operator, Ted Peppercorn, happened to be a friend of mine, so I headed for the station as soon as we went ashore, and spent a few hours having a natter with him.

We were more than happy to get away early next morning and head for the coolness of the highlands. The trip to Wessel Mere took exactly 2 hours 35 minutes, a short run compared to most of our operations. As we flew north, we could see several snowcapped peaks, reminding us that some of the mountains reached up more than 13,000 feet, sometimes covered in cloud. After a fairly easy run, we settled on the lake, threw out a few anchors and were taken ashore to the village by a couple of officials.

To our amazement we were greeted by a tribe of pygmies. Greeted warily, I might add. As soon as I saw the welcoming party my mind went back to about 1936, when I had read something of a story about explorer and patrol officer Jack Hides coming across a tribe of pygmies who had 'tails' attached to their bodies by a narrow band about the waist. The only other garment the men wore was a hollow shell gourd into which the penis was inserted. On top of the gourd was a tassel of Bird of Paradise feathers, giving the appearance of a feather duster.

The pygmies, no more than 4 feet 6 inches (137 cm) high, carried huge bows about 5 feet long, longer than they were tall. Most tribes had a ritual of qualifying for manhood that involved consuming human flesh. With this in mind, I felt a tad apprehensive as we stepped ashore, but warmed to them after an hour or so and succumbed to their willingness to trade, walking away with a bow and a couple of arrows.

We put aboard about twelve missionaries and set off. Alas, we just could not get airborne, not only because of the weight but because the lake was like glass, with not a ripple in sight. We needed a few waves to get air under the hull of the flying boat. Apart from that, the thinner atmosphere at that height was not conducive to lift-off. We off-loaded half the missionaries, spent a few minutes taxiing around the lake to stir up the water, creating a few waves, and made another attempt at take-off. It was a close shave, just missing the surrounding hills as we gained height, but from there on it was a pleasant trip back to that unpleasant place Merauke. I don't know how those we left behind got to Merauke.

Demobbed on 7 November 1945, I returned to civilian life and my interrupted career in broadcasting. By now developments in technology had taken radio far beyond the days of the cat's whisker. Tales of the new era, in which I was deeply involved until my retirement (sort of) from radio in 1972, do not belong with these stories of the early technologies, so I leave you with a final story. Stay tuned just a little longer ...

... and true? The Red Fleet surrenders

KEMPSEY, APRIL 1: Ten ships of the Red Merchant fleet in the South Pacific took refuge in Trial Bay this morning. The Commodore, Captain Ivan

Itzalieski, announced at dawn that he was surrendering the fleet to the Australian Government and the crews of all ships would seek political asylum. He also announced that about 200 of the crew of his ship, the *Joker*, had jumped overboard and swum ashore because they feared Australian authorities might shoot them as spies.

Units of the C.M.F. are now scouring swamp country west of the bay in a search for the deserters. Most of the seamen have already been taken into custody and are now being cared for at Trial Bay goal. Authorities say the operation has been peaceful and the men have been glad to give themselves up. Many are suffering from malnutrition.

The news of the surrender has stunned the Federal Government. Diplomatic circles in Canberra are in turmoil. The Red Ambassador is reported to have barricaded himself in the embassy and armed guards are patrolling the grounds.

The Acting Prime Minister, Mr McMahon, said in Sydney this morning he would make no statement until he had consulted the Prime Minister Mr Gorton, who is now in Washington.

No note received

He said he had received no official note from the Red Embassy or the commodore about 'anything untoward' and was not inclined to comment at this stage.

Mr McMahon ordered the Argus to 'kill' the story until he had received instructions from Mr Gorton or until the cabinet had met to discuss the political significance of the coup. The Argus declined to accept Mr McMahon's order because of the international significance of the surrender and its effect on the local economy.

Meanwhile, thousands of spectators, crowding the foreshores of South West Rocks are eyewitnesses to the most incredible capitulation since Drake took the Spanish Fleet. The first warning that units of the Red Merchant Navy were sailing toward Trial Bay came soon after midnight last night when a lone fisherman sent a radio message ashore.

The fisherman, Mr A. Witt, said he had been fishing about 20 miles off Green Rock when his line fouled a submerged object. Almost immediately, an unidentified submarine surfaced alongside.

Mr Witt said: 'I didn't wait to ask questions. I got for my life'.

The pilot at South West Rocks, Mr N. O'Keefe, put to sea at about 1 a.m. Some 15 miles off Laggers Point he sighted ten ships in line abreast, being shepherded toward Trial Bay by a submarine, a tug and a barque. Two helicopters flew overhead.

The *Looflirpa* heads fleet

The pride of the fleet, the M.V. *Looflirpa*, which has been in service on the clipper run for only a year, dwarfed other ships as she steamed slowly toward the Macleay coast. Bunting fluttered from the masthead and passengers threw streamers through the portholes.

The ships dropped anchor in Trial Bay just before dawn.

The store ship, *Titanic*, which has been operating in Asian waters disguised as a junk, ran aground when she attempted to berth alongside the breakwater at the old gaol. As this issue went to press she was shipping water in the forward section.

Cargo of narcotics

The *California*, an armed merchant ship believed to have a cargo of narcotics aboard, is standing by to rescue the crew if the *Titanic*'s list worsens.

Fearing an invasion, a leading citizen (Mr P. Rafferty) alerted the CMF and within minutes troop transports were hurtling down the river road toward the sleepy resort … [They] threw a barbed wire fence entanglement around the golf course (when it was learned that 200 sailors had jumped ship) and as this issue goes to press all but one of the Red merchantmen had been captured.

Army headquarters mobilised officers on the reserve and put them in immediate command of volunteers from the RSL.

The *Looflirpa* was the first to drop anchor, about one hundred yards offshore of the old terminal. A short while later Captain A. Prilfuski lowered the ship's ladder to welcome aboard an *Argus* journalist, and the tourist promotion officer, Mrs. V. Melville. The first to arrive had been the Chairman of the Oxley Regional Development Committee (Mr F. A. Slack) travelling by hovercraft. He is now in the bay assessing the tonnage of ships with a view to exploiting the bay's use as a deep sea port.

Hundreds of people in small craft have converged on the giant steamer, waiting for passes to board the ship.

In a message to Kempsey, the journalist said a vodka party was in progress in the captain's suite to celebrate the completion of the long voyage.

Mrs. Melville was then distributing tourist promotion pamphlets to passengers.

As the ships swung slowly at anchor in the bleak dawn light, the residents of South West Rocks were roused from their beds by the shark alarm and the tolling of church bells. They rushed to Point Briner to witness the surrender of the century.

So reported the local newspaper on the front page, with supporting pictures.

The year was 1969 when that dramatic event took place at Trial Bay near Kempsey on the mid North Coast of New South Wales. Headlined in the Kempsey district newspaper, the *Macleay Argus,*it was broadcast by local radio station 2KM with a vivid description by breakfast announcer Peter Bosley. The reaction was electric.

As dawn was breaking over the district, many concerned citizens were hot-footing it down to the Trial Bay seaside resort of South West Rocks, some to offer their services to those in need of a little comfort and a square meal, some just to gander at this massive defection. In response to Bosley's call for assistance in the form of blankets and hot coffee for the exhausted defectors, the Salvation Army loaded a truck with blankets and an urn of coffee and headed off too.

General Manager-Director of 2 KA and 2KM at the time, I was in my Sydney office in King Street. Munching away at a cut lunch lovingly prepared by my wife, I received a phone call from the Broadcasting Control Board in Melbourne. The caller immediately berated me for allowing the station manager of 2KM to contravene the conditions laid down by the *Broadcasting Act.* He made it known that if such an incident were repeated, the cancellation of 2KM's broadcasting licence could be considered.

Not being aware at this stage what the gent's complaint was, I assumed that somehow a profane word such as—dare I say it—'bloody' may have slipped into a broadcast, and I acknowledged his highly critical remarks with due docility. Then he told me the reason for the many complaints received that morning. Quite dumbfounded, and unable to think of a suitable explanation at short notice, I just breathed heavily into the phone as he continued to tear strips off me. Then suddenly, like a breath of fresh air, he changed tack and enquired about the weather in Sydney and my health, wished me all the best, and hung up—with a smile in his voice, I thought.

The Big Surrender was dreamt up by the editor of the newspaper, Patricia Riggs, fully supported by Peter Bosley. The many citizens who scurried along to South West Rocks to offer succour to the distressed, and suffered the ignominy of being made suckers on this day, the first day of April—April Fool's Day—1969. The trials of being in the media!

Epilogue

Looking back over the years at the extraordinary developments in the application of Hertzian (electromagnetic) waves—during the first three decades of the twentieth century in particular—I can't say they were the Good Old Days, yet they were romantic days for the radio pioneers.

Success was the outcome of improvisation, sufficient to place Australia but a footstep or two behind the United States, Great Britain and Europe in developments utilising Hertzian waves that have become dominating influences on our lifestyles, our methods of communication, and in the maintenance of our health.

Our part in these developments is all the more praiseworthy because Australia was then predominantly a rural nation suffering through two major economic depressions and two major wars. These disasters, which initially slowed progress somewhat, through necessity fostered many great technological achievements, many of which nowadays are given but scant attention–except on those occasions when one of them fails to function.

The German physicist Heinrich Rudolph Hertz would not have envisaged the widespread technical applications to which electro-magnetic waves have been put. He died in 1894, the year Marconi successfully propagated them to bring us wireless (radio).

No doubt the Scottish inventor John Logie Baird would not have persisted with his mechanical scanning method of transmitting television signals—which he began in1926—if he had been fully aware of the progress in the United States in the development of the cathode-ray tube, which was to become an integral part of the evolution of television as we know it now.

'The earth has been girdled, as it were, by a magic chain,' said Sir Hercules Robinson, Governor of New South Wales, in a speech at a grand celebratory banquet in Sydney in November 1872 to mark the successful opening of telegraphic communication with Europe. A section of his 'magic chain' was a single strand of iron wire suspended on porcelain insulators fastened to roughly hewn wooden poles spanning 3,000 kilometres of arid Australia from Darwin to Adelaide. This was known as the Overland Telegraph Line (OTL). Although messages were sent and received by Morse code, the OTL began a communication revolution for Australians at the time Wireless was unheard of.

Although these three snippets of history have little place in books and discussions nowadays, I harbour strong feelings of nostalgia and appreciation for the accomplishments of the pioneers in the field of communication, at home and abroad.

Maybe it's because I have lived through much of those times, before the coming of facsimile reproduction of sight and sound at the flick of a switch ... including the years when radio was the cat's whiskers.

Bernard Harte
March 2002

Appendix 1

Commercial life of Bernard Harte
1934–2001

1934/35 Music Masters Radio Co. Brisbane Employed in making 4-valve, 5-valve, 6-valve, 8-valve radio sets for local markets.

1935/38 Radio Station 4BH, Brisbane Technician, with some announcing duties.

1938/40 After qualifying by exam for Broadcast Operator's Certificate of Proficiency, sent to 4SB South Burnett, a powerful relay station, as Transmitter Engineer. Now graduate member Institution of Radio Engineers. September 1939 accepted by RAAF to train as pilot. Long delay for call-up had me worried that war would be over before started training, so accepted recruitment as Trainee W/T Operator.

1940/45 Royal Australian Air Force During this time qualified by exam for First Class Wireless Operator's Certificate of Proficiency (1942). Elevated to Associate Membership Institution of Radio Engineers (1942).

1945/47 Chief Engineer 4SB South Burnett with responsibility for transmitter at Wooroolin and studio at Kingaroy.

1947/50 Radio Station 2UW, Sydney Worked on installation of transmitting station at Concord West-Homebush. Remained on transmitter staff, completed course in business administration. Founded Paramount Recorded Productions after constructing my own 78 rpm disc and 16-inch recording equipment and studio at Epping.

1950/1966 Engineer/Manager 2KM, Kempsey Arrived in wake of 1950 major flood, which disabled transmitter and destroyed most of the facilities. Managed to get station back on air, then set about rebuilding new station on flood-free site. Meanwhile tornado struck Kempsey, destroying the now almost derelict transmitting aerial and wooden supporting masts. Operating from new site at Greenhill, soon became the 'Voice of the Floods', keeping up the morale of listeners during the severe floods which occurred in following years until 1963; the last one under my on-site management was preceded by a major drought. Broadcasting from studio, direct from mobile transmitter van and aircraft, kept listeners up to the minute with flood warnings and safety precautions.

Opened small studio at Port Macquarie and allocated landline time daily from that town. With the purpose of boosting the morale and improving the business activity of Kempsey, formed the Macleay Development Association, occupying the position of Foundation President. With input from New England University, the Association brought all established local organisations, not functioning since flood devastation, under the one umbrella, including the Kempsey Chamber of Commerce. When these organisations were strong enough to stand alone, encouraged them to do that. While remaining President of the MDA, took on the Presidency of the Kempsey Chamber of Commerce and Foundation Chairman of the Macleay Tourist Authority, using press and radio publicity to keep them alive.

Purchased large store in West Kempsey on behalf of company. Gutted it, designed and installed new studios and office. Established regional news service, the first country radio station to do so. Won Macquarie News Award.

Purchased 47 acres at Green Wattle Creek, South Kempsey. Large acreage required to carry directional transmitting station. Designed new system for new frequency allocated and installed same. Opened studio at Coffs Harbour—now receiving a 'local' signal.

Opened new studios in Port Macquarie, completing project to establish a mini-network, using one transmitter and three connected studios, plus permanent landline from 2GB-Macquarie.

This method of 'personal' broadcasting married the station to all mid North Coast and hinterland towns, and reduced listeners to the ABC to a minimum, as well as stimulating the development of resort towns and contributing to their commercial and tourist potential. Port Macquarie, now awakened from a long sleep, strode ahead commercially and in population

1966/72 General Manager/Director 2KM Kempsey and 2KA Katoomba
Operating from office in King Street, Sydney, administered both companies. Searched for a better 2KA transmitting site than existing site at Wentworth Falls. No suitable ground available, so set about installing transmitting tower on existing site, then supervised the tricky job of demolishing the now redundant antiquated aerial array.

Elected to the position of Vice-President (Country) of the Federation of Commercial Broadcasters and Chairman of the Quarter Century Club (a group of long-serving members of the industry). Organised several historic functions, including 50th Anniversary of Broadcasting.

1973/75 Resigned, and purchased interest in local 'free' newspaper. As Managing Editor published *The Observer* as a weekly, circulating in Kempsey-Macleay, Port Macquarie, Wauchope-Hastings and Nambucca Heads, Macksville-Nambucca districts.

After sudden death of my wife at Port Macquarie in 1974 and months later, my grandchild at Tully in North Queensland, decided to part company with *The Observer* and move to Sydney.

1975/77 Licensing Manager, Australasian Performing Right Association Work entailed visits interstate and to New Zealand. On behalf of APRA presented trophy to award winner Country Music Festival, Tamworth.

1977/79 Residing at Port Macquarie, appointed correspondent at *Port Macquarie News* and ABC. Also Channel 11 as on-camera interviewer for newly established regional news service. Wrote many historical features for *Port Macquarie News*.

1980/84 Public Relations Company   Established in partnership with the late Gilbert Mant and late John Moyes, engaged in production of the *North Coast Magazine* and *North Coast Weekly*. Gilbert Mant retired in 1981 but John Moyes and I continued to write many editorials, short stories and columns until dissolution of partnership. Continued freelancing for newspaper and on radio.

Founded Macquarie Radio Productions, then produced many historical audio cassettes, which lost popularity with the CD evolution. Donated my historical print and audio collection to Kempsey Museum and Port Macquarie Library in 1999 and 2001.

1991 Won FACB TV Award as presenter relocatable homes, Port Macquarie.

1992 Death of my second wife as result of car accident in North Queensland.

1993 Organised function in Port Macquarie to commemorate the 70th Anniversary of Radio Broadcasting in Australia.

2000/2 Last three years writing book on the history of radio entitled *When Radio Was the Cat's Whiskers* has overwhelmed my other activities. Sold home in Port Macquarie, and built new home near my daughter and her husband at Herberton, North Queensland.

Résumé of RAAF service career of 23086 Flight Lieutenant L. B. (Bernard) Harte 1940–1945

Musterings W/T Operator (Air), Wireless Operator/Air Gunner, Gunnery Leader, Staff Officer Radio Training.

1941
Trained West Melbourne Technical College and Point Cook. 6 May posted No. 1 Air Observers School, Cootamundra as flying W/T Op.

16 June Posted Seaplane Training Flight, Rathmines to undergo aircrew and marine training.

20 Oct. Posted 20 Sqdn. Port Moresby in Catalina A24-10. Operated out of Moresby, Gavutu (Solomons), Port Vila (Vanuatu), Noumea (New Caledonia), Suva and Lautoka (Fiji Is.)

4 Dec Picked up US VIP flight; aborted by bombing of Pearl Harbor by Japanese and entry into Pacific War.

1942
21 Jan. Attacked naval base at Truk, Caroline Islands. A24-10 skippered by S/Ldr Price.

23 Jan. Skipper S/Ldr Cohen operated Samarai-Moresby leg of evacuation RAAF personnel and some soldiers back from Rabaul. Rabaul-Samarai leg operated by Short Empire flying boats seconded fm Qantas.

1 Feb. Completed evacuation work. Bombing runs on Rabaul and Gasmata.

22 Feb. Continued missions until crashing out to sea Port Vila, Cat A24-10.

27 Feb. After emergency repairs flew 13 hrs 40 mins skippered by F/Lt. Thompson to Rathmines.

25 Mar. Returned to operational flying out of Moresby, Horn Island, shadowing Gull Force to Ambon.

6 Apr. Flying Tulagi (Solomons) to Moresby, diverted to near Woodlark Island to rescue remaining crew of US B-26, downed in sea. Crew included radio operator John Hamilton (USAF) and passenger S/Ldr Price, RAAF. Continued patrol flying Solomon Sea out of Guadalcanal.

11 Apr. Cat A24-21 damaged in heavy landing near Malaita. Skipper Terry Duigan's comment, 'Managed to bend her a bit!' Duigan suffering dengue fever at time. Flew A24-21 to Rathmines. Bombing practice/ferry trips Rathmines, Bowen, Cairns, until 29 May. Bombing strikes on Beluipe Is, operating out of Noumea and Tulagi. Skipper S/Ldr Price. Continued op. flying out of Vila and Noumea

4 Jun. Crashed in heavy landing Rathmines, coming in from Noumea A24-16

10 Jun. Crewed up with F/Lt Gil Thurston for test flights and ferry trips. Remained with Thurston for rest of his period with 20 Sqdn. Ferry trips Rathmines-Queensland north coast. Returned to operational flying out of Bowen and Cairns.

30 Jun. Bomb strike on Lae, Papua out of Cairns, also observation of Jap. Landing at Buna and Gona. Strike on Lae, then bombing practice out of Bowen. Test flights until

14 Jul. Resumed operational flying—patrols and search out of Cairns and Townsville. A24-21 then A24-4. Convoy and searches Cairns-Moresby.

27 Jul. Strike on Buna out of Cairns, trip time 15 hrs 50 mins.

29 Jul. Strike on Havana Harbour out of Cairns, trip time 17 hrs 45 mins.

30/31 Jul. Strike on Havana Harbour out of Vila, returning Cairns.

7 Aug. Strike on Buka Is (nth of Bougainville), trip time 19 hrs 50 mins.

16 Aug. Cairns to Darwin to prepare rescue attempt Commandos (Independents)

18 Aug. Darwin to Portuguese Timor (East Timor). Difficult assignment. Skipper Thurston in A24-4. Assignment also included evacuation of Portuguese Governor. Informed by Commander Governor was quisling (traitor). Decided not to evacuate this individual.

25 Aug. Back at Darwin to rescue Kittyhawk pilot stranded on beach, Anson Bay. Dispersed Haycock Creek for safe shelter against enemy air raid.

5 Sept. Operating out of Cairns on convoy and patrol missions until

8 Oct. Strike on Buka, next day on Rabaul, then back to convoy work

27 Oct. Strike on Buka Is, operating out of Cairns, trip time 17 hrs 5 mins.

29/31 Oct. Strike on Buin, trips 17.15 hrs and 15.25 hrs.

6 Nov. Night search Cairns -Papua coast -New Britain, trip time 21 hrs 30 min.

25/27 Nov. Night search Cairns-Buna-Lae and return, trip time 21 hrs and 19.20 min.

1 Dec. Night search Cairns-Gasmata-Buna and return, trip time 20.45 hrs.

3 Dec. Strike on Kavieng out of Cairns, trip time 18 hrs 20 mins.

6 Dec. Strike on Kavieng, then ferry Cairns to Bowen. Replaced A24-4 with A24-10, A24-30, A24-16.

1943

3 Jan. Convoy Cairns-Milne Bay, trip time 12 hrs 55 mins.

4 Jan. From Milne Bay, search-bomb strike Gasmata, return Cairns 16.15 hrs.

8 Jan. Search Cairns-Huon Gulf-Milne Bay, trip time 17 hrs 15 mins.

13 Jan. Search Cairns-Lae-Buna-Milne Bay, trip 16 hrs. Cat A24-16 & A24-2. Continued ops

17 Jan. Cairns to Horn Island thence Merauke (Dutch New Guinea) time 7 hrs.

18 Jan. Evacuation Merauke-Tanah-Merah, return Merauke then

19 Jan. To Horn Island with evacuees.

20 Jan. Horn Island-Merauke, then Wessel Mere Cat A24-30. To Cairns 22/1/43

23 Jan. Ferry work ports between Cairns-Brisbane.

18/19 Feb. Convoy work Cairns-Coral Sea A24-32, A24-35. Skipper F/O Robertson.

4 Mar. To 'leave'. Posted No 3 Wireless Air Gunners School, Maryborough 22/3.

8 Nov. Posted Cressy, Vic. for Gunnery Leaders Course

21 Dec. Posted No. 1 OTU, Sale, Vic. crew up/conversion course on Beauforts, 32 Squadron.

1944

27 Mar. Selected by RAAF HQ for staff officer course, Laverton, Vic.

7 Oct. Appointed Staff Officer Radio Training Eastern Area (Queanbeyan to Lowood based at Edgecliff, Sydney.

Posted to Hughes (Darwin). Took part in attack near Dili, Timor in B-25 Mitchell Bombers, 18 Squadron RAAF.

1945
28 Feb. Brief attachment, Rathmines, flying patrols Tasman Sea out of Rathmines.
19 Jun. Attached RAF Transport Sqdn (Royal Navy) for flight to Leyte, Philippines. Flew Camden-Mascot-Archerfield-Townsville-Milne Bay-Momote (Admiralty Islands)-Biak Is.-Peleliu-Morotai flying in C47, skipper F/O Phillips. Aggregate trip time 55 hrs 40 mins. Flying over Leyte Harbour saw biggest armada ever assembled or seen in history.
17 Jul. Posted to 11 Group Morotai as SORT.
14 Aug. Transport run Tarakan, Borneo, returned Morotai.
War ends.

Appendix 3

Popular tunes of the Twenties and Thirties

1915
Fascination (Romberg)
Jelly Roll Blues (Morton)
Kiss Me Again (Herbert)
She's the Daughter of Mother Machree (Ball)
Simple Melody (Berlin)

1916
If You Were the Only Girl in the World (Ayer)
Nola (Arndt)
Roses of Picardy (Weatherly)

1917
For Me and My Gal (Meyer)
Mason Dixon Line (Schwartz)
Some Sunday Morning (Whiting)
Tiger Rag (Dixieland Jazz Band)
Till the Clouds Roll By (Kern)

1918
K-K-K-Katy (O'Hara)
Oh! How I Hate to Get up iIn the Morning (Berlin)
Rock-A-Bye Your Baby with a Dixie Melody (Schwartz)
Somebody Stole My Gal (Wood)
Till We Meet Again (Egan)

1919
Alice Blue Gown (Tierney)
Swanee (Gershwin)

1920
Japanese Sandman (Whiting)
Mah Lindy Lou (Strickland)

1921
Ain't We Got Fun (Whiting)
April Showers (Silvers)
Kitten on the Keys (Confrey)
I'm Just Wild About Harry (Sissle & Blake)
Ma, He's Making Eyes at Me (Conrad)
Peggy O'Neil (Pease et al)

1922
Caroline in the Morning (Donaldson)
Georgia (Donaldson)
Toot Toot Tootsie (Kahn et al)

1923
Charleston (Mack & Johnson)
That Old Gang of Mine (Henderson)

1924
Fascinating Rhythm (Gershwin)
It had to be You (Jones)
Rhapsody in Blue (Gershwin)
Tea for Two (Youmans)

1925
Dinah (Akst)
If You Knew Susie Like I Know Susie (DeSylva & Meyer)

1926
Black Bottom (Henderson)
Bye Bye Blackbird (Henderson)

1927
Ain't She Sweet (Ager)
Diga Diga Doo (McHugh)
De Glory Road (Wolfe)
Jeannine, I Dream of Lilac Time (Shilkret)

1928
Lover Come Back to Me (Romberg)
Makin' Whoopee! (Donaldson)
Marie (Berlin)
Stout-Hearted Men (Romberg)

1929
Broadway Melody (Freed & Brown)
Singin' in the Rain (Brown)
Tip-Toe Thru the Tulips with Me (Burke)
When it's Springtime in the Rockies (Sauer)
With a Song in My Heart (Rodgers)

1930
I Got Rhythm (Gershwin)
It Happened in Monterey (Wayne)
Walkin' my Baby Back Home (Turk & Ahlert)
When Your Hair Has Turned to Silver I Will Love You Just the Same
(deRose)
You're Driving Me Crazy (Donaldson)

1931
Cuban Love Song (Stohart, McHugh & Fields)
Dancing in the Dark (Schwartz)

1932
How Deep is the Ocean? (Berlin)
Shuffle off to Buffalo (Warren)

Bibliography and resources

ABC Weekly, The Journal of the Australian Broadcasting Commission, Vol. 2, No. 29, 20 July 1940; Vo. 13, No. 25, 23 June 1951.

Bishton, E. *Diaries*. Unpublished manuscript.

Bisset, J. *Tramps and Ladies: My Early Days in Steamers*, Angus & Robertson, Sydney, 1959.

Bleakley, J. *The Eavesdroppers*, Kana, 1992.

Bolton, G. C. *Dick Boyer, An Australian Humanist*, ANU Press, Canberra, 1967.

Faiers, R. (ed.) *Evergreen*, Evergreen Publishers, Cheltenham UK, 1988. (Electrophone story and photos.)

Firkins, P. *Of Nautilus and Eagles: A History of the Royal Australian Navy*, Cassell Australia, 1975.

Fraser, B. & Weldon, K. *The Macquarie Book of Events*, Macquarie Library Pty Ltd, Sydney, 1983.

Gammage, W. *The Broken Years: Australian Soldiers in the Great War*, Penguin Australia, 1974.

Harte, B. Volumes of personal records, cassettes and files of a lifetime in Australia and the RAAF, 1940–2001.

Hill, P. Interview re wartime history of the Jehovah's Witnesses.

Hinckfuss, H. *Memories of a Signaller*, University of Queensland Press, Brisbane, 1982.

Jensen, P. R. *Early Radio*. Kangaroo Press, Sydney, 1994.

Johnson, M. *G-Pop. My Life and Work*. Privately published.

Marden, F. Interview

McCarthy, A. *The Dance Band Era*. Spring Books, UK, date unknown.

Moyal, A. *Clear Across Australia: A History of Telecommunication*, Telecom Australia Thomas Nelson, Australia, 1984.

Oliver, M.   Interview with widow and son, Alex.

Overseas Telecommunication Commission (Aust). *Information Broadsheet,* Sydney, 1977.

Penrose, G.   *The Blazing Stump: Story of an Australian Heritage.* Privately published, 1991.

Ross, J.   *Radio Broadcasting Technology 1923–1998,* Port Macquarie, NSW.

Slot, G.   *From Microphone to Ear,* Philips Technical Library, Eindhoven, Netherlands, 1959.

Smith, J. L.   *Sounds from Pythagoras to Laser—4000 BC to 1983 AD,* Century of Sound Music Museum, Port Macquarie, NSW, 1983.

Walker, R. R.   *The Magic Spark: 50 Years of Radio in Australia.* Hawthorn Press, Melbourne, 1973.

Wright, L.   *The Jack Davey Story,* Ure Smith Pty Ltd, Sydney, 1961

Index